Japan's Spy at Pearl Harbor

Japan's Spy at Pearl Harbor

*Memoir of an Imperial
Navy Secret Agent*

TAKEO YOSHIKAWA

Translated by ANDREW MITCHELL

McFarland & Company, Inc., Publishers
Jefferson, North Carolina

ISBN (print) 978-1-4766-7699-9
ISBN (ebook) 978-1-4766-3699-3

LIBRARY OF CONGRESS AND BRITISH LIBRARY
CATALOGUING DATA ARE AVAILABLE

Library of Congress Control Number 2020000412

© 2020 Takeo Yoshikawa. All rights reserved

No part of this book may be reproduced or transmitted in any form or by any means, electronic or mechanical, including photocopying or recording, or by any information storage and retrieval system, without permission in writing from the publisher.

Front cover images: Takeo Yoshikawa, aka Tadashi Morimura, a 27-year-old naval officer and Japanese spy (Library of Congress); Japanese World War II map of Hawaii, 1943; sailors rescue a survivor alongside the sunken USS *West Virginia* (BB-48) at Pearl Harbor (this is a color-tinted version of Photo # 80-G-19930 from the Army Signal Corps Collection in the U.S. National Archives); *background* December 7, 1941, chart of Pearl Harbor recovered from a Japanese midget submarine (official U.S. Navy photograph, now in the National Archives)

Printed in the United States of America

*McFarland & Company, Inc., Publishers
Box 611, Jefferson, North Carolina 28640
www.mcfarlandpub.com*

Table of Contents

Translator's Foreword	1
Preface to the Japanese Edition (1963)	5

Part One: A Letter

1. Ancient Light Hermitage	8
2. A Letter from a U.S. Soldier	11
3. Memories of Childhood and Growing Up	15
4. Navy Life	23
5. Returning Home to Convalesce	30

Part Two: Storm Clouds Over the Pacific

6. The Navy General Staff	34
7. Springtide	41
8. The Situation in America	46
9. Getting Ready	53
10. Aboard the *Nitta Maru*	58
11. Taking Up a New Post	62
12. An Overview of Hawaii	66
13. Getting Down to Work	70
14. Touring the Islands	74
15. Sending Telegrams	81
16. The Decision to Make War	86
17. The Hawaiian Climate	91

18. A Coral Sea	94
19. Airfields and Army Bases	99
20. The Secret Envoy	105
21. Activity in November	111
22. Cash for an Undercover Agent	118

Part Three: The Fateful Day

23. Activities in December	126
24. The Final Telegram	134
25. Pearl Harbor's Last Day	140
26. Life Under House Arrest	145
27. A Special Submarine	149
28. Remember Pearl Harbor	156
29. Triangle T Ranch	165
30. Carving	170
31. Rancher Tobacco	175
32. Leaving the Ranch	182
33. At a Crossroads	186
34. Navigating the Seas	192

Part Four: Returning

35. The Welcome	198
36. Longing for the Past	202
37. Interrogating Prisoners of War	210
38. Cipher Code and the Death of Commander Isoroku Yamamoto During Combat	218
39. Japanese Secret Code Before the War	223
40. Walking Away	236
41. On the Run	242
42. The Family Village	248
43. Green Vegetable Juice	255
44. War History	259

45.	CBS	268
46.	Filming	273
47.	Strolling Around Honolulu	279
48.	Returning to the Mountain	284

Chapter Notes   289
Index   297

Translator's Foreword

Although nearly eight decades have passed since the "Day of Infamy" at Pearl Harbor, United States citizens and others continue to commemorate those who paid with their lives and those who were injured during Japan's surprise attack. The USS *Arizona* Memorial in Pearl Harbor is a focal point for people wishing to pay tribute to the servicemen and civilians killed or wounded by the attack that started the Pacific War.

The battleship *Arizona* sunk after it was struck repeatedly during the attack, and most of its crew died inside the submerged vessel. Left in place in the harbor, the hull of the sunken battleship has been consecrated as a naval cemetery and now serves as a national memorial. The enduring popular interest in this memorial clearly indicates that the public has moved beyond recalling its soldiers' blood sacrifice as a toll paid along the road to victory. Modern war memorials such as the USS *Arizona* recall how the ravages of war brutally silence men and women and remind us that their lives are worthy of contemplation and remembrance.

Despite the modern tendency to commemorate sacrifices made in war in more comprehensive ways, many men and women who have fought for their nation and survived have failed to receive any recognition at all for their service. The ill-treatment widely meted out to Vietnam War veterans upon their return home shows that remembrance can be capricious. Although not generally recognized at first, the widespread mistreatment of Vietnam veterans is acknowledged by most Americans today. The gradual elevation of the social standing of these veterans did not come about by chance, however. It was brought on by the public airing of many Vietnam veterans' recollections of the war.

At the end of the Pacific War, Japan's ex-combatants found themselves met by the mistrust and scorn of their fellow citizens. Most Japanese were ashamed of their country's wartime actions and very reluctant to discuss the attack on Pearl Harbor. Instead, they hoped that the conflict might somehow be erased from the nation's collective memory.

Most of Japan's ex-combatants agreed with the idea that the Pacific War should be forgotten. Others, such as Captain Mitsuo Fuchida, felt the need to say that the war had been Japan's fault. Even so, Takeo Yoshikawa (1912–1993) questioned the popular views that the war could be blamed entirely upon the Japanese and that it was best forgotten. After working as a spy at Pearl Harbor during the nine months that preceded the outbreak of war, Yoshikawa felt compelled to reflect on his experiences and make notes about them. On the basis of those notes and reflections, he wrote his memoirs.

After serving as an ensign in the Imperial Japanese Navy during the early 1930s, Takeo Yoshikawa took on a role in intelligence gathering at the navy's headquarters. In March 1941 he was sent to work at the Japanese Consulate-General in Honolulu, under the alias "Morimura," and ordered to spy on the U.S. Pacific Fleet based at Pearl Harbor. Consequently, Yoshikawa not only witnessed many of the key events that led up to the outbreak of war, he was also a direct participant in the events that precipitated Japan's surprise attack on Pearl Harbor, an onlooker during that fateful attack, and a survivor of the Pacific War.

Yoshikawa's determination to better understand the singular and painful experiences he had endured and witnessed, both during and after the war, led him to research the causes of the war and the reasons for its eventual outcome. By 1960, public interest in his experiences led him to speak and write about his memories of the war, in defiance of his superiors' counsels. Soon after that, he wrote the memoirs that are presented here in English for the first time.

Since his memoirs have not been published in English until now, it is not surprising that Yoshikawa's espionage activities in Hawaii have remained little known in the USA or elsewhere in English-speaking world. A few English-language authors have written about Yoshikawa, though. Some have praised his work as a spy, others have dismissed Yoshikawa's spy work as "routine" or have insisted that he had many accomplices. Clearly, it is up to the reader to determine the truth of these competing views.

As Yoshikawa's memoirs include abundant details of his life before, during, and after the Pacific War, the suggestion that he should be defined by his nine months of espionage activity in Hawaii is in any case ill-founded. By writing so extensively about his recollections, Yoshikawa is able to tell his own story while describing the broader political and social changes that defined his life and times.

Although Yoshikawa's views are sometimes challenging, his eyewitness accounts of the pre-war period, the attack on Pearl Harbor, and the aftermath of the attack are compelling to read. In these memoirs the Japanese serviceman charged with the remarkable task of spying on the U.S. Pacific Fleet provides his readers with a unique perspective on the Pacific War.

This translation would not have been possible without the knowledgeable and helpful people who gave me their assistance. Takeo Yoshikawa's daughter Yoko and Mr. Matsufuji of Mainichi Wanz provided me with full access to Yoshikawa's text and I am very grateful to them for their support. Many thanks to Robbyn Swan, Alana Wilcox, and Henry Wilson. Special thanks to Ryoko Sumitomo for her valuable help. In addition, I am thankful to Mr. Soyama, Rachel Weeks, and Bud Hannings. I would also like to thank my family for their steadfast support while I worked on this project.

Andrew Mitchell
Toronto, Canada

Preface to the Japanese Edition (1963)

"East wind, rain." This cryptic message was broadcast by the Japanese government to its diplomatic missions overseas as the Pacific War broke out. "Japan is now at war against the United States," was its meaning. As Japan's Consul-General in Honolulu heard those words, Japan's air troops were releasing bombs like drops of rain upon Pearl Harbor and I was serving as an undercover agent in Honolulu.

This book contains a factual account of all of the espionage activities that I carried out during my ten months undercover in Hawaii. It also looks back at my experiences, both before and after the war, that were in some way connected to my intelligence reporting work. All of the opinions that I hold in this book, and indeed my recollections themselves, are subjective and thus have their limits. Yet while there are certainly some errors in my account, I have made every effort to faithfully record my experiences.

During the pre-war period, Japan didn't take the decision to go to war simply because of some arbitrary decisions made by Japan's military leaders. It happened because Japan lacked enough people of influence and the popular will necessary to forestall the march to war. Finally, without fully knowing what was happening, the country found itself feverishly embarking upon a fanatical war. Thus, the entire Japanese people (notwithstanding a small minority), whether they wished to or not, whether at the vanguard or the rearguard, poured all of their energies into the cause and propelled the war effort onward.

It was a time when everyone believed that there was only one way forward. I myself was one of those who helped our war effort and I had some extraordinary experiences while doing so. Yet I didn't pretend to understand the war right from the start, nor did I seek to take on the role of a spy. Nor had I, through any of my initiatives, hoped to take on any special role. I was simply swept up by the current of the times as Japan embarked upon the journey it seemingly had no other choice but to take.

Preface to the Japanese Edition (1963)

People often ask me, "What motivated you to work as a spy?" I am unsure how to reply, however. In order to answer this puzzling question, I've decided it's best if I change gears and begin by recounting some of my experiences from the time of my birth to the time that I joined the navy. I may then be able to provide reasons that explain why my taking on the role of a secret agent was inevitable.

In the recent past, many have criticized me for writing texts about the war. "Not even the Americans, the victors of the war, will say a single word about it," they say. "But you go around leaking state secrets. What sort of nonsense is that?" As a result, I am likely to receive further censure from every quarter soon after this edition is published. But now that modern-day Japan has decided to give up all warfare, I believe that it is absolutely necessary to reveal Japan's past state secrets in order to provide people with information that is cause for reflection, soul-searching, and repentance. It is, isn't it?

Although present-day Japan has taken a real turn for the better in comparison to that of the pre-war period, the wounds of war still remain fresh in people's hearts and minds. People remain tormented by introspection, remorsefulness, feelings of hate, and melancholy. I count myself as one of those troubled by such worries.

The telegrams presented in this book were actually sent by me. Furthermore, they were intercepted, deciphered, and translated by U.S. forces. I had no other choice but to use the deciphered cables and translate them back into Japanese. Although there are undoubtedly a few places where two or three words are not identical to those used in the original telegrams, this has in no way affected their meaning. I put enormous effort into drafting those telegrams and to this day I remember them with great clarity. It can safely be said that this text is currently the only Japanese source of those telegrams.

To conclude I wish to thank Mr. Michio Komatsu for helping to make this edition possible. I also offer my heartfelt thanks to Mrs. Furumori, Mrs. Tominaga, and Mrs. Yoshihisa for providing materials for this book.

        Takeo Yoshikawa
        6 November 1963
        Signed at the author's temporary residence in Tokyo

Part One
A Letter

1

Ancient Light Hermitage

When I wake up inside the Ancient Light Hermitage, I find it's already late morning. The shadow cast by the walnut tree just outside is already covering the window. I decide that it must be past ten o'clock. "It looks nice outside today," I tell myself loudly as I jump out of bed. "I should do my training exercises!" It has been raining non-stop for the past two or three days and I've been unable to train. My wrists are itching to get into action.

My so-called training is what's known as "knife throwing." It's an activity that looks somewhat like throwing a baseball and it requires that you use all of your energy to hurl a blade. That's all there is to it.

My only target is made out of thick planks. It's two meters across, three meters high and has been covered with straw matting. Concentric circles have been drawn on the target, the widest of which is 30 cm in diameter. I fling knives at the target from ten or fifteen paces away.

Although the knives are double-edged and look something like curling irons, they have been sharpened and can penetrate two traditional straw *tatami* mats (each roughly five cm thick). In fact, they are sufficiently sharp to kill a person. From an appropriate distance, it's possible to throw the tip of the knife right into the bull's-eye.

If you should ask me why I am interested in throwing knives, I would say it's because I feel that all athletic success comes down to the fraction of a second that's required to take command of the moment. It's because of the need to master this moment of opportunity that those athletes who wish to refine their dexterity, and learn how to take control, cannot stint on their training. This is especially true in knife throwing, which is a sport that involves primordial technique and dexterity. It's also a sport where hitting the target depends on actions decided upon and taken in a split second.

The courtyard is covered with a moss that has soaked up the morning dew and is as green as moldy bread. The maple tree has just begun to reveal its slightly reddish buds while the buds on the lespedeza bush are giving off a silvery shine.

With my left hand clutching ten knives, I follow the stone markers that lead to the training area. When I reach a spot 15 paces away from the target, I come to a stop. Facing the target, I become quiet and very calm. Then, in an instant, ten thousand thoughts are stilled.

I take hold of a knife with my right hand, I assume the throwing position and throw with a sweeping motion. The only sound I hear is a dull thud as the knife hits the bull's eye. I feel very satisfied with both the accuracy and speed of my throw. I know that if the first knife is thrown well, it will be quite easy to send the second and third knives into the bull's eye alongside it.

"It's really not going badly this morning!" I tell myself as I feel my happiness growing at the thought of just how much my throwing skills have improved. You might say that the rate of "direct hits" correlates closely with the knife thrower's state of mind.

At a distance of 15 paces, you can normally be fairly confident about hitting the target about 80 percent of the time. As you move further away from the target, however, the success rate falls ever lower. Since the knife rotates as it flies through the air toward the target, it sometimes fails to sink into the target when your timing is off. At such times, the knife may bounce off the target and onto the ground with a "ba-ta" sound. At other such times, the blade enters the target at an angle that does not allow the knife to hold on firmly. Then, even if the throw was on target, the knife is left drooping helplessly.

Normally, such silly games are only of interest to adolescents. Indeed, my wife furrowed her brow when she began to watch me throw knives. "You are always playing that childish game," she would say. "Forget about it! It's too dangerous!" Yet I have always been, and I am still, serious about practicing. What's more, I make and sharpen my own knives and have a few dozen of my own handmade blades stored away. I have been practicing knife throwing for many years now. My son, who is in his third year of high school, likes to practice the sport with me.

Having said all this, it only takes the fraction of a second when the knife leaves the hand to determine whether or not the blade will hit its target. There is no way to recalibrate once the blade has left the hand, nor is there any point in trying to "will" the knife into the target with mental energy. As it's not possible to explain the significance of that delicate moment when the knife leaves the hand, empty words alone would never suffice to teach a would-be knife thrower this art. The secret lies in surveying the target from a distance and correctly gauging the speed of the throw, the action of the rotation, and the direction of the blade. All of these techniques must come together in a single moment. Only then is there a chance that the knife will hit its mark.

I'm afraid that even a powerful computer would be helpless in the face of so many calculations. Yet man's natural intelligence is able to make these calculations in a split second. Man even has the potential to reach a 100 percent rate of success.

Knife throwing was the way through which I came to hone this kind of natural intelligence. Throw it, pull it out, and then come back. After returning, throw it yet again. You have to go back and forth like this until your body is covered in sweat. Only then can you find the sweet spot.

That morning in early spring, when I was out practicing, I heard my wife call out to me.

"There's a letter here for you, dear!"

"Where's it from?" I asked her while my eyes remained fixed upon the target.

"It looks as if it's from America, but I cannot say who it's from."

I decided to finish throwing the knives that remained in my hand. But as I had already lost my concentration, not one knife hit the target. Thus, I rolled down the shirtsleeve on my throwing arm and went back inside for some hot tea.

"Is it from a celebrity-seeker?"

"It seems to be, but there are so many words packed in there that I can't make heads or tails of it."

"There are some celebrity-seekers overseas who send me letters, so that wouldn't surprise me. Ha, ha, ha."

"Be careful! Sometimes even the silliest of situations can take a turn for the worse and bring you no end of trouble… Not long ago, yet another customer who had pulled up for some petrol said to me: 'You are a second-generation Hawaiian, aren't you Madam? Where did you and your husband tie the knot?' That sort of thing really makes you wonder."[1]

"What's that got to do with anything? Who has ever told you that you don't look Japanese?"

"No, it's not that. It's just that everybody accuses you of writing impossible stuff."

In fact, my wife really doesn't look Japanese. And soon after our son was born, he developed a most vexing boil. Then, after he had finished primary school, his hair turned dark brown. As a result, others increasingly regarded my wife as "mixed-race." Once this sort of rumor mongering has begun, it can be very hard to put an end to. Whenever I am out and about with all the members of my family, there are always lookers-on giving each other little winks or whispering in each other's ear.

Even though no one in our village doubts that my wife and I are of pure Japanese descent, people from elsewhere invariably take the news of my extended stay in Hawaii and connect that with my wife's exotic-looking face to reach the arbitrary conclusion that my wife is of mixed-race.

"You had better take a good look at this letter!"

My wife stood alongside and looked at me, perhaps dying of curiosity because she had tried to read the letter and couldn't understand a word of it. She then placed the opened letter on the table before leaving the room.

2

A Letter from a U.S. Soldier

The sender of the letter was a stranger from the United States; its small envelope hadn't been labeled with a proper mailing address. The envelope had become fairly dirty during its travels and it gave me the distinct impression that it had passed hands in various locales before finally arriving here.

The letter was written on five pages, all completely filled on both sides. On a sixth sheet of paper there was a pen-and-ink portrait of two soldiers, with a background that had been shaded in green. One of the two soldiers portrayed was the sender of the letter.

As this letter so clearly presents one side of the Pearl Harbor Incident story, I have included it here in its entirety:

Dear Mr. Yoshikawa,

In this letter, I want to talk about something that happened during the Second World War. In the summer of 1941, I was an army pilot based at Hickam Field in Hawaii. One day I was working alongside Sergeant Horner, a fellow serviceman (and a good buddy of mine), who hailed from Texas. On that day we had to make a fifteen-minute test flight out of John Rodgers Field. When the test flight was done, Sergeant Horner had some business to attend to elsewhere so I strolled over to the airfield's canteen on my own.

I remember clearly that it was in that canteen that I first happened to see you. At the time, I only saw a Japanese guy (who to this day, I still believe was you) sitting and eating lunch at a table at the east end of the canteen. I decided to sit down there as well.

That guy (who was none other than you) and I discussed lightweight aircraft and the technical aspects of flying. And I can still recall the guy's leather "Leica" brand camera case with the shoulder strap he was wearing over his shoulder. I also remember that the guy took my picture outside the canteen after we had finished our meals.

Can you still recall any of these details? At the time, I said to you: "My Army Air Force buddy is a big guy from Texas, with a big square face and two big hands. He is open and honest, like a child. He is also a sincere Christian and he carries his copy of the Bible wherever he goes. He couldn't join me for lunch today because he had other business to attend to."

I also said that I flew training aircraft, and that I circled over the Dole Pineapple Factory while making training flights.

Part One—A Letter

On December 7th 1960, Mr. Riley Allen (the editor of the *Honolulu Star*) sent me a clipping from his newspaper. In the clipping was a report with the headline "Concerning Japan's December 7th 1941 Surprise Attack on Pearl Harbor and the Spying Incident Involving the Japanese Consulate's Vice Consul, Tadashi Morimura."

After reading the article, I remembered you. I clearly remembered having run into you at the airfield on two or three occasions.

I am now forty-two years old. Sergeant Horner died at the Queen's Hospital on the day after the air raid (8 December). At the time of the air raid he was at Hickam Field, somewhere between the Number 11 and Number 3 aircraft hangars, which were both bombed. His arms and legs were blown off.

Through sheer luck, I managed to escape the attack unscathed. But, at around eight o'clock, I witnessed the bombing of the soldiers' canteen in the northeast corner of the base.

To this day I have never wished to say anything spiteful towards you because of your role in the Pearl Harbor attack, but I can't understand how at that time (or at the present time) it could be possible for someone in plainclothes to enter a restricted zone on a military base. How could such a person casually take photos of strategic sites, whether at ground level or at higher elevations? And how could such a person be allowed to make use of the local press or other sources to compile intelligence reports?

Moreover, you were a Japanese citizen and you actually ran around the military air base taking pictures at will. How was it that our military authorities somehow managed to turn a blind eye to your activities? In the final analysis, we were too stupid! Both our officers and our soldiers were completely apathetic.

That morning, I noticed a squadron of "Zero" fighter planes storming into Pearl Harbor. And even though I did all that I could, by shouting "Those are Japanese aircraft!" and explaining that I could make out the "Rising Sun" symbol under the wings of the planes that were flying over the Officers' Club, nobody wanted to listen to a word I had to say. They just wouldn't believe that something terrible was happening.

Mr. Yoshikawa, I want to give you the title "Gentleman Spy." You certainly did your job and you did it well!

During the air raid, the Colonel asked me to take down the sign that was hanging outside the camp's HQ. In the midst of falling bombs, the sound of bombs exploding, and awfully thick, billowing smoke (try to imagine it if you will), I somehow managed to climb up to the sign. I was just twenty-three years old at the time, the same age as Sergeant Horner. Horner was at that moment in front of the Number 11 aircraft hangar, replacing the tires on a B-18 bomber. We were both pilots of medium bombers, flying B-18s with the 11th Bomber Squadron.

As I recall, we were preparing for war in the summer of 1941, but by December there were rumors that war was not going to break out after all. As a result, we let our guard down.

I have been trying so hard to figure out how to convince the Soviets, the Americans and the American navy, and Queen Elizabeth of Great Britain, to throw away their plans for making war—and it's making my head hurt. Yet I believe that even if Moscow and America can come to terms, there will still be another "Pearl Harbor Incident." And that means there will probably be another World War.

There were some other events that took place on the day of the surprise attack on Pearl Harbor that I still find hard to forget:

At 08:05 I was with the first-lieutenant, our sergeant, and rank and file soldiers,

2. A Letter from a U.S. Soldier

taking cover inside the quarters at the northern end of Hickam's new barracks when we came under machine-gun attack from a Japanese "Zero" aircraft. The marksman aboard didn't aim well and the bullets fired from the aircraft missed us by about one meter, hitting a nearby coral reef instead and sending up a plume of smoke. None of us was injured by the attack.

But when the aircraft was making to leave the scene, the pilot directed his plane right at us. As he drew near to us, he raised his thumb up just in front of his nose. We replied by making the same gesture at him (The gesture means that a challenge has been made and shows scorn for one's opponent.)

At 08:30 I was helping to evacuate women and children from the officers' quarters at Hickam Field.

At around 09:30 there were large numbers of the dead and wounded who needed to be transported to Honolulu or Ford Island. While the huge air base was in a state of total disorder and confusion, I was ordered to make the roadways passable for the trucks.

Mr. Yoshikawa, I have always felt that you did the most splendid of jobs on the field of battle. But whenever I remember 1941, it doesn't matter to me if you did well or even if the American military did well. Both sides were simply playing at spying or at making war, nothing more.

I say this because the American military didn't believe that there was going to be a war and because you were strutting around sightseeing with a camera. It was all too easy for you to fulfill your duties as a spy. In truth, what you did at Pearl Harbor was a most despicable, sordid piece of double-dealing. But in the end, we lost everything.

I have already mentioned my Air Corps buddy, James Horner. I was told that while he was in the Queen's Hospital he said: "Charles I won't be seeing you anymore! Almighty God has just told me 'It's your turn to go!'" And after that, we never did see one another again.

As I think back to that time, I see that you accomplished the mission that was given to you in the most outstanding way. Likewise, I did my utmost while doing what I was told and I even earned a medal for doing so.

Today, I sincerely believe that both Japan and the United States need to work together to build a free world. We need to meet together in all places, cooperate, and dedicate ourselves to the task of building a lasting peace for all mankind.

Charles Mason
6 San Jose Street
Missouri, USA

After I finished reading this very long letter, I felt as if an old wound had been reopened. Charles Mason, the sender of the letter, said that he was now 42 years old. As a man in his forties, he was part of the generation that now formed the backbone of America. I believe that he was candidly expressing his generation's worldview and philosophy. From the style of his letter, it was easy to tell that he was not a man of any great culture or learning. He was just an ordinary citizen and nothing more.

In his letter, he quite surprisingly put forward the idea that the guy he had run into in the summer of 1941 was me. That was a ridiculous idea! Although people did not have a heightened sense of vigilance at that time, I'm afraid that no spy would have been so brazen as to stroll around a restricted military zone while carrying a camera. All the same, I could understand what he wanted to say.

For some time now, people have been trying to persuade me to write my story and I have written down a few notes to make a record of it. I have also accepted invitations to appear on radio and television to tell my story. Despite this, in my heart of hearts, I know that I have never sought to boast about my activities as a spy. All I have ever wanted to do is truthfully detail all that I did to carry out the burdensome responsibilities I was charged with during that momentous era.

Whenever I reflect on the massacres and destruction that my activities as a secret agent helped to bring about, I also remember that my efforts to help save the homeland perversely helped to bring about its crushing defeat. All of which, quite naturally, leaves me feeling desperately ashamed and bereft of any place to hide. Despite the fact that I was following orders, I know that there is no escaping my responsibility.

I have always felt that if the opportunity were to arrive, I would return to Pearl Harbor to apologize to those who were killed there and to all those who suffered from the calamity.

I am "Morimura," the very man who took on the role of secret agent at Pearl Harbor. Nearly two years before the war began, while in Japan, I agreed to go undercover in Hawaii. At the end of March 1941, I took up my official duties as a secretary at the Japanese Consulate-General in Honolulu and unofficially began working as an undercover agent. From the date of my arrival there to 8 December 1941, the day when Japan launched its bombs upon Pearl Harbor, I worked day and night to send telegrams to Tokyo about the strategic positioning of the U.S. Navy.[1]

I was the "man behind the curtain" who guided Japan's air fleet into position for the surprise attack. And yet, I was simply a 28-year-old naval officer retired from active duty. So why exactly was I obliged to take on this task, which was to decisively affect Japan's fate? What did I have to do to carry out my enormously important responsibilities? And just how much mental anguish did the carrying out of those duties cause me?

In order to answer those very questions, I have decided to embark upon this process of recollection. Perhaps the reason for my doing so has a lot to do with the fact that more than 20 years of astonishing change has already taken place since that day when Japan's destiny was decided.

3

Memories of Childhood and Growing Up

A person's place of birth is important and ought to be taken seriously. In some countries, an individual's place of birth not only determines their citizenship but also has a bearing on their personality and temperament. As a result, one's place of birth is usually essential on passports, CVs, and questionnaires.

When speaking with foreigners, I am again and again asked the same questions about my place of birth:

"Where were you born?"

"Were you born in the countryside or in the city?"

"Near the mountains or near the seaside?"

When the person making the inquiries happens to have been born in the same sort of place, they are usually quite pleased by my reply.

Whenever I'm asked, "Were you born near the mountains or near the seaside?" I always have to think carefully. For those accustomed to living inland on a large continent, every place in Japan seems close to both mountains and the seaside. Yet those born in Yamanashi Prefecture, or in one of the prefectures traversed by the Hida Mountains, will undoubtedly reply, "Near the mountains."

Since I was born in the city of Matsuyama, in Ehime Prefecture, it's not so easy to reply. That's because it's only 30 minutes from the seaside by public bus and just ten kilometers on foot from some of Shikoku's mountains. "It's a small city that's not far from the sea," is my usual reply. When I reply in this way, my answer seems to satisfy everyone's expectations quite nicely. They will usually respond to this news by saying: "That's what I thought. That's why you're good at swimming. You must have wanted to go out to sea ever since you were a child. That's why you joined the navy, isn't it?"

Actually, I come from a small village in the countryside. When I was small, we only went to the seaside once or twice a year to bathe in the saltwater. As for the mountains, we only went there to collect sticks, wild fruit or flowers, and that was it. You could say that although I grew up near the coast, I never really had a great affinity for the sea. And though I was born in Matsuyama, my ancestral village is a small farming village called Shigenobu in Ehime Prefecture's Onsen District. My family has lived there since the time of my paternal grandfather.

Apparently, my paternal grandfather got rid of his pregnant wife (my paternal grandmother) and eloped there with his lover. They arrived in the village walking hand-in-hand and quickly made a home for themselves there. My paternal grandfather was a simple, straightforward man who liked to look after others. He soon won the respect and trust of the other villagers and became successful in business.

After my father was born, his mother raised him until the age of five. After that, he was raised by his stepmother and he soon began to help with the family chores. As my father did not get on well with his stepmother or her relatives, he decided to set off and make his own way in the world when he was a young man.

Not long after he left home, the Russo-Japanese War broke out and my father was called up for military service. He was subsequently injured in the northeast of China, at Jiguan Mountain. After that, he obtained a low-level government post and began working in Matsuyama.

It was around that time that I was born. My mother was a country girl from a village near Matsuyama. She was eleven years younger than my father and extremely impatient. I don't think that their marriage was an especially happy one, but they did have four children and they spent their lives together. Both of my parents were frank and upright common folk. I seem to have inherited my father's physique and my mother's temperament.

I was born in the final year of Emperor Meiji's reign, on 7 March 1912.[1] I was, right from the start, a difficult infant who refused breastfeeding. I required cow's milk and rice gruel instead. In addition to that, I suffered from frequent stomach and intestinal troubles and I cried often.

By the time I was a small child, I began suffering from the effects of malnutrition. I am told that I was so unhealthy that the doctor refused to treat me on several occasions. Eventually, my parents themselves grew resigned to the idea that I wouldn't live long because I was so ill.

One day, while holding me in his arms (emaciated, tiny, and deathly pale as I was), my father looked into my eyes and had a sudden inspiration. "Perhaps you aren't going to live much longer," he said. "So why don't we see what happens when we get you doing some exercise! If that doesn't work, and you die an early death, it won't be for lack of trying and you should die contented!"

After my father had resolved to do this, he cut off all contact with the doctor and refused to give me any more medicine. He then began to put me

3. Memories of Childhood and Growing Up

through very intensive exercise sessions. Though I was still walking to school hand-in-hand with my mother, as my gait was a bit unsteady, my father soon had me climbing up the nearby hills, running in the school playground, and taking a wooden scythe to the riverside to cut flowers. He hoped that all of these activities would help make me stronger and more curious about my surroundings.

I soon began to run with my father. Although this left me white-faced and tired I still followed him, huffing and puffing. At the time, my father was just 30 years old. He was in top physical condition and had gone through military training, while I was a small boy just two or three years old.

Now that I think about it, his decision to put me through military-style training exercises does seem a bit cruel. From a modern perspective, however, the techniques that my father adopted might be described as a combination of hard physical exercise and naturopathy. By using such techniques, he turned me into a healthy child of the sturdiest sort.

I have quite vivid memories of something that happened around that time. My father had told us that he needed to go far away on business and he was not at home for some time. When he finally returned, he gave me a small Japanese toy boat that was made with sheet metal. My elder sister was very pleased then, as I recall, because my father had returned with a present for every member of the family. Actually, we were all very happy because we rarely had any toys to play with.

That toy boat was shiny, it had a glistening golden yellow hue, and was obviously very posh. I attached a cotton string to the boat and placed it in a drainage dyke. After I had pulled lightly on the string, it quickly made waves while moving straight ahead. That gently rocking, golden-yellow boat really was wonderful! As I watched the boat gently glide across the water, I felt surprised. I went from one end of the dyke to the other, pulling it from this side to the other and then from the other side back to this side. Time and again, I found myself asking the same questions:

"Why is the boat able to float like that?"

"How does it move forward so smoothly?"

When I pulled gently on the string, it created a series of waves that were close together. When I pulled with force, it made a series of waves that were spaced further apart. Yet all of the waves that it produced were of the same size. "What is the reason for that?" I wondered.

Later on, I came up with the idea of taking the boat to a small river some distance away to float it on those waters. When my mother said she wouldn't allow it, I hid the boat under my arm and stole off!

At the time, a period of heavy rain had just ended and it was beginning to clear. The rain had stripped the gravel road of its heavier stones and exposed many small, sharper ones. My bare feet were badly gashed as a result.

I caught a small crab that was trying to scurry off the road and into the tall grass at the road's edge and then I put it inside the boat. I found the sound of the crab scurrying back and forth on the boat's sheet metal bottom most interesting.

Before long I was at the river's edge, kneeling upon a wooden bridge that was some three meters in length. I had hoped to put the boat right down and watch it float on the water. Yet after the rain, the river's current had become much stronger than usual. The tea-brown waters were up to the top of the riverbank and the river had become a raging torrent. Although the sight of the river gave me pause, I soon decided to place all my hopes on my boat.

I was only just able to see my boat floating under the billowing waves of water. It seemed like a large ship cleaving its way through stormy seas. When I pulled tightly on the string, I could feel vibrations as the boat tossed in the water. I was soon completely caught up in a world of fantasy. I had previously seen pictures of steamship skippers on the high seas, sailing for foreign lands, and they all had the same spirited expression that I was wearing that day. I too had become a captain. I felt a kind of carefree energy that is difficult to describe.

Even though it was my first such experience, I fixed my gaze on the boat and caught its every movement. I skillfully maneuvered the vessel by using both hands to pull on the string and change its direction. I seemed to have become the most expert and experienced of navigators. I was delighted by the game I was playing because it felt so very real.

Just when I was feeling happiest about my game, I heard a shout coming from behind me. I turned my head back with a start and suddenly the pressure from the string that I was holding in my hands increased enormously. The string couldn't take the pressure from the boat's hull and it broke unexpectedly. The happy vibrations that I had felt in my hands stopped abruptly and the boat was swept off in the spray!

I hastily pulled in the string with the thought I could bring the boat back, but it was no use. The boat was floating further and further away. I couldn't believe my eyes! In an instant, I was drained of energy. It felt as if my entire being had been soaked by coldness and disappointment simultaneously.

"Boy! It's too dangerous there! The riverbank is going to fall. Get back here quickly!"

"Hey… Over here! This … side!"

A group of people wearing straw sandals and clothing made of rushes were squishing though puddles of stagnant water as they approached. They were common folk, risking their lives trying to shore up the riverbanks. I had no idea that the wooden bridge that I was standing on was about to be swept away. I was still gazing at my boat as it floated ever further away. And that is my first memory of a boat.

3. Memories of Childhood and Growing Up

Thanks to the fact that I had begun intensive physical training during my early childhood, I got used to sleeping whenever I was tired and eating whenever I was hungry. My day-to-day routine was disorganized, if not haphazard. Consequently, when the time came for me to begin primary school (with all its rules and its mission of instilling self-discipline), I felt extremely uncomfortable and frequently skipped my lessons. This meant that my grades were not good and that made me hate school all the more.

So, after I had left home for school in the morning, I would run over to the extensive, hallowed woods that stood beside a nearby Shinto shrine. Once in the woods, I would play with magical tortoises and fish all day long before returning home.

While I was in the woods by the Shinto shrine, I would sometimes end up helping the soldiers who did their training exercises there. I might carry a bag of pastries that their commanding officer had given them or keep an eye on the stuffed bread and sweets that they had brought with them.

My father used to flog me whenever he learned of this. He would flog me until he was out of breath. He would even tie me to a pillar and leave me outside all night. Despite this, I never once thought that I had done anything wrong.

As my mother soon began to worry that her little boy was going to turn into a bad egg, she would drag me to school nearly every day while I protested vehemently all the way there. On one such occasion, I bit my mother's hand. She endured the pain and managed to drop me off at the school, though she wasn't able to wipe the blood off her hand until then.

My father's income was quite low, so my mother had to take on various casual jobs to earn a bit of extra money for our household. This was during the First World War, when Japan was experiencing very high levels of inflation. Our family's financial situation was proving to be quite difficult around that time and rice riots were breaking out all over the country.[2]

When I was attending my classes at school I used to hear stories about arson, murder, and all sorts of other things, but I didn't actually understand what any of it meant. I was inattentive and my thoughts often carried me far away to the countryside with its flowers, plants, dragonflies, and butterflies.

Whenever a dragonfly was around me, flying back and forth, I wanted nothing more than to find a way to catch it. To be completely honest, I myself found my wild nature somewhat odd. I suppose it has always been a part of my personality, though.

One day, there was a group of foreigners going over to the military parade grounds. As I recall, Matsuyama's air squadron was celebrating "Military Flag Day" just then. Before long, the news that airplanes were going to take part in an air show caused a commotion that spread all over town.

That was the first time that I had ever seen an airplane. Looking its yellow fuselage and the many steel cables that stretched between the upper and lower wings was such a special experience. It was very nice to see.

Soon enough, I saw a foreigner in a strange uniform make his way through the crowd to get to the airplane. He waved to the crowd as he climbed into the aircraft. And then there was a thunderous roar as the aircraft spat out black smoke and promptly began to taxi. At that very moment, I heard my younger brother start to cry. When I asked him what was wrong, I learned that the great gust of wind produced by the airplane had blown off his hat and sent it rolling behind us.

With great difficulty the two of us managed to move through the crowd and recover the hat, which had been so trampled upon that it didn't even look like a hat. By the time I had just about coaxed my brother to stop his crying, the airplane was already very high in the air and far away.

"Big brother, let's go!"

It seemed that my physically weak younger brother was not only uninterested in the noise and bravado of the spectacle, he actually felt a bit intimidated by it. I had no choice but to leave the crowd as it wildly cheered the aircraft. Greatly disappointed, I led my little brother away from the parade grounds and back home again.

My younger brother suffered from a strange food allergy that prevented him from eating rice or vegetables. At every meal, three times a day, he ate only a piece of tofu. Father and mother tried everything possible to get him to eat some rice congee or vegetables, but he would always refuse to eat such things. If he tasted just a little bit of green onion, he would throw a tantrum and spit it out. If he was served tofu that was covered in rice, he would pick off every last grain of rice before eating the tofu plain. Yet he would happily polish off every last bit of tofu when it was served plain. As for pastries? He wouldn't go near them.

Since he suffered from this strange aversion to food, he was physically weak. When he was five years old, in the springtime, he came down with a very bad cold and couldn't get up from his bed. After a week, the doctor said that he was probably suffering from pneumonia.

"My tummy hurts, big brother! My tummy hurts!" he kept saying during his last two days.

Finally, while crying out in agonizing pain, my little brother died. My family hired several rickshaws and my brother's coffin was carried to the Buddhist burial grounds on the mountainside. There he was laid to rest in a rectangular grave that was very long and very deep. As I peered into the freshly dug section of the visibly hard and shiny red earth, I noticed that there was a little water at the very bottom.

Then some people gently lowered the white wooden coffin, which had been secured with thick straw rope, into the grave. I couldn't stop myself from feeling most unhappy, even though my brother might have found the place cool and shady.

"Close it up," said one of the adults supervising nearby. "Put the earth over it now!"

When I heard those words, a wave of sorrow entered my heart and I couldn't stop myself from sobbing.

I remember that as I was gently picking up a small piece of earth to throw into the grave, a large clump of earth fell from the grave wall and onto the coffin and it landed with a loud thud. When I heard that thud, I imagined I could hear my brother speaking to me: "Big brother! That really hurts!"

Without intending to, I fell to my knees beside a mound of earth and began to wail. "Waaaa!"

"It's all right! It's all right! Don't cry! We have to fill it in now!"

Some of the adults began using spades and hoes to fill in the grave.

"Hey! It looks like that little troublemaker can actually feel unhappy."

"We never thought that little rascal would cry, did we eh?"

Many people were discussing me, but I bit my lip and pretended that I couldn't hear them.

Not long after that, my lovely little brother had become a child with the "feeling and wisdom of Zen."

That's what was written on his white wooden grave marker.[3]

My younger brother's death was a turning point for me. In an instant, I grew up. I became an introspective, diligent son and I was mischievous no longer. In the third term of my third year at school, I served as the classroom monitor. I also I won a prize for my composition "The death of my little brother" in an essay competition held across the whole prefecture. My teacher thought highly of me and my parents both stopped worrying about my behavior. From then on, I put all my energy into doing well in my studies.

My father was a very upright man who was extremely serious and highly disciplined. His personality made it impossible for him to try to curry favor with the powerful and influential. As a result, he decided to retire and return to his village when he was in his forties. He then took up hunting and fishing and, because he was a gifted swordsman, he began teaching me the art of swordsmanship when I was ten. Even though I was still but a child, he took no account of it when we were practicing. All I could do was take up my bamboo rod, put on my bravest battle face, and counter him. It didn't matter whether it was midwinter or the summer holidays, we always had to practice. I even had to take a beating from him on school days for an hour before I was allowed to go off to school.

At times he would knock me over and I would fight back my tears while getting up again, at which point he would set upon me with more blows. If

I have an unyielding personality, you might say that it has something to do with this training.

I still didn't know how to swim when I was that age, so one day my father took me out to learn how. We waded into the river together until the water was up to my waist, but then I became frightened and let go of my father's hand before hurrying back to shallow water. As a result of which my father told me that I had no guts and grabbed hold of me, paying no attention whatsoever to my crying, before dragging me to a place where the water was higher than my head. From there, he pushed me into even deeper water.

Then and there, at risk of losing my life, I learned how to swim. Fortunately, I had always been the stubborn type. This, and my sudden resolve to conquer the water, helped me to stay afloat. I didn't merely swim in the river after that, I also practiced swimming whenever I went to the public bathhouse to bathe. I was sometimes reprimanded for this by the bathhouse manager, but I continued to practice there on the sly. During the winter, I often filled a large bowl with water and put my head right inside it so as to practice holding my breath underwater.

Over time, all of my efforts had the desired effect. The following year, I took part in a long-distance swimming event that covered a distance of two nautical miles. The year after that, I took part in the local swim meet and won first prize.

4

Navy Life

After finishing my studies at the village school, I entered a middle school run by the local prefecture in Matsuyama. Every day I went to school and back home again on the same sort of small fire truck that is described in Natsume Sōseki's novel *Botchan*.[1]

Although I wasn't the most brilliant student at my middle school, I worked hard to complete all of my assignments and I proved to be an exceptional athlete in both track and field and swimming. I did not strive superficially for grades, though. Instead, I always tried to thoroughly grasp the very heart of a subject. I put all my effort into getting a complete education.

In 1930 I wrote and passed the entrance exam for the Naval Academy.[2] Although my father was very happy that I was going to be a military man, in my heart of hearts I was far less pleased about it. I particularly enjoyed the natural sciences and I was especially interested in mineralogy. I had initially hoped to continue my studies at a top-level professional academy where those entering the mining industry were trained, but I was unable to persuade my father about this wisdom of this. In the end, I complied with his wishes.

Passing the entrance exam for the Naval Academy was no easy matter. At that time, putting yourself forward as a candidate meant competing against more than 4,000 other candidates for one of only 130 places at the academy. It's fair to say that the candidates were talented youths from all over the country. Whenever I remember those days while looking at pictures of my fellow students in my photo album, I also think of my own mediocre abilities and feel amazed that I too was destined to have a place within that brilliant group.

The Head of the Academy was Admiral Osami Nagano, who would later serve as Chief of Staff at the Navy General Staff.[3] As the main aim of his pedagogical stewardship was to motivate students to study independently, our instructors only covered the key points and central themes during our lessons. This meant that my fellow students and I were obliged to carry out further investigations and test our assumptions on our own time. As I was not exactly the brightest of students, studying at the Naval Academy left me feeling quite drained.

As a result of the restrictions imposed by the so-called 5:5:3 Treaty, the Imperial Japanese Navy was clearly inferior in strength to its U.S. and British counterparts.[4] Therefore, it was always stressed to us that the Imperial Japanese Navy needed to "make the most of" its natural intelligence, energy, and enthusiasm to compensate for its relatively inferior strength in vessel numbers. This slogan practically became a directive within the navy. Of course, the same held true for all of us at the Naval Academy. We were expected to carry out our course work and other duties with the "make the most of it" spirit at all times. Whether we were getting up in the morning, studying, or retiring for the night, we always had to adhere to the most rigorous rules and regulations.

Moreover, all of the sports and competitions that formed a part of our training (rowing, mountaineering, team jousting, open-air war games, practice drill competitions held aboard ship, and so on) were selected so as to imbue participants with the "fight to the bitter end" spirit of a "never-say-die" warrior.

In order to gain entry to the Naval Academy, students needed to be graduates of traditional preparatory schools, all were required to pass a series of rigorous academic exams, and all had to undergo physical fitness testing as well. The number of recruits accepted by the academy in any given year depended on the specific requirements of our navy. For example, in the middle of Emperor Taishō's reign (the years just before and after 1918) when Japan's "Eight-Eight" naval fleet plan was underway, about 300 recruits were accepted into the Naval Academy each year.[5] Yet by the time Emperor Shōwa's reign began (around 1930), the number of recruits accepted by the academy was down to approximately 130 per year.

Although the majority of the aspiring students who wrote the entrance examinations for the Naval Academy came from Tokyo and Kagoshima, each prefecture was only permitted to put forward two candidates for admission.

Students studied at the Naval Academy for a period of three years and eight months, but were allowed to return home for the summer and winter holidays. With the exception of these periods, students were completely cut off from outside social contact since the island of Etajima was generally inaccessible to the world beyond its shores.

Student life at the academy was extremely busy. We were expected to spend every possible minute with the other members of our work group, from the moment we got up to the moment we retired for the night. This meant that there wasn't even enough spare time to read a newspaper. The curriculum at the academy included all the courses typically required by university programs, especially the applied sciences. Apart from that, there were courses on navigation, torpedo operation, gun operation, radio science, and more. In each course, students were expected to become completely familiar with all of the topics covered.

4. Navy Life

At the Naval Academy, great emphasis was placed upon our moral education. The behavior and style of each student during the exchange of salutes in war games exercises, while marching, or simply in the general carrying out of work duties, was considered highly important. In fact, every occasion was considered equally important in this regard.

Our instructors also aimed to instill their students with both the "spirit" and "moral compass" of a warrior. This was so very characteristic of the navy and particularly challenging for us. In order to cultivate a sense of obedience, an understanding of one's superiors, and a familiarity with the needs of their roles, separate work units that each numbered 40 students (with ten students from each year) were formed. Since the students in the units were chosen from senior and junior years, working together involved discipline, training, and hammering (or being hammered) into shape. Some students were members of the royal family and all of them were enlisted in the same work unit. Their unit became known as "Their Royal Highnesses' Platoon" and every one of its members was filled with pride.

Within the Imperial Japanese Navy, tradition saw to it that the two underlying principles that summed up the spirit of the navy were passed down through the generations. These were: (i) lay down your life for your country and (ii) attack first to subdue. You might say that the Naval Academy was built so that these two principles could be passed down.

There wasn't a day when the Naval Academy didn't stress the need for future servicemen to be prepared to give up their lives. Students were told to accept the principle that as soon as you realized that the nation needed your sacrifice, you had to sacrifice your very life to protect it. Every morning when getting up from our bunks, we carefully read the "Imperial Rescript to Soldiers and Sailors." This text was given to the troops by Emperor Meiji himself in order to instill them with heartfelt loyalty to their sovereign and a love of their country.[6]

At the start of my time at the Naval Academy, I didn't really have much of an idea about what believing in the sailor's "bounden duty" meant. I had certainly acquired an awareness of what that meant by the time I graduated, however. That was because I had been living the life of a naval recruit for a considerable period of time. Life at the academy not only strengthened my loyalty to the sovereign and my patriotism, it also deepened my understanding of the serviceman's bounden duty and made me respect that duty very highly.

Whenever I found myself looking at photographs of Naval Academy graduates in the exhibition hall, especially those who had lost their lives during the First Sino-Japanese War and the Russo-Japanese War, I was filled with reverence and admiration and I wanted to sacrifice my own life for my country. Yet to be perfectly honest, I was also terribly afraid of death. Despite having been given a very strict upbringing, along with physical training that was at times quite violent, I couldn't completely free myself of the fear of death. To free myself of this worry and cultivate my inner-self, I decided to take up Zen meditation. Consequently, I have read many books about Zen Buddhism. Zen teachings continue to greatly influence the way that I look at life.

The idea of "attacking first to subdue" has been an important element of so very many military strategies all across the ancient and modern worlds, in both East and West. Thus, the emphasis the Japanese place on dealing the first blow really isn't unique. Every country's military has adopted this principle to some degree. At the Naval Academy, great importance was attached to teaching the philosophy of "taking the battle to the enemy in order to debilitate him" while "going on until your dying breath." The strategic thinking that prevailed in the Imperial Japanese Navy was built upon the concept of controlling the enemy by taking the initiative. Indeed, the attack on Pearl Harbor was conceived, guided, and planned on the basis of this idea.

At the Naval Academy, all of the pole jousting practice, open-air war games exercises, individual swordsmanship competitions, boat races, and the like that we participated in were, without exception, designed to put the "Take the initiative!" philosophy into practice. The use of the surprise attack at Pearl Harbor at the war's start, as well as in subsequent maritime and air attacks elsewhere, proves just how deep-rooted this attack-first-to-subdue thinking was within the navy. It automatically dominated the strategic outlook of every commanding officer.

Although this "take the initiative" mindset was hardly unique to our navy, it was of the greatest importance that the Imperial Japanese Navy's vessels attack with utmost vigor and that they keep on doing so until the last of their sailors' dying breaths. Anyone who is committed to the idea of keeping on until his dying breath can quite often turn something that's *impossible* into something possible.

For example, some recruits at the academy didn't know how to swim when they began their studies there, but after two months of strict training even they were able to participate in a long-distance swimming event over six nautical miles in the sea. Furthermore, they made it all the way to the finish line along with all of their classmates. For the *Shaba* outside the Naval Academy, such an accomplishment would have been impossible to imagine.[7]

Yet another example of this was the small sailboat competition that the academy held every year, a race that covered 15 nautical miles of open sea. After reaching the finish line on Miyajima (Itsukushima Island), students had to climb Mount Misen. But in order to reach that mountain's summit, they were obliged to negotiate about 2,200 meters of mountain paths. Every year that this event was held, several students collapsed upon reaching the top of

4. Navy Life

the mountain. I too endured this ghastly training exercise in November of 1933, just before my graduation.

Right around that time, some recruits had behaved a bit unwisely and this caught the unwanted attention of the media. Consequently, when the members of our graduating class set off for duty in China, we wanted to live up to the academy Head's exhortations about "doing your utmost to fulfill your bounden duty" while "not getting caught up in the confusion of public debate."

Apart from traveling to every part of Japan during that voyage, we also traveled to Hsinking. Although the new capital of distant *Manchukuo* was still under construction at that time, we paid a courtesy call on its ruler Puyi while we were there.[8] We left for Shanghai soon afterwards and we saw the vestiges of the fairly recent "Shanghai Incident" when we sailed up the Yangtze.[9] Seeing the remains of that attack made a very deep impression on us and it left us with the feeling that the way ahead was going to be anything but smooth.

In March of 1934, we left China and returned to Tokyo. There we had an audience with the Emperor before immediately setting off on a long-distance voyage for Paris. Our warships navigated the Indian Ocean, the Suez Canal, and the Mediterranean Sea at 12 nautical miles per hour. At that speed, it's possible to get a good sense of the atmosphere in the foreign countries that you are traveling past. Yet for those of us newly responsible for using the stars to chart our position, taking turns at the ship's helm, and doing other tasks necessary to navigate the high seas, it was certainly not a relaxing voyage.

The two vessels that we took on that expedition, the *Asama* and the *Iwate*, were older cruisers and both were fueled by a mixture of coal and heavy oil. As a result, it was necessary for us to stop and take on more coal at Aden. We were forced to brave the summer-like heat there, alongside the local "coolies." Together, we spent an entire day transporting coal aboard ship.

Soon afterwards, I felt something like a fever coming on, along with abdominal pains. When the ship's medical officer examined me, he discovered that I was suffering from appendicitis. He immediately determined that surgery was the only thing that could be done for it.

The ship had already entered the Red Sea by that time. There wasn't any wind, it was scorching hot under the deep blue sky, and the ship was maintaining its speed at the usual 12 knots per hour. Although the conditions ensured that the ship was very stable, undergoing surgery on such a hot and muggy ship was an almost suffocating experience. To make matters worse, the anesthetic was largely ineffective. So, this was what I heard:

"How is it that this surgical knife is unable to make an incision?"

"Oh, it's rusty!"

"Wipe the sweat off my face and my hands, quickly!"

Part One—A Letter

"Bring another electric fan here!"

"The sweat is dripping off the surgical blade and right inside. Disinfect that well!"

Then, I again heard the Officer-Instructor giving orders:

"Lieutenant-Commander Doctor, take your hand and feel the affected area!"

Standing over me were two or three intern doctors who were doing their training aboard ship. Soon enough, each one in his turn was stretching out a hand to feel the area where I was suffering great pain. Each time they did so, I felt such pain that I needed to shout. Yet as I was afraid of being seen as a serviceman who was unable to endure a little bit of pain, all that I could do was grit my teeth and bear it. All the while I was thinking, "It's bad enough to have to endure getting my appendix cut out, but in addition to that I have to suffer this indignity!"

Through sheer luck the wound left by the surgery didn't fester, which spared me from the misfortune of getting buried at sea. By the time our ships had passed through the Suez Canal and were entering the Dardanelle Straights, I was already able to walk on the main deck.

At Istanbul Turkey, we toured the Dolmabahçe Palace and saw jewelry on display that served as a record of the Near East's past civilizations. In Greece, we were reminded of Persian legends as we rubbed shoulders with sailors from the Greek Navy. In Italy we were received by Mussolini, the flourishing young country's new dictator. At the Louvre in Paris, we encountered the gorgeous art objects that formed part of Western Europe's beautiful and dazzling cultural heritage. All of us left the museum with a new perspective. It was an eye-opening experience.

Japan was already drawing closer to the other Axis powers by that time. As a result, the Japanese navy's maneuvers were beginning to attract a great deal of scrutiny from around the world. Nonetheless, during the course of our travels it was evident that the people we came into contact with really did not know much at all about Japan since we were most frequently mistaken for Chinese citizens. "You are Chinese, aren't you?" people often asked us.

Through this it became clear that Japan was, at best, considered a small country in North-East Asia that was hardly worth mentioning. More often than not, it was simply considered to be one of China's many constituent parts. Japan was proud of its alliance with the other Axis Powers, its Shinto religion, and its unrivalled Imperial Japanese Navy, so it pained me to feel that Japan had nowhere near enough economic power to dominate the world's economy. Nor did it have the ideology or culture suited to leading the many nations of the world.

Despite this, I also noticed during the course of our long voyage that the people living in many of the countries along the Indian Ocean and Mediterranean Sea were very poor. The vast majority of the people in these colonized lands nursed grievances about the occupation of their countries, yet all were in awe of the power of the occupying armies and feared their repressive force. Thus, they found themselves in a helpless position.

In summary, after going on this long journey our understanding of the world was broadened tremendously. Yet I was still in very delicate shape after the surgery that I had undergone. Its detrimental effect on my physical constitution would soon oblige me to petition for early withdrawal from active service.

Several years later, it was because I had been on this extensive voyage that the Navy General Staff decided to reconsider an initial decision to send me to Singapore, as it was thought possible that someone there might recognize me. Consequently, they decided to send me off to a land that was completely unfamiliar to me: Hawaii.

5

Returning Home to Convalesce

When our voyage ended in August 1934, I was assigned work as a communications officer aboard the *Yura*. It was a light cruiser that served as a supply ship for the submarine fleet. In my wildest dreams I never could have imagined that everything I was learning about translating, encrypting, and decrypting messages aboard the *Yura* would play a part in my work during a later posting in Hawaii.

After our training aboard the *Yura* had been completed, I entered the Submarine and Mine Academy at Yokohama to complete some technical courses. I subsequently moved to Kasumigaura where I joined a practice flight team. However, my time there was cut short because I fell ill. I was then moved to the Navy Hospital at Tsukui in Tokyo for a short time. From there, I returned to my village to convalesce over a two-year period.

This period of convalescence in my village produced a dramatic change in my well-being. When I arrived back at home I was a dispirited wanderer, but soon enough I was once again enjoying the warm embrace of Mother Nature. As I strolled along the local hills and riverbanks, I felt as though I couldn't get enough of the joyfulness that came to me from the natural sites in the area.

This two-year period gave me the opportunity to read books on military history and it allowed me to study English. Furthermore, at the local library, I read extensively about the history of Iyo Province (our prefecture's former name) and I studied many of the key texts, both ancient and modern, about naval strategy and maritime battle operations.[1] In short, I read about the most important naval battles from Salamis right up to the First World War.[2]

I read about Lord Nelson. I also read about the battles fought by Jean Bart and other naval officers at the Dogger Banks, as well as the German naval blockade that was contested there. These lessons in naval history made a deep impression on me and I still remember all of them to this day.

Before long, I was studying English with a foreign teacher at a missionary school and I continued my studies there for a year. Every day, no matter what the weather was like, I used to take the train to the school more than 15 kilometers away. After a year of English study there, I was able to read and understand Arthur Conan Doyle's detective novels.

By that time, my elder and younger sisters had both gone away to live with their spouses and I was the only child still living at home with my parents. I was spending a leisurely and relaxing time there while regaining my health. As far as I was concerned, that was my life's golden era. Yet after the Manchurian Incident and the Marco Polo Bridge Incident, my father had noticed that conditions in Japan and abroad were steadily worsening and he was very worried about how my future was going to pan out.[3]

My health problems still remained a concern by the time the waiting period for further orders had exceeded the two-year time limit. I knew then that I would not be able to return to a post aboard a warship, so I reluctantly decided that I would have to take early retirement from active duty in the navy.

In order to perform one final service before taking my retirement, I thought I would go to every neighboring locality and do public relations work for the navy. I began by visiting primary schools to speak to students and then I visited war veterans' groups and local fire halls to deliver speeches. In these places, I discussed the nervousness our nation felt about its national defense.

My speeches covered topics such as "If Japan and America go to war," "The present-day state of the Imperial Japanese Navy," "Strategic advantage and weakness on the Pacific Ocean," and "Navy life." All of these were very warmly received. In addition, I discussed what a future war between America and Japan might look like and I hypothesized about the sorts of situations that might arise during such a war:

"Dark clouds loom over the Pacific as the U.S. Navy finally draws near to Japan. The ships from the U.S. fleet are sailing in a wheel-shaped formation. Our navy, which is without equal, sends out some patrol boats. Soon afterwards, our warships are deployed in battle formation and move in fiercely to engage the enemy fleet. They are determined to meet the enemy and fight a decisive battle there and then on the high seas.

"In the end, because of the support provided by Japan's submarines and speedy destroyers, the Imperial Japanese Navy carries the day and completely destroys the enemy."

When I think back to the ignorant assumptions and arrogant claims I made during my long-winded speeches, I feel ashamed of myself.

Then one day, a naval officer in charge of personnel matters (a captain, who was also from Shikoku) came to my village to give a speech about the political situation. I brought along the village head and several other local gentlemen to listen to the speech. As soon as we saw the captain, they followed my lead as I ordered them to give him a friendly salute.

Yet when the captain noticed that I was wearing the uniform of a naval officer, he reacted with evident displeasure. "Things are so busy in the navy today that there isn't any time for pleasantries," he told me. "We don't have the manpower for all that needs to be done. Yet here you are, a young naval officer, relaxing and having a lovely time in this small village. It's truly shocking, isn't it?"

I told him my story and then I asked him to use his connections within the navy to find a position that would be suitable for me, given my physical condition.

Not long after that, I received a letter from the Navy General Staff that notified me of my new appointment: "Imperial Japanese Navy Ensign Takeo Yoshikawa, you are ordered to report for reserve duty as soon as possible. Please confirm your receipt of this document and your identity by reporting to Bureau 3."

In addition to these instructions, there was another page with details about my salary, future salary increases, and uniform.

When I accepted this appointment, which represented a real step forward on my life's journey, I never suspected that a subsequent posting would see me working as a spy! Yet making this move meant retiring from active duty in the navy, and that was a very painful step for me to take. The thought of going to live anonymously in some big town, which meant leaving my former brothers-in-arms behind, left me feeling vexed.

After I graduated from the Naval Academy, my greatest hope was to be able to make some sort of useful contribution to the nation. I really hadn't planned on using my years in the navy as a way of advancing my career. From the time of my graduation to the day I learned that I was being thrown into a big city's great abyss of anonymity, my outlook hadn't changed. Consequently, I felt some satisfaction about my new appointment. I decided to accept whatever new role the navy had seen fit to give me. I was going to put all of my energy into making a success of it.

I was subsequently moved into my own apartment on the outskirts of Tokyo. Every day, I traveled from there to Kasumigaseki to work at the Navy General Staff.[4]

PART TWO

Storm Clouds Over the Pacific

6

The Navy General Staff

The Imperial Japanese Navy's General Staff Office was located in a two-story red brick building alongside the Navy Ministry. Although the Navy General Staff was structured along the same lines as the Army General Staff Office, a lot of people were unclear about the significance of these shared quarters. Some wrongly believed that the Navy General Staff and the Ministry of the Navy were one and the same thing, while others thought that the Navy General Staff was a branch of the Navy Ministry. In fact, the Ministry of the Navy was a branch of government while the Navy General Staff was under the command of its own Chief of Staff. The main responsibilities of the Navy General Staff were the management and control of naval defense operations.

The Navy General Staff was divided into four Bureaus:

1. Operations (Command and control of all defense operations)
2. Armaments and Supplies
3. Intelligence
4. Communications

The Chief of Staff at the Navy General Staff, the commanding officer there, was always a naval officer of the highest rank (either an admiral or vice-admiral). The Bureau Heads were rear admirals, while the Section Heads within each Bureau were officers of a lesser rank, such as captain. The majority of the personnel within each section, those who did most of the practical work, were either commanders or lieutenant-commanders. Furthermore, each Section was provided with additional personnel such as assistants, translators, etc.

The post I took up was in Bureau 3 (the Intelligence Bureau), Section 8 at the Navy General Staff.

Bureau 3 had four Sections (Section 5, Section 6, Section 7, and Section 8). Section 5 was responsible for military intelligence reports about the United States and Latin America; Section 6 was responsible for intelligence reports on China; Section 7 was responsible for intelligence reports on Europe and the Soviet Union; and Section 8 was responsible for intelligence reports on Great Britain and the Commonwealth countries. Each Section had five special staff officers, one of whom was also the Section Head.

On their jackets the special staff officers each wore a shiny badge, which denoted their superior status. They worked quietly and with great solemnity. As I wore civilian clothes to work and served only as an assistant to the staff officers, I couldn't help but feel a bit awkward when I was around them. My work within Section 8 consisted of "compiling facts about military zones" and "compiling maps of those zones." I was also responsible for maintaining the files kept on Britain's Royal Navy, which included investigative reports about the positioning and likely movements of that navy.

By 1937, Japan had begun preparations to expand its zone of influence in order to adapt to the new world order. At that critical juncture, our political leaders had already fallen under the sway of the military because the politicians didn't seem to have the faintest idea about what to do. What's more, because our army found itself bogged down in China, the navy was expected to take on the task of expanding Japan's power base and its sphere of influence.

Consequently, the navy proposed a plan to enter regions far to the south of Japan. To make the nation more powerful, a great increase in the production of military supplies was required. In order to do that, sufficient supplies of raw materials (such as steel, rubber, tin, lead, cotton etc.) and finished goods were needed.

As we prepared for the time when the colonies and semi-independent states of those regions would be placed under Japan's rule, Section 8 was charged with learning all about the natural resources that were found in each corner of Southeast Asia and the South Pacific. We were also charged with finding and ascertaining the viability of zones that could serve as staging posts and strongholds for Japan's forces during their movements throughout those regions.

Many great leaders of industry and various consultants paid visits to Section 8. One such regular visitor was Ōtani Kōzui.[1] He frequently came by looking to speak to the Head of our Section, to whom he hoped to expound various "grand ideas" of his own design. Through his plans, he felt it would be possible to link the Malayan Peninsula, the Caroline Islands, and the Marshall Islands along a single line of supply. Once this line of supply that he proposed was established, some very ambitious military and economic policies could be carried out.

"Japan's politicians and the staff officers with rocks in their heads at the army headquarters actually take the East China Sea to be the only possible theatre of operations for our navy," our Section Head could frequently be heard grumbling. "It's unbelievable!"

Not long after this, Captain Horiuchi became our new Section Head. He then put forward the very ideas that the former Section Head had discussed.

"What exactly should we call this lifeline within the Pacific region?" he asked us. We thought of quite a few names for it: The Greater East Asia Sphere; The Greater East Asia Social Sphere; The Greater East Asia Economic Sphere; and the final suggestion, which ultimately began to appear in the newspapers, The Greater East Asia Co-Prosperity Sphere.

At around the same time, I was making use of a stockpile of disparate military documents about Burma, the Malayan Peninsula, and Borneo to draw up a map of the Malayan Peninsula and the other territories around the South China Sea. On this military map, several important items were detailed. Those items were:

1. The air and sea routes used by foreign nations (including civilian airports that could be converted into military bases).
2. Foreign military bases (Naval, army, and air installations were all noted separately, yet the notes provided about air bases were the most detailed.)
3. Commercial shipping lines.
4. Dockyards and harbors.
5. Areas that could serve as temporary airstrips and sites where forced landings might be made.
6. Important cities and towns.

Since most of the maps that we were basing our work upon were very old and were not drawn up to the same scale, and as most of the navigational charts for the area were unreliable, we also made use of the Royal Navy's nautical maps. After that, those responsible for waterways at the Navy General Staff were asked to draw up the map. Finally, we added some notations in various colors, along with critical data.

After the map had been printed, it was classified as "Secret" or "Top Secret" and sent out to every ship in our fleet. It had taken nearly half a year to produce this military map, yet even then it was not entirely accurate. Nonetheless, at a time when there were no other reference materials of the kind, it was a very high-quality map with useful references for the purpose of coming to grips with the lands around the South China Sea.

However, in the middle of the Second World War, a fleet of ships entered Borneo while relying solely upon this map. They subsequently contacted the Navy General Staff with the complaint that the map showed the Kuching airport on the right bank of the Sarawak River when in fact it was located on the left bank. This made those of us involved in the map's production feel very ashamed.

By 1925, near the end of the Taishō Period, the Navy General Staff had begun to recruit sailors, tourists, and expatriates stationed in the countries of the South Seas to gather intelligence about this region. I was able to ascer-

6. The Navy General Staff

tain this on the basis of the dates stamped on the supplements attached to intelligence reports that were piled in stacks. The greater part of these stacks of intelligence information was composed of fragments that had not been placed together in any sort of systematic order and had instead been shelved haphazardly in a storage room, left simply to gather dust. Nevertheless, the information collected about Singapore was relatively detailed. This might have been because the Royal Navy's Far East Fleet was stationed there and was so conspicuous as to attract a great deal of attention.

And yet not a single thing was known about the situations in Borneo and Celebes Island at that time, even though the Navy placed a great deal of importance on their oil resources. It was because of this that many Japanese firms began setting up shop there, under the pretext of entering the cotton trade. They traveled right across those lands and then set up cotton plantations. Without doubt, they were in close contact with the Navy General Staff as they did so.

As there were only five special staff officers (including the Section Head) available to lead the hunt for intelligence information about so vast a zone, we were too busy to manage. Yet in addition to this, there was an unwritten rule in the navy: "If you haven't got several years' experience at sea on active duty, you won't get promoted to a higher rank." As a result, the special staff officers would only work in the Section for two or three years and after that they would go back aboard ship. This was called an "honorable transfer" to active duty.

Whenever a special staff officer's position was left vacant in our Section, the rest of us (the so-called "non-regulars") were entrusted with filling the breach. Thus, we were considered "staunchly loyal guardians" of the Navy General Staff. In short, we were the white mice who had remained there. Our principal work consisted of constantly updating dossiers and maps about military zones and making inquiries to learn about the positioning and movement of the Royal Navy's fleet.

Trying to keep track of the movement of an entire fleet is a very difficult thing to do, as navy fleets are usually on the move and often don't stop for long stretches of time. As far as charting the movements of the Royal Navy was concerned, we were largely able to do that thanks to *The Navy List*, a document published at the beginning of every year by the Royal Navy. This document was sent to us once a year by our attaché at the Japanese Embassy in London, who probably used some legerdemain to get hold of the publication for us. Sometimes the document was slow to arrive and the Navy General Staff would order that its delivery be expedited.

According to that attaché, the Navy General Staff's very highest authorities demanded the document. He was thus obliged to overcome every obstacle and obtain it by hook or by crook. Of course, we also received intelligence reports about naval vessels, commercial vessels, aircraft, and more from our agents stationed abroad. By using both the Royal Navy's annual inventory and this additional information, we were able to roughly work out the positioning and movement of the Royal Navy's fleet.

For a more precise picture of the movement of their fleet, we also relied on other intelligence reports about repairs to naval vessels, ships going to dock, ships that had been called home, and new submarines being launched. Therefore, we frequently corrected or revised our records. By contrast, gathering intelligence about the deployment and transfer of troops was very difficult because such information is kept secret by all countries.

As for our intelligence reports about each navy vessel's armor, the caliber of its guns, the type of shells used, its specific capabilities and so on, there were always some discrepancies with the publicly stated figures. Consequently, whenever such precise technical information was required, it was necessary to ask one of our technical officers stationed abroad to provide it.

At the time, there was nothing especially novel about the methods we used to estimate the sizes and types of ships deployed by the Royal Navy or the types of weaponry that they had aboard. The same could not be said about aircraft, the production of which was growing by leaps and bounds. This made the work of estimating of the numbers of aircraft deployed by Britain in the Near East, the Middle East, and India very challenging.

Gaining a clearer picture of the state of a country's military armaments also required a thorough understanding of that country's political situation, its international relations, its economic weight (especially its trade relations), its energy supplies, and more. Consequently, we collated press reports, official telegrams from our embassies, and reports sent in to each Section by our intelligence agents and commercial field operatives on a daily basis. When stacked together, these reports would form a pile more than 12 inches thick. We had to sift through these intelligence reports to find useful information, and then we had to place those reports into various categories before collating and filing them.

In addition, we kept dossiers on Britain's leading political figures and military leaders. These included their full name, experience, current post, duties, and so on. We had to make the necessary changes to a dossier whenever a professional or personal change occurred in the life of one of these leaders.

Such was the nature of the work that I performed in Bureau 3, Section 8 for five years. Then one day in May 1940 our Section Head, Captain Horiuchi, asked to have a word with me:

"Mr. Yoshikawa. Could you please go to see Captain Yamaguchi, the Head of Section 5? There is a matter he would like to discuss with you."

I was still feeling quite surprised about my Section Head's request when I reached the office belonging to the Head of Section 5. Both Section 5 and

6. The Navy General Staff

Section 8 shared the same large office space, so I was on familiar terms with Captain Yamaguchi.

"Mr. Yoshikawa, we are preparing to send you to Hawaii. What do you think of that?"

As I didn't know a thing about what I was supposed to be doing there, I didn't know what to think. I assumed it was for some sort of trivial task, like that of a messenger. I'd go, make contact, and then I'd come back.

"Sure, I'll go," I replied.

"All right then, starting today I want you to study everything there is to learn about the U.S. Navy's fleet! In a few days, we will be in contact with the Foreign Ministry. You must not discuss this matter with anyone, not even your parents or your siblings."

"Understood."

"Do you have any worries concerning your family?"

"None."

"Well then, that's good."

I gave the Captain a salute and left his office. As I did so, I figured that I might be required to perform an important duty on this trip. I still hadn't acquired the spy's ability to grasp a situation intuitively. Many of us at the Navy General Staff were in fact doing spy work and the place itself was, broadly speaking, the base camp for all of our spies. Yet although I was working in a tense atmosphere each and every day, I did not yet consider the inherent dangers of our work to be of any great importance.

As I left that meeting, my heart was overcome by a very strong feeling. My morale was so high and my feelings so strong that my face was momentarily subject to hot flushes.

"I am going to have to go all out to fetch a most valuable intelligence report!" I told myself.

A few days later, Captain Yamaguchi called me into his office and gave me orders to report to the Foreign Ministry to receive my instructions. Then he lowered his voice and told me:

"Mr. Yoshikawa, you will be going to Japan's Consulate-General in Honolulu to serve as an official there. You'll be living there for a while. The Foreign Ministry is taking care of all the formalities. Just follow your instructions on this assignment!

"In order to guarantee that you can be sent out, it will be necessary to change your identity. You will have to start playing the part of an official from the Foreign Ministry as soon as you get there. Your mission is to find out all that you can about developments at Pearl Harbor, which we don't understand very well.

"However, as I'm sure you are aware, Japan-U.S. relations are very tense at the moment. Moreover, one of our special agents has just been detained on the U.S. West Coast. If you happen to be caught by the FBI, it will certainly lead to some serious repercussions for Japan-U.S. relations. Not only that, it will put your own safety very much at risk. You'll have to be very careful in going about your business.

"Only one or two people at the Foreign Ministry will know your true identity. You'll have to be very discreet and do your best to get along with all your colleagues. Don't create any friction.

"Finally, you should know that the Foreign Ministry is not very pleased about the idea of taking you on.

"Anyway, as the saying goes, 'if you want to deceive your enemy, you must first dupe yourself.'

"Be careful, and go and do your work."

My head was lowered respectfully as I listened to these exhortations from the Section Head.

"Oh, that's right! You had better shave off your hair, and keep it like that. Okay!"

The Captain then pointed to the calendar. "You'll be there until the end of the year," he added. "Can you stay there until then?"

These events occurred in May 1940.

7

Springtide

    I had been living on my own since the day I first arrived in Tokyo. As I was not tied down to anyone, I had moved into and out of several flats. I would live in each flat for just a year and then move on, either for my own convenience or because someone had convinced me to change flats. Finding a new flat back then wasn't anywhere near as difficult as it is these days and my attitude was one of simple resignation. I accepted whatever the future would bring. Under the strong influence of this fatalistic outlook, I moved house once again in the summer of 1939.

    I moved into Nagata Manor, a tranquil tower block that was a short distance from the Prime Minister's official residence. I very much liked the place since it wasn't far from my office. And it was convenient to study there because it was so quiet. Since my superiors had begun planning to send me to Singapore, I was already preparing to be posted there. Subsequently, after considering the long-distance journey by sea that had taken me to Singapore, Batavia, and Manila, my superiors began to fear that I would run into someone I had met on my travels and that they would reveal my true identity. Thus, the decision was made to send someone else to Singapore.

    It was around this time that I met a woman. One day, as I was leaning through an open window and enjoying the sight of the flowers of a calabash plant that had nearly grown up as high as my windows, I suddenly heard a great noise coming from the flat next to mine where a couple lived (both were Thai students). Soon afterwards, I heard the familiar sound of feet running up from downstairs.

    It was another neighbor, Mr. Matsuo. He was huffing and puffing as he gave me his news.

    "Mr. Yoshikawa, some new neighbors have just moved in next to me. Two real beauties! Why don't you come downstairs and see?"

    Mr. Matsuo was a notorious lecher. He had very thick lips and spoke with a heavy Osaka accent. I am repulsed by the very thought of it.

    "Why haven't I seen them? When did they move in?"

    "It's been a week now!"

"Why haven't you said anything all this time? And you call yourself a friend?"

"Haven't I just invited you over? I'll invite the sisters over to listen to some records and you can come over too. It would be strange if I were to invite them to visit me on my own."

"If what I hear is true, the delivery girls from the restaurant have all given you the brush off. So will you go over to the restaurant and buy some nice things to eat?"

"Sure, sure!" Matsuo replied with a laugh. He then hurried off and ran back downstairs.

Later, Matsuo had completely tidied up his flat, set up the record player, and presented the food appropriately. He had even put each and every cushion neatly into place.

"Well then, should I call on them now?"

"You don't know if they're at home, do you?"

"Yes, they are. I'm certain!"

"It's as if you're hunting rabbits!"

He went out for a moment and came right back.

"Well, what's going on?" I asked impatiently.

He replied with a single word: "Coming!" He was obviously feeling quite pleased with himself.

And then the three female guests arrived.

For some reason, men always feel much older and somewhat distracted when meeting pretty and gently perfumed women of that sort. So, the three guests seemed a bit restrained at first.

But after the tea was poured and we got to know one another, they began to laugh. "Hee hee. Ha ha."

The elder sister was called Chika, she was around 22. The younger sister was called Mika. Their girlfriend's name was Midge. It seemed as if they had discussed what they were going to call themselves since all of their names were composed of only two syllables and they all sounded quite similar. This actually made you feel that they had come up with their names as a way of toying with you.

Chika was dressed from head to toe in Japanese clothing. She was very well-mannered, and sat quite solemnly, but was in every respect considerate and thoughtful. Her eyes sparkled with intelligence and her remarks were often quite witty and suave. She seemed to have taken on the role of "leader" among the three. No, that's not quite right. Put simply, her solemn but gentle mien and utterly correct behavior made her seem a queen.

Midge was a round-faced beauty. She was full-figured, white-skinned, and very attractive. She was wearing a western-style outfit made of very fine material. You might say she was delicate and charming. In addition, she sported a beautiful head of soft, unruly hair, which was enough on its own to make men fall for her.

The younger sister, Mika, was a modern woman. She had a pair of gleaming eyes, rosy lips, and you couldn't help but love her. Yet her manner was somewhat restrained. That must have been because she couldn't be seen to let herself go while in the company of her elder sister.

Although all three were good-looking, to me the most beautiful was Chika.

From their discussions, I gathered that the two sisters were the daughters of the owner of a posh restaurant in Akasaka. The two had been sent to live temporarily in a flat at Nagata Manor as a result of some family matter.

Once I had learned that three such beautiful and distinguished women actually existed in Tokyo, and that they could be invited to dance, to listen to music, to watch films, and go to plays, I couldn't help but feel amazed. Yet as I always wore a severe expression at that time, it was hardly surprising when the three young ladies all said that I was a "far too serious" and "somewhat depressing" person. This was because my arduous work responsibilities left me feeling as if I was carrying a heavy burden, which in turn dampened my spirits. I had, of course, already had some contact with women. I had been through several romantic relationships and seen women from all around the world, so I was not completely naive. Despite this, I never expected that I would come across someone like Chika. She had knocked me off my feet.

From then on, the two of us would find any excuse to meet up. Naturally, Chika's female intuition had picked up on my feelings for her. But when I was still working up the nerve to find some excuse to ask her out, she was also finding it difficult to show her true feelings for me.

Then one day, I thought of asking for a photo of her.

"And what exactly do you want my photograph for, hmmm?" she asked half-jokingly, while tilting her head back slightly so as to better gauge my response.

"It's because of my parents, who live in a small village. Since they always urge me to get married every time they send me a letter, I'd like to have some grounds for refusing their request. Maybe this isn't something you want to hear, but … you must give me a photo. Any one will do," I implored her earnestly.

"What you mean is that you've already found a sweetheart?"

"That's right. And she's you!"

"You do nothing but tell lies!" she said, while laughing loudly.

As Matsuo and Midge were sitting right next to us, she could have believed that I was only joking. Nevertheless, my words were heartfelt. In fact, in her heart of hearts, she was hoping that I would bring up the question of marriage.

As my parents knew almost nothing about my situation at that time, they worried that their young bachelor son in the big city might fall into a life of debauchery. Every letter that they sent urged me to marry; only then would they stop fretting about me. "By the way, I wanted to mention so-and-so's daughter. You know her. Well, she's from such-and-such a family and she's a really nice young lady." The letter would then ask me to go back to the village to make up my mind.

While one part of me felt that I had no reason to get married with those women, another part of me felt I was fated to die for my country and that my prospects were gloomy. Rather than reveling in the simple pleasures enjoyed by the citizens of some small town, I thought it so much better to separate myself completely from all that and get on with it. Thus, I was not in any hurry to marry.

Matsuo was an expert skirt-chaser. First, he made a move on Mika and then he was drooling over Midge. On those summer evenings, the three of them always wanted to go out together for a stroll and soon enough this became something they did every day. Sometimes they went to the woods beside the Sannō shrine for a heart-to-heart chat, at other times they walked past Akasaka-mitsuke and all the way over to Yotsuya. Weary, and with tired feet, they would pause for a rest at a tea house. Once their spirits had been restored, they would go to Shimizudani Park where they would dance under the shade of the trees. On occasion they would get so carried away enjoying themselves that they wouldn't return until the middle of the night.

I always made plans to meet with Chika instead. Sometimes we would go to see a film, or we would go out for a meal. At times, we went to the outer moat park at Yotsuya. There we would sit on one of the long benches, quietly looking at the streetlamps and watching the lights of the tram cars paddle across the water and then disappear.

I could never make up my mind about confessing the love I felt for her and asking her to be mine. So our mutual passion, which had developed so quickly, began to drain out of us like water rushing out of a reservoir after its wall has been breached. This left her feeling hurt and emotionally scarred.

Things turned out that way because of the thoughts that I had about my likely fate. I resolved that it would be best for her if we kept our relationship at the platonic stage. Not getting myself any further involved with her was the manly attitude to take. Yet she too had her own bottled up feelings. She had been hoping all along that I would say the words that I never uttered. She herself never said a word of this, but chose quite understandably to get away from the uneasiness that had arisen between us. Although the two of us continued to see one another, whenever we did so we were always joined by our mirthful companions.

However, I still wanted to go out with Chika alone to theaters, concerts,

7. Springtide

to places where people gathered in crowds, and to the other places we always used to go to. Deep down, I still loved her. But after the summer had long since passed and the arrival of cold winds announced the passing of late autumn into early winter, I suddenly stopped seeing her.

Some time afterwards, I ran into Chika's sister.

"Hey! My sister is married now!" Mika told me.

8

The Situation in America

The steel filing cabinets at the Navy General Staff contained piles of documents that our predecessors had researched, summarized, and classified. In those documents, which dated back to 1907 in some cases, the United States was treated as Japan's foremost "hypothetical" enemy. Efforts to research the U.S. were intensified after Japan-U.S. relations reached a crisis point in 1934. Before long, Rear-Admiral Yuzuke and others began pouring all of their energy into compiling classified materials on the U.S. The materials they produced were hidden away in the Navy General Staff archives once each file had been stamped with the words "Secret Military File" and wrapped with a red paper-strip seal. If placed in a single stack, those files would have stood over two meters high.

The U.S. Navy's forces were deployed in two large, yet distinct, zones by that time. The naval troops deployed in the first zone were part of the U.S. Pacific Fleet and based in Hawaii. Those deployed in the second zone were part of the U.S. Atlantic Fleet, which was charged with protecting America's East Coast and the Panama Canal (the link between the two oceans that was considered America's lifeline).

While the numbers of vessels and troops allocated to each of these two zones did vary somewhat, they were never equal in size or number. Troops were allocated on a 3:1 basis, the greater part of which was obviously allocated to the Pacific Fleet. What's more, the Navy General Staff had determined that if the U.S. Pacific Fleet were to find itself faced with an emergency situation, it would only take the Atlantic Fleet ten days to join up with it.

We were able to get a fairly detailed picture of the U.S. Navy's capabilities thanks to the material sent from our naval attaché based in Washington, material taken from the U.S. President's address to both houses of Congress, drafts of the U.S. Navy budget, the roster of U.S. Navy officers, the U.S. Navy Regulations, openly published information concerning navy reviews and the navy's ports of supply, specialist magazines about the U.S. military, and other sources.

We knew everything there was to know about the organizational struc-

8. The Situation in America

ture of the U.S. Navy, the first and last names of the commanding officers, the deployment of the fleet, and the stage of construction of the vessels that were going to be added to the fleet. We were even able to forecast the relative strength of the U.S. Navy two or three years down the line. We could even say "a warship of ---- type will be launched in ---- month of ---- year."

We also knew about the defenses at Pearl Harbor, which was called "impregnable" and "indestructible." We were completely clear about the number of troops garrisoned by the harbor, the military installations there, and the caliber of the guns within the fortifications that overlooked the harbor (although their exact numbers may not have been clear to us).

Apart from all of this, we had thoroughly investigated the strategic military sites that were spread across the zone that contained the Hawaiian Archipelago at its center and extended north to Dutch Harbor and Kiska Island, south to Manila and Guam, and from there as far east as San Diego, San Pedro, San Francisco, Puget Sound, and so on. Our data was so thorough and so systematically maintained that we had no trouble in making the necessary changes or adjustments to keep it up to date.

Despite this, given the constant changes that were then underway, some crucial questions concerning Pearl Harbor still needed to be answered if the Navy General Staff was going to direct our war operations effectively:

How many American naval vessels entered and exited Pearl Harbor?

How many military aircraft were moving through the airfields there?

What were their missions?

Yet regardless of the country, and whether it's at peace or at war, information about the movement of troops is always kept top secret and is strictly controlled. If you are able ascertain the number of enemy troops, where they are going, and what they are doing, then you can easily determine what their strategic plans are.

Every nation uses its embassies, secret agents, newspapers, media broadcasts, secret intelligence reports, and all manners of artifice (risking both life and limb) to gather intelligence about the movement of the enemy's troops. Moreover, the work of gathering this information is not something that can be done all at once and then stopped. Such work must be carried out continuously, over decades. As the Chinese military strategist Sun Tzu once put it: "If you know yourself and you know your enemy, you will win every battle."[1]

In a word, this is why each side must gather information about the enemy. Conversely, the enemy must do his utmost to keep such information secret. As a result, getting to stage of "knowing each other" is no simple matter. The Hōjō school's military strategy puts this in somewhat different terms: "Look, watch, and check to determine the enemy's intentions."[2] "To look" requires the use of your eyes. "To watch" requires the use of all five senses. "To check" is to go and investigate thoroughly, which means you must go and perceive, in a state of great doubt and worry, in order to draw inferences from what you have learned.

I gradually read my way through all of the secret files in Section 5. Since I had already taken on a fair number of challenges within the Navy General Staff by then, I really didn't mind tending to those files. In fact, I found all of them very interesting. After several years of learning as I went along, the Navy General Staff continued to hold surprises for me. I had come to see it as a lair of sorts for the specialists who were ensconced there, day and night, mulling over the art of war.

Before I set off, I had to memorize all the types and classes of vessel within the U.S. Navy's fleet. I needed to get to the point where I could cast an eye over a vessel and immediately recall its type and class. I was greatly helped in this work by a book that was published in London, which listed the naval vessels of various countries.

It was obviously necessary for me to be able to catch sight of the silhouette of a warship and know instantly that it was a certain type of ship, as well as all of the various characteristics that were specific to it: the cannons installed, its maximum speed and range, and so on. I also had to be able to spot the slight differences that distinguished a given vessel from earlier or later versions of that vessel, as well as any differences in function, operational parameters, and more.

While all of this was going on, I was taking a preparatory course for future diplomats and preparing for the Foreign Ministry exam. Furthermore, I was studying English and International Law at university. I also began to work mornings at the Foreign Ministry, where I was known as "Morimura" (I always signed the ministry's employee register as Morimura.) In the afternoons, I returned to the Navy General Staff where I was once again called Yoshikawa.

I had adopted the alias Morimura for my work with the Foreign Ministry because I felt that foreigners would find it hard to pronounce and difficult to remember after they'd heard it. After choosing my new name, I decided that using it at the Foreign Ministry would allow my ears to get accustomed to being called by that name. When you want to deceive your enemy, you must first dupe yourself.

In September 1940, Japan, Germany, and Italy formalized their Tripartite Pact.[3] Our army had been the main backer of this alliance, which had been concluded thanks to its backroom dealings. Meanwhile, our navy had refused to endorse the pact. Consequently, there were many discussions inside the Intelligence Bureau at the Navy General Staff on the day this was announced.

"They did it in the end anyway! I truly can't understand it. How will shaking hands with Germany, so far away as it is, be of any use to us?"

"Germany's military is land-based. Not only will they be unable to help our navy, they will on the contrary be expecting our navy to shoulder their burdens at sea. What a bunch of scoundrels!"

While the staff officers who worked in the American and British Sections of the Intelligence Bureau loudly cursed those who had been behind the decision to join the alliance, those staff officers who worked on German intelligence in Section 7 made every effort to defend the idea that Germany was superior:

"No, no, no. It's not necessarily a bad thing. If we start by sharing intelligence reports with one another, our cooperation might enable us to get hold of the most advanced German machinery and armaments. And that would be quite advantageous for Japan. At present, Germany in the process of building a new order in Europe. We shouldn't miss out because Germany's air fleet and its submarines are really quite extraordinary."

In the Intelligence Bureau, all the young staff officers who specialized in Germany, America, or Britain sat alongside one another at tables in a large hall and each one could freely express his opinions about this matter. Yet once it had become official government policy, every man was obliged to align his views with those of the government and do his utmost to aid the cause.

Not long afterwards, the first intelligence report from Germany arrived. This intelligence report concerned the deployment of the U.S. Navy in the Atlantic Ocean. However, as we had long since learned all of the information it provided, it was of no use to us. As a result, the report served to buttress the arguments of those who held the negative view that while Germany was a country with land forces, its navy was still very weak. If they didn't know much about the situation in the United States, we wouldn't take much notice of their intelligence reports.

And yet, because our counterpart had already reported his "plum" to us, we were obliged to return the favor by responding with a "peach." Therefore, we replied with a report that provided the key ratio of 3:1 (i.e., the ratio that described how U.S. troops and armaments were allocated to the U.S. Navy's Pacific and Atlantic Fleets respectively).

"It doesn't matter what sort of intelligence reports we give them, any will do. But we will never get any German arms or machinery if we don't send them a little something," said Lieutenant-Commander Tsukada. He was a staff officer who specialized in German intelligence and I had often seen him asking questions of colleagues who worked on gathering military intelligence about Britain and the United States. With this sort of demand being placed on us, we had no choice but to report a bit of information on the Royal Navy's Mediterranean and Far East fleets.

Even though the next report that we sent hadn't been fabricated, it was slightly out of date and of little practical use. This was how we dealt with one another at the time. Although the information sent to the other side wasn't falsified, it wasn't of any great value either. It was right around this time that something happened that would have pleased Hitler.

While reading an intercepted intelligence report from Australia one day, I discovered that a flotilla of cargo ships had left the port of Fremantle and was on its way to Britain. By then, the Navy General Staff was gathering considerable numbers of intelligence reports from Australia that had been transmitted on shortwave and longwave radio. Telegrams sent out regularly by the Australian military and by the many diplomatic legations there were collected too. With such large numbers of reports in hand, it wasn't easy to cast an eye over each and every one.

I had taken this intercepted intelligence report, studied it carefully, and learned:

    i. the date that the flotilla of cargo ships had left port
    ii. the speed of the vessels
    iii. the date of their estimated arrival on the west coast of Africa
    iv. the duration of their voyage up that coast

I immediately wrote down the following telegram and gave it to Lieutenant-Commander Tsukada:

"Extremely Urgent Decoded Telegram. From a flotilla of 24 cargo ships. Have already left Fremantle and now en route to Great Britain. Estimated time of arrival along the West Coast of Africa ---- Day of ---- Month."

We then hastened to send this telegram to our counterparts. Soon afterwards we received their reply: "On the basis of your valuable telegram # ---- , this flotilla will be intercepted and sunk when it reaches the vicinity of the Azores. We hope you can continue to provide intelligence reports of this sort."

Near the end of 1940, not long after the Tripartite Pact had been formalized, the Navy General Staff decided to station an officer in Seattle in order to strengthen our network of intelligence operatives on the West Coast of the United States. I had often noticed a certain Lieutenant-Commander K at the Navy General Staff, until he stopped coming in to work. I soon concluded that he was the officer who had been sent overseas. If that were so, the Imperial Japanese Navy now had two active officers stationed on America's West Coast. Both were tasked with gathering intelligence (Commander Y, the other officer, had long been posted in Los Angeles.) As for the Hawaiian Islands, that region was to be my area of responsibility.

I had already shaved off all my hair by this time and everything else had been made ready for my departure. I just needed my marching orders before I could set off. However, those orders were taking a long time to come down to me.

Soon after the Lunar New Year in 1941, a telegram message from Germany informed Japan that it had just dispatched a shipment of machine tools

8. The Situation in America

as a goodwill gesture that was meant to recognize the value of the intelligence information shared between our two nations. The shipment had been sent by road to Spain. The *Asaka Maru* (a vessel owned by Japan's NYK Shipping Company) was then commandeered by the navy to ship these machine tools to Japan. It was renamed *Special Service Ship Asaka* and hurried off to Spain under the command of a naval officer.

In order to hasten the arrival of the cargo, the Japanese navy contacted the U.S. government to request that the ship be allowed to transit the Panama Canal. However, the U.S. government replied that it would be necessary to send uniformed U.S. military personnel aboard to supervise the transit of the ship and ensure the safety of the vessel. The Japanese government responded that it did not agree with the idea of having foreign military officers on board its ship, as it was felt that this would violate the generally accepted rights of naval vessels and damage the nation's honor. Although the government maintained that its vessel deserved free, unsupervised transit through the canal, its request was denied. After subsequent negotiations, it was agreed that the crew of the Japanese ship would invite uniformed U.S. military personnel aboard and then the ship would be allowed to transit the canal.

Although a mere passage through the Panama Canal was not worth so much aggravation, Japan believed it was worth using every possible means to investigate the state of America's readiness in that key military zone. Thus, the Japanese authorities had persisted with the matter. What's more, Japan's naval attaché in Washington went to Panama during the same period on the pretext of having some business to attend to there.

Immediately after that, while the *Nishin Maru* was moored at San Francisco on 20 January 1941, an incident occurred during which American officials seized a book of cipher codes. Those officials had taken control of the vessel after alleging that they had to check if anything on board needed to be quarantined. They then asked the captain to open all of the strongboxes so that they could check for the presence of cocaine or any other illegal goods aboard.

While the ship's captain was opening the strongboxes, an American inspector caught sight of a tightly-guarded book, *Cipher Codes for Ships and Boats,* as well as other secret documents. Although the captain risked his life trying to stop the U.S. officials, they simply snatched up the code book and documents and quickly left the vessel.

After the Japanese Consul-General received the captain's urgent report about this, he immediately lodged an official protest with the Americans. Though the code book was returned to the ship a few hours later, the contents of the book had without doubt been photographed (and thus stolen) by the Americans. This meant that the cipher codes in the book had lost all of their usefulness. In addition, the photographed book would furnish the U.S. Navy with a lot of very useful study material on how to break Japanese codes. All those at the Navy General Staff felt extremely angry with the U.S. over this contemptible act.

Shortly thereafter, on 23 January 1941, our new Ambassador to the United States, Admiral Kichisaburō Nomura, took up his post. Many in society were placing the highest of hopes on Admiral Nomura as he began his new role because he had served as Japan's naval attaché to the U.S. while Franklin Delano Roosevelt was serving as Assistant-Secretary of the U.S. Navy. As the two were old friends, and because the Admiral had many other contacts in America, it was thought that he would certainly be able to return Japan-U.S. relations to a more peaceable state.

It was then that Captain Yamaguchi at the Navy General Staff told me in secret that I should prepare to follow in the new ambassador's wake. Soon afterwards, however, my departure was postponed. This was because many feared that if my true identity were discovered, it would cause the ambassador a great deal of trouble. Consequently, those in charge at the Navy General Staff dithered and I stayed put.

Finally, on 20 March, I boarded the *Nitta Maru* at the docks in Yokohama. I arrived in Honolulu on 27 March. From that day to the day of the attack on Pearl Harbor, I was actively gathering intelligence there.

After leaving the Navy General Staff, I obviously knew nothing more about naval officers being dispatched to the U.S. West Coast. However, I did hear afterwards that the Japanese army attaché's office in Washington had been placed under tight surveillance by the FBI (the Federal Bureau of Investigation) in April and that a senior figure in our armaments industry was investigated by both police and U.S. Navy officers on the basis of trumped up charges.

In June, the previously mentioned Commander Y was caught in possession of an intelligence report given to him by a low-ranking officer from the *Pennsylvania*, the U.S. Pacific Fleet's flagship. He had been caught in a "double-agent snare" and was promptly arrested. Subsequently, after Ambassador Nomura had lodged special appeals about the matter, the U.S. government released Commander Y one day before his trial was to begin, on the condition that he leave the country.

The navy attaché's office took this matter as a warning and recalled Lieutenant-Commander K to Washington since he had been in regular contact with Commander Y. Thus, our naval attaché's office in Washington found itself in an awkward position because it had been caught trying to acquire intelligence reports about the U.S. Pacific fleet and because both of the naval officers posted to the U.S. West Coast had been uprooted.

As a result, after he'd been thrown into the turbulent waters where the U.S. Pacific Fleet was based, the secretary known as "Morimura" would become the Navy General Staff's one and only active secret agent.

9

Getting Ready

As time went on I became increasingly aware of the significance of my undercover mission at Pearl Harbor. Consequently, I came to feel I had been condemned to die for my country and that I could do very little about this other than accept my misfortune. Yet I also felt very excited because I had been charged with the task of lifting the veil that concealed the U.S. Navy in order to reveal its true face.

I was fully aware that even the slightest mistake during the course of my mission would not only put me in a perilous position, it would also damage the Japanese government's prestige. Furthermore, it would harm the good faith that formed the foundation upon which Japan's international diplomatic relations were based. When the Director of the American Office at the Foreign Ministry took me aside and repeatedly stressed the importance of this question to me, I completely understood the concerns behind his exhortations.

However, I sensed that Japan's diplomatic authorities were somewhat too cautious regarding the U.S. When dealing with America, which was many times more powerful than Japan, it was of course necessary to avoid any diplomatic incidents that could offend the other side. This became imperative after the Lytton Report was published.[1] British and American attitudes towards Japan had worsened rapidly after its publication and the flames of war that continued to rage between Japan and China threatened to place the U.S. Pacific Fleet in a dangerous spot.

In light of these perilous developments, it would have created a lot of trouble for those carrying out diplomatic negotiations in Washington if it were discovered that an employee at a Japanese consulate in America was a spy. That could even have scuttled those negotiations. The Foreign Ministry had evidently thought long and hard about this before deciding to proceed very cautiously.

For their part, those charged with leading our war operations at the Navy General Staff believed that it was necessary to adopt every possible measure to achieve success, even if that meant taking some risks. Thus, the Navy General Staff compelled the Foreign Ministry to prepare the way for a diplomat operating under an assumed name. I was then asked to go through all the various steps necessary to prepare for the role in order to ensure that there would be no slip-ups.

Before sending an undercover agent off to a foreign country, you must first consider the following questions:

1. Will the agent will be able to deliver intelligence reports in a timely fashion?
2. Will the agent follow orders?
3. Will the agent bring expert knowledge to the role and be able to judge the situation on the ground accurately?
4. Will the agent be able to work independently and avoid getting caught up by networks designed to ensnare him and bring about his downfall?
5. Will the agent be able to hold up under repeated interrogations conducted by the enemy and resist efforts to turn him into a double agent if captured?

While this may seem to be a lot of questions, I believe that all of them ultimately refer to the character of the person under consideration. In other words, you have to determine whether the person who is to serve as an undercover agent is going to do so for the money or because of his personal beliefs and convictions.

As for the matter of whether or not an undercover agent will succeed, I suggest the following adage: "Man proposes, God disposes."

Of all the numerous books about espionage that I have read, from both East and West, *Lawrence of Arabia* is the one that has made the greatest impression upon me. Lawrence knew all about the risks involved in his work as an undercover agent. He also knew that his death would not be heroic, but rather miserable and tragic. Yet despite knowing all the while that the path he had embarked upon could prove to be fatal, he continued along that path for the sake of his country. What's more, he believed that such a destiny was the sort that any real man should hope for.

By that time, I had received the approbation of my superiors. I had to see that as a great honor and push forward with all of my might. It was no time to retreat. As the old saying goes, "A gentleman is always willing to die for his friends." I was a serviceman sworn to giving everything that was mine, even my life, for the homeland. That is the serviceman's bounden duty.

I frequently had trouble getting any sleep at night due to the excitement that thinking about my important mission initially caused me to feel. After reflecting on this, I decided it was important that I not allow myself to be dominated by excitement. I realized that in order to successfully complete my mission I needed to go about things in a calm and steady way. Only then could I prepare for everything properly.

9. Getting Ready

Although I was about to experience a major change in my life, there wasn't anyone close to me that I could speak about it with. I was obliged to keep quiet about it all, even with my family. Even so, I wanted my parents to live with me, if only for a very short while, because I felt that my life was not going to last very much longer. So, I made arrangements to rent a small flat.

After my mother arrived in Tokyo, she was full of the idea that her son was preparing to get married. As a result, she was especially happy. Consequently, I had a word with her one day: "Ma, I wanted to ask you to live here with me for a while, for about six months or so. Could you speak to Dad about this and ask him to look after himself temporarily? Tell him that it's quite likely that I will be transferred far, far away for my work."

"Really? Is that right? What kind of place are you going to?"

"Well, about that… I'm still not quite sure," I managed to sputter. "Maybe to a foreign country, or perhaps down in the south somewhere," I added vaguely.

After hearing that, my mother looked dispirited and fell into deep thought.

"Wherever you want to go, just listen to your heart and go," she then said. "If it's an order from your superiors, you may go, wherever it is… However, you must be careful about your health. I can live here temporarily. I'll just write your father a letter and tell him about this. Everything will be fine."

Her calm response was completely unexpected. I had thought that persuading my mother would be extremely difficult. I never imagined that the matter would be resolved so smoothly.

Let me return yet again to the subject of Japan, which had gone on the attack on the Chinese mainland in 1937. Although it was possible to seize control of certain areas and territories, there was simply no way to completely subjugate all of China. As a result, Japan began slipping ever deeper into a quagmire from which there was no way to extricate itself.

The Japanese government was deeply worried; all its members believed that a new order in East Asia had to be established with utmost haste. There had to be a quick end to the pointless waste of troops in useless battles on the mainland, otherwise Japan was doomed to find itself falling behind in the new world that was taking shape. As a consequence of all of this, on 31 March 1940, Japan helped to prop up a regime headed by Wang Jing Wei. Following that, on 17 July, Wang Jing Wei's second cabinet issued a statement declaring that it would not accept Chiang Kai-Shek's presence at the negotiating table. That statement was in fact an attempt to put an end to the Second Sino-Japanese war, but it was made in vain.

The war was causing great hardship by that time. Essential products were in short supply and our citizens were suffering terribly. Economic conditions were grim and black marketeering was rife. The rich could use the black market to obtain some goods, whereas the toiling masses found their stomachs filled only with the grumblings of hunger.

While my salary provided me with just enough to allow me to support my mother, our short time together was one of the most beautiful periods of my life. I took a great clod of earth and planted many flowers in it. I also planted a pumpkin next to some bamboo fencing and it began to flower there, which delighted me. On Sundays, I sometimes took my mother out of Tokyo and into the surrounding countryside and villages to sightsee. Sometimes, we stayed within the city and visited sites such as the Royal Palace, Roka-kōen Park, and the Tama river. On other occasions we went much further afield, to places such as the Musashi Imperial Graveyard and Jindai-ji Temple. The only thing I bought of any value during this period was a simple traditional wooden bathtub made from Japanese cypress. I have very fond memories of that as well.

On 1 August of that year, the U.S. suddenly passed the "Export Control Law." This was aimed at restricting the shipment of iron, steel and petroleum to Japan. By that time, the Imperial Japanese Navy's stockpiles of petroleum could meet the requirements of its attack-ready, high-speed and quick-to-deploy fleet for only one year. As a result of this, the navy had no choice but to adopt the strategy of going on the attack in regions to the south of Japan. Once in the South, Japanese forces would seek out petroleum and other natural resources.

Consequently, the Navy General Staff dispatched undercover agents to Singapore, Hawaii, and Batavia. It also dispatched some of its functionaries to those territories in order to inspect the situation on the ground. Japan then began to undertake a series of measures designed to respond to the U.S. embargo. On 23 September, Japanese forces entered the northern portion of French Indochina for stationing there. Then, on 27 September, Japan, Germany and Italy held an official ceremony in Berlin to celebrate their Tripartite Alliance. On 12 October, Japan established its Imperial Rule Assistance Association.

At home and abroad the situation had suddenly become very tense. The political scene was marked everywhere by great unrest, while ordinary citizens were forced to deal with trials and hardships and yet somehow find the ways and means to carry on.

By October, my hair had already grown back. Originally, it had been thought that I would set off in the middle of November. However, for various reasons I still hadn't embarked on my journey by that year's end.

With the coming of the new calendar year the Japanese government decided it would send Admiral Kichisaburō Nomura, an old friend of President Roosevelt, to serve as Special Ambassador to the U.S. Then Japan and the United States began a round of diplomatic negotiations aimed at securing the

9. Getting Ready

peace. Not long after Special Ambassador Nomura had hurried off to Washington to take up his post, I was given secret orders to board the ship *Nitta Maru*. It was to depart Yokahama for the United States on 20 March.

At that time Japan was neither at war nor at peace, it remained between the two. While in this position, it chose to show patience and maintain a dignified attitude. Yet within ten months, Japan would finally cast peace aside and set out on the road to war.

Once I had received my passport for official business and my visa, I went to the Nippon Yusen Shipping Company's offices to book a first-class cabin. After that, I began to put my things in order and pack my bags. As a precaution, everything that I packed for my journey to America was new. There was not one old article among my belongings because my name had always been stitched to my work clothes. I feared that someone at the local laundry would discover this and expose my true identity.

Owing to the shortage of goods of every sort, it was impossible to buy a pure wool suit. I could only buy a suit made of synthetic materials. The shoes that I bought were also synthetic. Needless to say, I very carefully wrote the initials of my pseudonym, T M, on my briefcase and suitcase.

When I went to Bureau 3 at the Navy General Staff to say my goodbyes, Captain T gave me six 100-dollar bills. Each bill was crisp, clean, and seemed new. He told me that the money was to cover my temporary living expenses and that I was only allowed to spend it once I had arrived in Hawaii. At the time, the Yokohama Specie Bank would exchange Japanese Yen for U.S. dollars at the rate of four Yen to one dollar. However, the maximum amount you could exchange was $50 U.S. I took the $600 and safeguarded it in a money belt that I wore around my waist.

Once everything had been properly prepared and all the arrangements had been made, it was time to "do my best and let the heavens take care of the rest." While pulling my newly purchased leather suitcase along the dimly-lighted streets, my steps grew heavier as I made my way closer to home. I felt utterly forsaken. I didn't know what I was supposed to say to my mother about my mission. In the end, I just spoke in general terms about it. After that, I told my mother to gather up all of our belongings and return to our village as soon as I had gone. It grieved me when I told my mother that I might not be able to write to her again. Inwardly, my mother was crying.

And so it was that Morimura, a secretary at Japan's Consulate-General in Honolulu, was born.

As for me? In the next instant, I just disappeared from Tokyo.

10

Aboard the *Nitta Maru*

The *Nitta Maru* was a newly built and sumptuous 20-ton steamship. Two days before our departure, it was already moored to the docks. I completed the all the required formalities for boarding well in advance and then checked into the Hotel New Grand, where I had decided to wait out the two days that remained before we set off. Although this decision had been made in part so as to allow me one last taste of the finer things in life before leaving my homeland, it was also a tactical move. After I had realized that there would be many foreigners among the passengers waiting to board, I vowed to do my utmost to avoid being seen by them.

When I took a taxi to the docks, there obviously wasn't anyone with me to see me off. Nevertheless, I didn't feel alone as I stepped onto the ship's deck. I was overcome by a tremendous feeling of courage.

"Well Morimura, it's just you," I told myself inwardly. "Now that you've got your battle face on, you absolutely cannot bring shame to the servicemen of the Imperial Japanese Navy! It goes without saying that if you fail, you will never again see this harbor. But seeing it again is exactly what you've pledged to do, isn't it?"

Aboard ship there were very many foreigners who were being evacuated from Japan. Very few of the passengers were Japanese going to the United States, though. It was perhaps because of this that the foreigners on deck, all of whom were wearing colorful clothing, seemed quite wealthy. As I was accustomed to kimonos and prickly work clothes, and because Japan had totally forgotten about color, these men and women all seemed to be good-looking.

The gong that signaled the ship's departure sounded and then the massive hull of the *Nitta Maru* quietly moved away from the docks at Yokohama. As the paper bunting slowly began to rip apart, piece by piece, you could hear people sobbing everywhere on deck.

When looking back at the docks, you could see the people gathered there waving white handkerchiefs in the air with all their might. While I was holding fast to the side-railing with both hands, my eyes fixed on the tall buildings

10. Aboard the *Nitta Maru*

in Yokohama's Naka district that were slowly slipping away, I suddenly heard someone call out to me from behind.

"Mr. Morimura!"

The feeling that had come over me as I left my homeland behind was gone in a flash. I was quite startled by that shout.

I whirled my head back.

"I'm sorry. You must be Mr. Morimura, aren't you sir?"

It was just one of the stewards, he was addressing me politely as he approached.

"May I offer you some tea? It has already been prepared."

"Ah. Thank you," I replied with a nod.

"Also, I have prepared your cabin for you. If it pleases you!"

"Hmm?"

I followed the steward's lead and went with him below deck to the passenger cabins. Once there, I let out a deep sigh. It was true. I had finally become Morimura. From this day forward, no one would ever call me "Yoshikawa" again! I had taken on the character of another person and been reborn.

Just now hadn't I taken that photograph of "her," which I had been loath to part with, and thrown it into the billowing waves? She and I had seen our fates so toyed with by the gods that I didn't know whether to laugh or cry! Earlier that morning, while I was sitting on a tramcar as it traveled between the city's outer limits and the docks, I quite unexpectedly noticed Chika cradling an infant on a tram station platform. In an instant I was totally stupefied! My breathing seemed to come to a stop. Then, without giving me a moment to think, the tramcar moved on. All I could do was to close my eyes and say a prayer to wish her happiness. Soon afterwards, the focus of my prayer moved from mother and child to our ancestral land. I prayed for the happiness of the homeland.

The cabin I had been led to was one of the most luxurious aboard the ship. Perhaps that fellow from the Navy General Staff who had telephoned to say that a "farewell dinner" had been specially prepared for me had arranged it! I accepted this bounty graciously, but inwardly I felt a certain distaste for it all. I couldn't help but feel that it had been prepared as a sendoff to a certain death.

"Oh, what the hell!"

While I thought this over, I remembered an old saying: "A spy should beware of money and women." If you don't take this stricture seriously when working as a spy, you will fail. The examples that bear this out are simply too numerous to mention. Men are enticed and enchanted by money and women, and they are hard to brush aside. Wasn't I just remembering Chika? And hadn't I let my thoughts run wild? Wasn't that tantamount to suddenly becoming a careless fool and forgetting all about my alias? I needed to watch myself. Oh boy, I needed to watch myself carefully! I changed my clothes, climbed onto the bed, and sank deep into thought.

After a time, the ship was rocking quite violently from side-to-side. It had probably entered the high seas.

"Hello! How are you?"
"Hi! Come down here!"
"Nice sunshine!"
"Yes!"
"Do you like the sea?"
"Yes! And you?"

I often went to the lower deck to practice my English. There I met some second-generation overseas Japanese students who had been pulled out of Japan. They would either sit atop the heavy ropes and bask in the sun, stand on deck and look out at the vastness of the ocean, or sit and read books.

After sunrise on the second day of our voyage, I stood on the deck and scanned the ship's surroundings in every direction. The waves were surging around us and the sea and sky seemed to merge together. It didn't matter in which direction you looked, the horizon was always the same. It was perhaps because the vast blue ocean gives people a feeling of emptiness that everyone quickly found themselves on warm, affectionate terms with others.

There was a young lady who told me that she was returning to her parents' home in Nebraska. Although she had been in her second year at a university in Japan, she felt compelled to give up her studies and leave the country because she was afraid that there wouldn't be any more ships going back to America before long. The young lady was very concerned about the situation she saw developing all around the world.

"Do you like Japan?"
"I very much like it. However, Japan isn't an easy place to find yourself a good opportunity."
"What sort of opportunity do you mean?"
"…For example, finding a job… First of all, finding someone to marry is not easy at all… I don't trust them and I can't get them to trust me either. In Japan, every opportunity seems to fit into a ready-made pattern and it's really hard trying to see what that pattern is when you are fumbling around in the dark!"

It seemed as if those second-generation Japanese-Americans shared an outlook and temperament that was very Japanese, but there was something else about them that made them incompatible with the Japanese.

There were four people including myself in our section of the ship. The first was the president of the Silver Fox Company, while the other two were business executives. The company president was on his way to Argentina to buy up furs and pelts that were not finding any buyers at that time. I joined

10. Aboard the Nitta Maru

him the in the common area for two or three games of Japanese chess (also known as "Go") and he sounded worried when he told me that he didn't know if he was going to be able to return to Japan.

Apart from these people, there was an American missionary who left a very deep impression upon me. Both of us often went up to the ship's deck to take a stroll. We only nodded politely when we first saw one another, but after a little while we found ourselves talking and soon we were on friendly terms. Apparently, he had lived in Sendai for well over ten years.

"The Japanese authorities began to insist that I was a spy," he told me. "And they forced me out of the country. How could something like that ever happen? I really don't understand what this new Japanese government is trying to do!"

When I heard his words, a wave of fear entered my heart and gave me a start. Then I began to wonder if he might actually be sizing me up. Yet it appeared that my suspicions were unfounded because I couldn't find any other clues that justified them. In fact, from the time that I got to know him to the time that we disembarked, I was always the one who took the initiative to suggest that we play another round of mini golf on deck together. I couldn't help but smile a bitter smile when I later remembered a slogan that was popular in Japan at the time: "There is a spy right beside you!"

Passengers aboard the *Nitta Maru* seemed to share the philosophy that even mortal enemies should help one another in the face of a common danger. Each passenger had their own individual thoughts and desires. Each had a destiny. None of which mattered to the ship. Heading due east, it continued to steam straight ahead.

11

Taking Up a New Post

As the *Nitta Maru* gently glided to a stop alongside the docks at Honolulu on 27 March 1941, a choral version of "*Aloha-Oe*" ("Goodbye!"), a sad, gently modulating melody of farewell, was played non-stop over the P.A. system.

Local women were greeting the newly arrived visitors, hurrying here and there with bare feet while carrying large necklaces made of flowers in their arms. Local youths mixed in with the crowds as well, walking back and forth and calling out loudly to advertise their wares. All of this gave that early morning on the docks a feeling of great vitality.

I stood on the deck and looked down at the crowd. Standing off to one side was a group of three or four people watching the passengers who were making their way down the ship's gangway. As soon as I had concluded that they were staff from Japan's Consulate-General, I reminded myself that I was going to have to look the part. I absolutely could not let them see my true self.

"Excuse me gentlemen, are you from the consulate? My name is Morimura."

"Welcome! Welcome! You've had a long journey!"

"Thank you very much for your assistance!"

After we had exchanged our greetings, we climbed into the car that had been dispatched from the consulate-general and I continued to worry someone would notice my manner was that of a serviceman.

During our journey everything that I saw and heard gave me a completely new feeling for Hawaii, where all four seasons are summer. As I looked out at the huge verdant green trees, red flowers speckled with emerald green, lawns as thick as heavy carpets, and the tall, slender coconut palms, I was reminded everywhere of the eternal joy of spring. There was so much beauty there that it overwhelmed me. I felt very deeply that I was not worthy of this paradise in the Pacific.

I truly was envious beyond measure when I saw that this isolated island, situated thousands of nautical miles away from my homeland, was a dreamlike paradise with so many people of different skin colors living peacefully

11. Taking Up a New Post

together. Yet from that day onwards, I had no choice but to treat all of the people in that peaceful place as the enemy. I had to live the life of one who dupes himself in order to deceive his enemy. My thoughts were racing as I sat in the car, my mind was in a tumult.

Halfway along Nu'uanu Avenue, the car stopped in front of the Japanese Consulate-General. I soon caught sight of the extensive lawn, the flower garden, and the office building sitting within the grounds. Set within the brickwork high above was a very shiny emblem displaying a chrysanthemum, the symbol of the Japanese Empire.

I was led into the consul-general's office.

"I am Morimura, I have come to report for duty."

"Do come in, and please sit down!" said Consul-General Nagao Kita, after I had extended the usual courtesies. He was blinking very frequently as he motioned for me to sit in the chair facing his (I learned afterwards that this was a nervous defect he suffered from.) After that, he smiled and lowered his voice in a way that suggested we were sharing a private joke:

"So, you are Mr. Yoshikawa! I do know. The Navy General Staff has told me all about it."

"Oh, really?"

Those few words from Kita made me feel very much at ease. I felt right away as if I could freely speak my mind with him.

"Now … what's the situation here at present?"

"The situation is extremely perilous! I've only just arrived myself, on the last boat, so I don't have a very detailed understanding of the situation here. However, the FBI is definitely keeping watch over us. There's no doubt about that Mr. Morimura, sir. It's best that you be careful! Ha, ha, ha!"

Kita let out a hearty laugh.

"But, consul-general, you have seen Pearl Harbor, haven't you sir?"

"No, I have not. That side of things will depend entirely upon you. All right, first of all, lighten up a little and have some fun! You and I are the only bachelors here. Ha, ha, ha!"

"Consul-General, I have been carrying $600 in U.S. currency with me on this journey. I have kept it close to me at all times, whether I was going for a walk on deck or taking a shower. I haven't dared to do anything careless with the money. Could I ask you to look after it for me?"

"No, that's all for you. And I will reimburse you for any expenses you run up in the course of gathering information for your reports. It doesn't matter how much those expenses are, you can spend whatever it takes.

"As for your duties here, I would like to ask you to deal with matters concerning those who are renouncing their citizenship. I am going to brief the others about this. You need to remember that. Naturally, none of the others know about your true background so you'll need to be careful!"

"Understood. Thank you. Please give me more such advice. Sir."

"In the residence, just behind you, there is a room that has been made ready for you. You can live there. It is just too dangerous outside!"

"Thank you very much, sir!"

From then on, all of my tasks and activities were carried out in accordance with the consul-general's instructions.

Consul-General Kita had arrived aboard the ship that had docked before mine. Shortly before I left Tokyo, I had heard that he had been transferred from Guangdong. He was apparently one of the "hardliners" among the current generation of diplomats. A hard-drinking sort of man quite accustomed to dealing with those from the military, he had been specially chosen for transfer from Guangdong to understand, guide, and help me, blunt and impulsive as I was.

Under international law, every consulate-general was permitted to send coded telegrams to its Foreign Ministry for reasons of diplomatic secrecy and some opted to take advantage of this special right. In fact, this was the reason behind the decision to send me to the consulate-general. My intelligence reports were to be sent from the consulate-general to the Foreign Ministry. From there they would be dispatched to the Navy General Staff.

Other than Consul-General Kita, there were several employees at the consulate-general. There was Vice-Consul-General Okuda, Secretary Tsukikawa, Mr. Aburashita, Mr. Seki, and myself. In addition, there were three second-generation Japanese-American clerks, a typist, two drivers, three garage/warehouse workers, and the family members of the employees. With the exception of the three second-generation Japanese-Americans and Secretary Tsukikawa, the staff members and their families all lived in residence at the consulate-general.

The room given to me was on the second floor, at the western end of the residence building. It had a balcony next to three cocoa trees that were burdened with countless fruit. The balcony also overlooked the expansive lawn that extended far beyond that side of the building.

After I'd had a bit of a rest, I followed the instructions given to me by Vice-Consul-General Okuda and introduced myself to every one my new colleagues. Afterwards, I sat down at my desk and Consul-General Kita made a show of handing over the "work" that was ostensibly mine to deal with. With the help of some instructions given to me by a Japanese-American clerk, I learned all about the wonderful job of dealing with applications to renounce one's nationality. It was a completely routine sort of job. All that was required was that you put the applicant's full name on a form and then complete the rest of the application. Following that, you simply needed to report this information to the Japanese government.

As was commonly known, all second-generation Japanese-Americans were considered Japanese citizens under Japanese law because they had been born to Japanese parents. Yet under U.S. law, all those born within the United States were entitled to claim U.S. nationality. Second-generation Japanese-Americans were therefore both Japanese and American citizens. However, there were some who worried they might be distrusted during the course of their work or military service, or that their Japanese nationality could cause them other problems. Consequently, many second-generation Japanese-Americans decided to renounce their birthright of Japanese nationality in order to become "pure" U.S. citizens.

For its part, the Japanese government had long taken the attitude of a loving parent in allowing its citizens to make up their own minds. Thus, all applicants were permitted to renounce their Japanese nationality. This marvelous work was the only job assigned to me during my stint at the consulate-general.

On 27 March, a local newspaper printed some details about my arrival to take up a post at the consulate-general. It also reported that the *Nitta Maru* had set a speed record from Yokohama to Honolulu. The ship had made the voyage in just 5 days and 20 hours.

12

An Overview of Hawaii

The overall situation in Hawaii is very much what one would expect. It is a paradise in the Pacific where all four seasons are an endless summer. The shoreline at Waikiki, the paddling of canoes, surfing, Hawaiian guitar, Hawaiian folk singing, the traditional clothing worn by Hawaiian women and their hula dancing ... these are but some of the things that make people long for Hawaii.

Yet the vast majority of people don't realize that there are two mountains that rise higher than Mount Fuji in Hawaii, nor are they aware that the U.S. Navy's huge Pacific Fleet is based there. Pearl Harbor, located on Oahu, sits right in the middle of the Hawaiian Archipelago.

Allow me to provide a basic description of the archipelago. Twenty Hawaiian Islands are located in the middle of the Pacific Ocean, either slightly above or below the parallel at 23 degrees latitude north that demarcates the Tropic of Cancer. When traveling across the archipelago from east to west, one sees several large islands: Hawaii (The Big Island), Maui, Molokai, Oahu, and Kauai. These five islands are often grouped together with three others of similar size and collectively they are known as "The Big Eight."

The total surface area of the Hawaiian Islands is roughly equal to that of Japan's Shikoku Island. The Hawaiian Archipelago is spread out over 1,500 miles, from Kure Atoll in the northwest to Hawaii in the southeast.

In the past, it would take about seven days to travel by ship from Yokohama to Honolulu and another five days or so to travel from Honolulu to San Francisco. Nowadays, thanks to the jet aircraft, one can substitute hours for days when calculating the time required to travel the same distances.

All of the islands of the Hawaiian Archipelago were either formed through volcanic activity or produced by coral reefs. Among the local volcanoes are Kilauea (an active giant volcano on Hawaii) and Haleakala (a giant volcano on Maui). These volcanoes, the Leprosy Settlement on Molokai, and Oahu's Pearl Harbor, are well-known tourist sites.

The first inhabitants of the islands came from Polynesia and the name "Hawaii" was given to the archipelago in honor of Hawai'iloa, the man who was said to have discovered and subdued the island chain. Subsequently, the famous British explorer Captain James Cook introduced Hawaii to the world.

In 1795, Kamehameha and his forces defeated the local warriors in fierce combat by the slopes of Oahu's Nu'uanu Pali. Kamehameha then became ruler of the entire Hawaiian Archipelago. Soon after his victory, Kamehameha established his court on the coast at Waikiki. The court was then moved a short distance inland to the site of present-day Honolulu, which Kamehameha III later designated the capital of Hawaii. Waikiki was where Kamehameha landed when he first traveled from Hawaii to Oahu in a wooden canoe and it subsequently became the place the kings would go to whenever they wanted to take a pleasure cruise. Gradually, it became as it is today with its rows upon rows of houses, hotels, and tower blocks. Waikiki is now a well-known scenic area and a bustling, highly developed hub of commercial activity.

Although Captain Cook had decided to call the archipelago "The Sandwich Islands," Kamehameha III, the monarch who drafted Hawaii's first constitution, didn't like that term.[1] In 1840, he formally changed its name to The Hawaiian Islands. Hawaii is also known as the "Paradise in the Pacific" and more recently it has been called "The Aloha State."

The only royal palace in the United States, Honolulu's Iolani Palace, is located in Hawaii. The King's throne is still kept there today as a tourist attraction, though some of the State's administrative offices now occupy the building.

Captain Cook noted in his logbooks that archipelago's population numbered around 300,000 at the end of the 18th century. These days (in the 1960s), the total population of the Hawaiian Archipelago is more than 600,000.

Although the Hawaiian Archipelago was made a territory of the United States in 1900, the bill to make it a fully-fledged state was not passed by the U.S. Congress until 12 March 1958. On 21 August of the same year, President Eisenhower signed the bill into law and this finally granted the citizens of Hawaii that which they had anticipated for more than 50 years.

Some 75 percent of the total population of the Hawaiian Archipelago is based on Oahu. The state capital, Honolulu, has a population of 30,000. The total ethnic Japanese population living in the Hawaiian Archipelago is 150,000. Of that population, 83,000 are based on Oahu. There are roughly 110,000 telephones on Oahu.

During my time in Hawaii, there were four main areas of economic activity within the archipelago. Those areas of economic activity and the revenues they generated were as follows:

1. Sugar production $130 million
2. Pineapple production $130 million

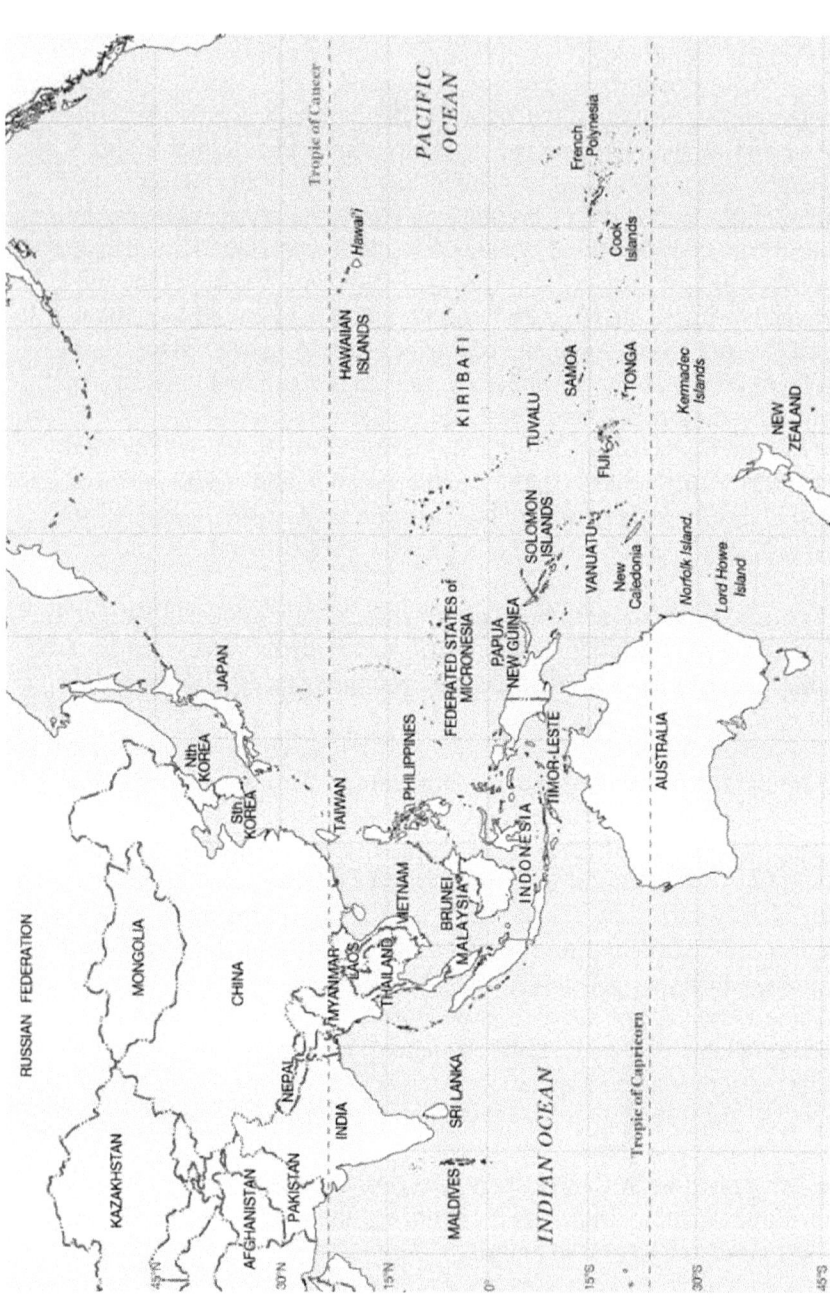

A map (2011) of the Pacific Ocean showing East Asia, the Philippines, and Australasia. Reproduced with the permission of CartoGIS Services, ANU College of Asia and the Pacific, the Australian National University.

3. Tourism $110 million
4. Military $340 million

In total, the annual revenue generated by all economic activity in the Hawaiian Archipelago amounted to well over $700 million. From that time to today, this figure has not changed by much. Nevertheless, the archipelago is a truly beautiful region. No matter the island you go to, all are endowed with lush green sugarcane farms and fields of pineapple.

13

Getting Down to Work

I began to get down to work soon after I took up my post. Whenever I went out "sightseeing" I wore olive khaki trousers, a floral Hawaiian aloha shirt and a Hawaiian hat. I frequently took a ride in a taxi over to Pearl Harbor. Once there, I pretended to be doing some sightseeing when I was in fact working.

"I think I ought to go out and do a little sightseeing. I may as well take in some of the scenery here so I'll have something to talk about later on." From my first day onward, whenever I was about to leave the office, I would never forget to repeat this script to dupe my colleagues.

One of them, who knew nothing of my true background, gave me a warning: "It's best that you don't go over to Pearl Harbor. If you're picked up by any of the sentries there, that will surely cause you trouble."

Hmm! How did he know that was precisely the site I needed to check out? I wondered.

"Well then, I think I'll go for a stroll along the seashore at Waikiki."

After heading down Nu'uanu Avenue past the busy downtown area, and then continuing along the avenue as it curved west, we entered a much wider road. The right side of that road looked onto the foot of a mountain where the sugarcane crops stretched off into the distance as far as the eye could see. On the left side of the road was Hickam airfield. Pearl Harbor was located roughly 40 kilometers further down that road.

Although I was making a concerted effort to seem as if I was most interested in the sugarcane plantations, all of my energy had long been concentrated on the scene on the opposite side of the road where the naval base was. I did this so that the driver wouldn't think I had any knowledge whatsoever about the military.

"Hey! There's a great big plane over there. Is that for tourists?"

"No. That's a B-17, a 4-engine bomber that arrived here recently. Now right at the very end there, you'll see a dome-shaped structure. That's an airplane hangar… And that large-sized seaplane is a tourist aircraft. It takes off and lands in the water, just beyond Pearl Harbor. You'll get a good look at it if you turn your head now."

13. Getting Down to Work

The driver seemed to be very familiar with the situation there as he explained these things to me.

After we had continued down the road a while longer, we saw Pearl Harbor. Lights were flickering all over, making it look like an enormous starfish. Previously, while at the Navy General Staff, I had only been able to contemplate the harbor by looking at a small-scale replica in a sandbox. Now it was right there, stretched out before my very eyes. Two or three fighter planes were taking off from Ford Island in the middle of the harbor just then.

To the east of that island, there were several battleships moored alongside one another. To the island's west, aircraft carriers and heavy cruisers were grouped together. At anchor near those warships were other vessels of various types, positioned according to their size and class.

In the industrial zone along the shore, there were occasional flashes of light along with plumes of white smoke from the welding that was being carried out there. One look at the place was enough for anyone to see that Pearl Harbor was the scene of tremendous activity.

As we drew near to Pearl Harbor, the driver greatly increased our speed. He was evidently quite familiar with the rules of the zone.

"Wow, there are so many boats here."

"This is a restricted military zone. You aren't allowed to stay and look around here. Cars aren't allowed to drive slowly here either. Take a look to the left and to the right. Do you see those people standing there? They are sentries."

"Oh, really?"

"A few days ago, there was a Japanese tourist who didn't notice them and was taking pictures from his car. He ended up being grabbed by the guards… Anyway, it's 'No pen!' and 'No camera!' here."

He almost seemed to be singing those two phrases and he shrugged as he did so.

Pearl Harbor was surrounded on all sides by wrought iron fencing. Within the fenced-in enclosure there were great big petroleum storage containers. Armed sentries stood guard in every key area of the compound.

The policemen who were hidden on either side of the road, lying in wait, were much more troublesome than the sentries according to the driver. If a car so much as stopped for a moment, they would immediately set upon the car, interrogate the driver, and then forcibly escort him out of the zone. In a word, when driving through this area you had to simply look straight ahead and keep right on driving.

Given that this was the state of things around there, how exactly was I going to complete my mission? In addition to all of that, the wrought iron fencing, the petroleum containers, and the buildings at the site all blocked my line of vision and made it very difficult for me to differentiate between ships of the same class or determine the size and weight of the ships.

There were four different types of battleship in the U.S. Navy's armada and there were two versions of each type of battleship. If you were unable to determine what sort of battleship you were looking at, you couldn't accurately judge the current deployment of the fleet.

When I was in Japan looking at photographs and sketches, I could always remember the name and class of ships with tall masts. But out in the field I wasn't playing a game of soldiers any longer, I was obliged to judge what I could actually see. It really wasn't at all easy.

"Mister, would you like to go and see a large-size tourist airplane?" said the driver, just as I was beginning to sink into deep thought.

"Sure, let's go! But are we allowed to go there?"

"It's okay!"

The car wound its way around Pearl Harbor, passed a promontory and Pearl City, and continued along a peninsula toward the ocean. Streets lined with houses surrounded by trees stretched out from either side of the road, yet few people were to be seen along those streets. The area was very peaceful.

Just then, I began to feel a bit uncomfortable. Was this guy beginning to notice that I was just a little bit suspicious? Had he decided to bring me to this place because of that? Although he was a second-generation Japanese-American, that was no reason to get careless. Perhaps he had some contacts at the FBI? Just as my misgivings were beginning to grow about the circumstances I found myself in, we suddenly reached a spot where we could see the ocean.

We got out of the car and then the driver began to introduce me to the area. He explained a lot of things about the large flying-boat passenger plane, exactly how it landed in this lake-like bay, on which days of the week, on which days of the week it took off again and so on. Though none of that had anything to do with my specific interests, I was listening patiently when he said: "It's like a white swan when it's taking off. It's really nice to look at."

Those words left a deep impression on me and I still remember them very clearly.

"Hey, let's go over there and drink some Coca-Cola!" he suggested.

"Hmm. Okay!"

I thought to myself that I might as well listen to him on this sightseeing tour, rather than blindly feeling my way around. This outing gave me the opportunity to understand exactly in which areas ordinary citizens were allowed to come and go freely.

The car followed the road as it curved one way and then the other, again and again. Halfway down the road, there was a curve to the right and then we reached the peninsula's summit. From there we had a clear view over the aircraft carriers and the heavy cruisers. You could even see sailors on the docks loading small motorboats with fresh fruit, vegetable and other foodstuffs.

13. Getting Down to Work

There were some docks just a short distance away and not very far from them was a quaint little teashop that sold Coca-Cola and sweets. I looked on in amazement, and then recoiled in my seat, as I watched the driver walk up to the tea shop without the slightest care in the world. "Mr. Teashop," he said. "I've brought you a customer. He's taking a tour. Give us some cold drinks and snacks, will you?"

He began to wave me over as he was speaking. The teashop was apparently run by an older Japanese couple who took turns manning their business, which catered almost exclusively to sailors.

"Isn't this a restricted zone?" I asked.

"No, no. Over here it's okay. I often come here."

"Oh, really?"

"The old boy is a really kind-hearted man!"

The U.S. Navy must have overlooked that place, and it was a major oversight!

It made me extremely happy to know that I would be able to come back to that spot, because it was an ideal vantage point. Pearl Harbor appeared to be closely-guarded only along its front flank, yet it was wide-open along its rear. It was so good to know this!

I told myself that I would be returning there frequently.

14

Touring the Islands

Pearl Harbor was not the only military base on Oahu, there were many others. Some of those bases were being expanded, while others already stood completed. Each one needed to be thoroughly scouted out to determine its relative state of completion, troop movements, and capacity for reinforcements.

I was determined to complete a thorough reconnaissance report about every island in the archipelago, starting with Oahu. When vowing to do so, I also promised myself that I would remember the name of every site that I visited. Yet since all Hawaiian place names come from the local language, and because every such name contains vowel sounds, it is quite difficult for someone from Japan to pronounce them correctly. Nevertheless, it was absolutely necessary that I remember them all in order to differentiate between places whose names sounded similar.

At that time, Pearl Harbor's conventional forces included:

Navy

8 Battleships
10 Heavy Cruisers
12 Light Cruisers
3 Aircraft Carriers
100 Other Assorted Vessels

Army

1 Division of Troops
Air power: 300 Aircraft
Installations: Docks, shipyards, dry docks for repairs, petroleum
   storage tanks, and more.

The decision to give a 28-year-old guy the task of finding out everything possible about such huge numbers of troops and their deployment was completely mad. Basically, it wasn't going to work. It occurred to me then that if Japan were to confront this enormous military machine, and if the conven-

14. Touring the Islands

tional rules were followed, we could send our entire armada and yet have absolutely no chance of securing victory. Recent events in Europe appeared to bear this out. Although Hitler possessed the upper hand in air power, he wasn't able to get his forces across the English Channel.

I didn't think that there was a single country that could attack distant Hawaii, which was situated thousands of nautical miles from anywhere, and make a success of it. Hawaii had been called an impregnable and indestructible fortress, and not without good reason. Nevertheless, I had to challenge its enormous military might. This was something I would do primarily by "knowing the enemy" (ferreting out all the details about the enemy's forces that had hitherto remained unknown).

Consequently, I came up with the idea of touring each of the Hawaiian Islands. Using Oahu as my base, I would roam all around each island. My first objective was of course Oahu itself, the total distance around which is roughly 100 nautical miles. It took about four hours to circumnavigate the island.

A June 1941 photograph showing Ford Island (foreground), Navy Yard (upper left) and the Waipio Peninsula (right center) (Naval History and Heritage Command).

So as to not arouse any suspicions, I pretended to do the work assigned to me at the consulate-general during the day and then I would go out for a stroll after work. In the evenings, I would make my way over to the busy downtown area to seek out some of the white-uniformed sailors who mobbed the streets and invite them for a drink. Through making some inquiries, I would get details about the local situation from them. When I returned to my residence in the middle of the night, I wouldn't undress. I'd just go straight to sleep. And that was how I usually whiled away my days.

I often got back to my room on the second floor of our living quarters long after the Japanese-American attendant had gone home to her family. On such occasions, I didn't manage to get much rest before I had to go and get that day's local newspaper, browse through it, and read between the lines to glean a few clues.

I read advertisements aimed at recruiting workers to active construction sites on military bases, news about ships and shipping, stories on celebrities with links to the military who had come to visit, articles questioning whether or not Japanese language schools should be allowed to remain open, where and when the Overseas Japanese Residents' Association should convene its upcoming meeting, and so on. I had to take clippings of all such articles and then research them.

Once, while I was reading the announcements of upcoming weddings (a section of the newspaper that was five pages long and filled with very detailed information), I discovered some rather interesting news:

> On ____ day of ____ month at ____ place, a local young lady from such-and-such a family is going to be married to an officer who is in command of ____ on the battleship *West Virginia*.

I read it very carefully and took notes. Armed with this news, I hurried over to Pearl Harbor that day to check it out. Sure enough, there was a warship at anchor there. I came to the conclusion that it was the *West Virginia*, the battleship whose presence had been leaked by the newspaper.

After adopting this method of collecting crumbs of information day after day, I was finally able to identify all the ships by name even though I had initially been unsure about those names for the most part. I kept the useful newspaper clippings in my desk at the consulate-general and burned all the others.

When it occurred to me that I should try to find someone to assist me in my work, I went (fully aware of what I was doing) to meetings of the Overseas Japanese Residents' Association, to Japanese chess (Go) tournaments, to amateur baseball games, and other such activities. There I did my utmost to come into close contact with Japanese expatriates and with second-generation Japanese-Americans.

14. Touring the Islands

During that period, I was certainly able to determine that so-and-so, and so-and-so, were sympathetic to the Japanese cause. Yet after spending some time monitoring them and putting them to the test, I discovered that most of those people had no knowledge of military matters. They were full of talk, but of no practical use whatsoever. Furthermore, it was very difficult to guarantee that they wouldn't divulge secrets.

Due to these experiences, I was forced to accept the truth that those of us in the business of espionage cannot depend on outside help. We can only depend on our own strengths and abilities to meticulously reconnoiter our targets. Apart from that, there are no shortcuts. Consequently, I abandoned the idea of finding an assistant.

Having to depend on my own strengths and abilities to do the job meant that I had to go everywhere myself to scout things out. However, if I were to go to Pearl Harbor every day for a stroll it would attract too much attention. How could I deceive the eyes of others so that they did not see me? I began racking my brains to answer that question.

There was a street in front of our living quarters and on the opposite side of that street there was a private home. Whenever I left our living quarters and went out to that street, a person within the private dwelling would contact the FBI and they would send someone to follow me. When I exited the consulate-general's front door to get to the wide avenue it faced, many people were always coming and going and it was quite easy to find yourself being followed there too. This occurred despite the fact that few private residences were to be found nearby. As it seemed that neither of those two exits was very convenient for my purposes, I set about finding, and found, a third exit. I would cross the consulate-general's large grounds, hop over a wall, cross a stream, get to the main road, and then hire a taxi.

There was yet another way to avoid catching anyone's attention and that was to go out in disguise. As a result, I frequently went to shops during the workday to buy formal evening-wear, suits, sportswear, aloha shirts, leather shoes, hats, work wear, lunch pails and so on. Afterwards I would simply return to work, which meant that I sometimes ended up wearing three different outfits in a single day. Yet in so doing, I repeatedly incurred the censure of my colleagues.

"Morimura. You ought to take your work seriously, don't you think?"

"Yes!"

"It's been decided that we will have a party to welcome you formally this evening. All the employees will be there. We will meet at six o'clock sharp in front of the consulate's main building."

"Really, I don't deserve such kindness."

Beforehand I had a bath, changed into some nice clothes, and then strolled outside onto the grounds. I felt unusually relaxed, as if my spirit had been set free. I then stopped on the lawn and stood there while scanning the verdant greenery of the surrounding woods and enjoying the flower garden's sweet fragrance. Evening time in Hawaii truly was a most intoxicating hour.

The priest from the neighboring Catholic Church, clad in his black vestment, had come outside for a stroll just then. I noticed that he was stopping and standing from time to time, as if he were thinking of something. The white cross that hung from his neck was particularly eye-catching in the midst of so much greenery.

Our eyes met and we exchanged a silent greeting.

"That was very impolite of me a few days ago."

I had been hitting a golf ball around the grounds two days earlier, until I hit it too fiercely. It then bounced off the top of the wall and hit one of the church school's window frames, which made a very loud noise and gave him a fright. I was now apologizing to him in person.

He smiled and replied softly, "Don't worry about that, it was nothing!"

I too was smiling, as I nodded my head.

It was just before six o'clock when I reached the main building. I was surprised to see Consul-General Kita following the Japanese chefs (a husband and wife duo specially brought over from Japan) as they directed a team of female assistants setting up the food tables.

I was then told that evening's invitees included the following guests of honor: an official from the Italian Consulate-General, the Director of the Overseas Japanese Residents' Association, and the President of the Association of Commerce and Industry. By that time, the scope of Japan's diplomatic activities had narrowed considerably and our Consulate-General had practically broken off all contact with the other consulates, apart from the Italian Consulate-General.

Seated next to me at the dinner table was the official from the Italian Consulate-General, a very chatty and good-natured sort of man. At times, he gestured wildly when speaking and was obviously quite agitated. When he was in this state, he took to using Italian. At other times he was quite obviously dispirited and used a very heavily Italian-accented English instead. I didn't catch much of what he was actually saying, but I did manage to understand that they were soon going to up sticks and return home.

A few of the Japanese expatriates said that they were worried about the worsening of Japan-U.S. relations. Although their words were quite circumspect, they also said that some second-generation Japanese-Americans were not at all concerned about the situation. After enlisting in the U.S. armed forces, these young Japanese-Americans had dragged their elders to their farewell parties so they could see them off. Moreover, after the young Japanese-Americans had recited the pledge of allegiance in front of the American Flag, they insisted that their elders make a speech to congratulate them. The elders didn't know whether to laugh or cry.

14. Touring the Islands

Everyone found this quite amusing.

At that time, overseas Japanese and the Japanese at home kept up the same tradition. Whenever young Japanese enlisted in the military, there would always be a grand sendoff party held for them in a public place such as a theater or a meeting hall. This practice is almost exclusively Japanese, apparently. It is seldom observed in other parts of the world.

"Morimura, let's go find some place where we can have another drink!" Consul-General Kita said to me once the banquet was over and the guests, staff, and their family members had all gone home.

"Yes!"

"I want to have a welcoming party, for you and you alone!" Consul-General Kita added with great enthusiasm.

He then told Ozaki, the chauffeur, to get the car ready. Ozaki was a very dependable member of staff with more than 20 years' experience. He had worked for several consuls-general. Furthermore, he was highly respected by U.S. officials because he had served in the U.S. military as a young man.

The car rolled out into the darkness of the night and followed Nu'uanu Avenue uphill. Before long we turned right, just as we reached the Shunchoro Teahouse in Alewa Heights. This was the first time that I had been to the Japanese teahouse and tavern.

"Oh my! A most rare visitor! Consul-General, sir, you've arrived with another guest. Who might this gentleman be?"

"This is Mr. Morimura."

"Ah, did you arrive recently to take up a new post? Welcome!"

After the landlady had led us upstairs to the dining room on the second floor, we exchanged more courtesies.

The wide-open and very spacious dining hall looked out to the southwest. You could see tiny lights shining out there. I was certain that they were lighting Pearl Harbor and Hickam Field.

Inwardly, I let out a sigh. "Hmm."

"Hey, Mr. Morimura. The FBI agents that followed us here are probably in the dining room below ours, huh!"

"Ha, ha, ha!"

The two of us then began to drink to our hearts' content.

"Consul-General, sir, I was wondering if you have done the tour of this island."

"No, I still haven't. Shivers, the chief of the local FBI bureau, came to visit a few days ago and asked me if I had 'gone on a tour of the island.' But I replied, 'I'm not going anywhere because I hate it when you guys follow me.' 'How can that be?' he said. 'Please take a tour whenever you like.'"

"Ha, ha, ha."

While we were laughing loudly and drinking our whiskies with soda, several beautiful young ladies appeared before us. Hanako, Yuko, Okinu, and others still, were following Sweetie's lead. All of them were wearing Japanese kimonos.

Sweetie was unashamed of hailing from the Shinbashi district in Tokyo.[1] She was a geisha who had studied abroad and knew how to play popular tunes. By contrast, the two of us were both a bit rough around the edges and possessed no artistic talent whatsoever, apart from drinking booze.

Everyone somehow seemed to have the gift of the gab. Thanks to the influence of the ever-sociable Consul-General Kita, the dining hall was soon buzzing with energy and became a happy sort of place.

After three rounds of drinks, Yuko and Okinu began speaking to one another.

"Oh my, this waistband is pulled in so tight. It feels as if it's trying to kill me!"

"Would you mind if I took it off?"

"All right. And I'll take yours off too!"

I was amazed to see these two young Japanese-Americans take their waistbands off, thereby revealing the aloha shirts that they were wearing underneath.

"All right, all right, now we can relax! Please have some beer! Morimura!"

I was quietly sizing up the situation. If I was going to be able to come back to that lookout point, I would have to: (i) Make friends with the geisha girls. (ii) Find a pretext to return on a regular basis.

Very late into that night, my mind was brimming with ideas as I looked over a peaceful and sleepy Pearl Harbor.

15

Sending Telegrams

Every year, invitations were sent out to locals and expatriate residents for the celebration of the Emperor's birthday at the Japanese Consulate-General on 29 April. Over the years, this annual celebration had become something of an event. That year, however, a group of rarely seen visitors was also in attendance. The group was comprised of more than ten young naval officers from Pearl Harbor, each of whom was wearing an all-white uniform. They made quite an impression when they were gathered together. Never before had so many U.S. naval officers been welcomed to the consulate-general at the same time.

Naturally, they had received a special invitation from the consulate-general. Yet from that day to the day of the surprise attack on Pearl Harbor, they never invited us to pay them a visit in return. I believe that they had taken advantage of the occasion to scout out our consulate-general.

I say this mainly because there were so many rumors making the rounds at the time. For example, an old Meiji-style nationalist expatriate came running in to the consulate-general to say that the U.S. Navy was installing dozens of cannons "as wide as church bells" at Diamond Head. Then someone else came running in to the consulate-general to make a special petition. He and some others were going to go into the sugarcane fields and would set them on fire as soon as the Japanese Army entered Oahu. These fires would send a signal to the entire Japanese expatriate community that they should to rise up and join our army's attack. He then asked if arms and ammunition might be stored in the consulate-general's basement in preparation for such an attack. Soon after that, rumors about dozens of machine guns and rifles being hidden inside the consulate-general were widespread.

All of this is borne out by FBI chief Shivers' post-war recollections:

> By then we had compiled a list of several thousands of people who were in league with hostile forces and we were ready to round all of them up within 24 hours of a declaration of war. However, Morimura was not actually on that list. If we had known before the war that he was the person sending the (coded) telegrams, we definitely would have arrested him.

He seems to have regretted this forever after.

After the formal gathering came to an end, the guests were invited to enjoy the gardens. There, quite naturally, the task of looking after the U.S. Navy's officers fell to me. Generally speaking, Japanese people are not very good at socializing. Even Japanese housewives, who bear the responsibility of welcoming guests, are unlikely to receive visitors. Consequently, the garden party was an utterly dull affair. It was perhaps an augur of the dismal prospects that the Japan-U.S. peace talks would soon be facing.

However, I did my utmost to converse with the naval officers and I urged them to drink and drink some more. I was trying my very best to speak in a civilized tone with them when I told them how much I hoped that the Japan-U.S. negotiations would allow our countries to reach some sort of compromise. I also explained that all we really wanted was peace in the Pacific and so on.

I understood, of course, that they weren't particularly focused on those questions, but I had my reasons for speaking to them in that way. I was hoping to gauge their reactions to my words by carefully following their conversations and manner. However, they too were hoping to find some clues about our true position by listening carefully to what we were saying. As a result, our discussions remained fixed at the level of diplomatic niceties and lacked any sort of understanding or warmth.

To try and cheer things up, I even brought out some woodblock prints and decorative fans used in dance that had been imported from faraway Japan and I offered them to the officers as mementos. However, they politely refused. "We have received orders from our superiors not to accept any gifts from Japanese people," they said. They had already made up their minds. In that instant, I felt the strength of their resolve.

If both expatriates and second-generation Japanese-Americans were unreliable, it went without saying that my chances of finding a bosom buddy from the American navy were slim to none. I realized then that the more painful things got for me, the more I had to rely on my own efforts to gather intelligence. There was no other way forward.

In addition to participating at such events, I had been scouting around Pearl Harbor for more than 40 days by then and I had come to understand much about the naval vessels moored in the harbor. Consequently, I drew up and transmitted my first telegram on 12 May.

12 May 1941
From: Consul-General Kita, Honolulu
To: The Minister for Foreign Affairs, Tokyo

1.
On 11 May the ships anchored at Pearl Harbor were:
11 Battleships: *Colorado, West Virginia, California, Tennessee, Idaho, Mississippi, New Mexico, Pennsylvania, Arizona, Oklahoma, Nevada.*

15. Sending Telegrams 83

5 Heavy Cruisers: 2 of Pensacola-class, 3 of San Francisco-class.
10 Light Cruisers, 37 Destroyers, 2 Destroyer Flagships, 1 Submarine Flagship,
11 Submarines, and roughly 10 or more other naval vessels including cargo ships.

2.
The Aircraft Carrier *Lexington* is now cruising in the seas off the east coast of Oahu, accompanied by two Destroyers.

Soon afterwards, I sent the two following telegrams:

26 May 1941
From: Consul-General Kita, Honolulu
To: The Minister for Foreign Affairs, Tokyo

On 24 and 25 May, the following vessels were anchored in Pearl Harbor.
6 Battleships: *California, Tennessee, Pennsylvania, Arizona, Oklahoma, Nevada.*
5 Heavy Cruisers: 2 of Pensacola-class, 3 of San Francisco-class, 7 Light Cruisers, 19 Destroyers, 1 Destroyer Flagship, 5 Submarines, 1 Submarine Flagship, 2 Large Oil Tankers, 5 Cargo Ships.
Aircraft Carrier … (What remains of the text is unclear.)

14 June 1941
From: Consul-General Kita, Honolulu
To: The Minister for Foreign Affairs, Tokyo

On 11 June, 2 refitted cruisers from the Royal Navy entered Pearl Harbor. They are now berthed at the old docks.

Tokyo responded to this telegram with the following instructions:

In order to maintain secrecy, reports concerning vessels anchored at Pearl Harbor in May, June and July are only to be sent once every ten days. As long as there are no major changes observed there, that will suffice.

My excessive enthusiasm had led me to send reports too frequently and for this I was reprimanded. Furthermore, I received these additional instructions: "Great caution must be taken with the wording of each report."

The message here was that Japanese government policy still had not reached the point where the decision to attack Pearl Harbor had been taken, so we were to avoid inflaming sentiments on the American side. This meant that I had a chance to get out into the field and toughen myself up during the three or four months that followed.

Consequently, every evening when night fell I would run over to the bars downtown or to the Shunchoro Teahouse up on the hill to have fun. I was determined to get the most out of all that Hawaii had to offer. I subsequently became arrogant and self-satisfied. I thought to myself that there was nothing to the work of a secret agent. With just a little effort, my abilities would certainly prove to be more than sufficient to get the job done.

Yet after I sent Tokyo a cable report about the naval vessels at anchor on the next prescribed date, I quite unexpectedly discovered some discrepancies when comparing it to the previous two reports I had sent. I found that the numbers of vessels at anchor had changed and that the names of the vessels listed were different as well. Furthermore, for some of the days detailed, the cable failed to note the presence of a single battleship. I then found myself thinking about the situation over and over.

Where was the U.S. Navy fleet? What was it doing? When did it return to the harbor? When did it leave? When the fleet was out conducting exercises, what battle formation was adopted? What speed did it travel at? And in what sort of order?

It then occurred to me that if I could find the answers to these questions, I could clarify how the U.S. Navy's exercises were conducted and what sort of preparations were underway to make ready for war.

At that time, I still didn't believe that Japan was going to take any action against Pearl Harbor. Yet I did believe that the U.S. Navy was quite likely to set off from Pearl Harbor and attack Japan or a target somewhere in the South Seas once it had completed its preparations. Therefore, I felt that sending timely reports to Tokyo about the movements of the U.S. fleet was my most important mission.

When one takes a casual look at the vessels berthed in a harbor, there appears to be little difference between a ship that has just returned from a journey of several thousand nautical miles and another ship that is about to leave harbor. Yet from the point of view of military strategy, there is a great difference between those two ships. This led me to believe that I should also serve as an "oracle" of sorts by gathering up all the available evidence to deduce the enemy's troop strength, his targets, and his plan of action. For our forces, this sort of understanding of the enemy's situation was absolutely critical.

However, even though this was what I believed, I didn't receive any further instructions from Tokyo. In fact, it looked as if they were somewhat fed up with my telegrams, which I found absolutely incredible. It actually seemed as though they thought that an immature and inexperienced fellow such as myself had no business whatsoever dealing in these weighty matters. I was apparently supposed to avoid rashly making a case for my views, carefully follow my instructions, and keep a steady eye on developments in Pearl Harbor.

It was because all of this was weighing on my mind and causing my mood to swing up and down that I decided to chase away my low spirits one day by booking a room at the Shunchoro Teahouse. Early the next morning when I was opening the window, which looked out toward Pearl Harbor from the second floor, I couldn't help but feel a great shock.

Wasn't that the U.S. Navy's enormous Pacific Fleet right in the midst of leaving port?

Beyond the harbor, several destroyers were already aligned in battle formation and the heavy and light cruisers were in the process of getting into their formations. Five or six battleships were slowly steaming out of the harbor.

The streets of Honolulu were empty and the city still fast asleep, but the immense Pacific Fleet was stealthily leaving peaceful and quiet Oahu behind. It gradually disappeared from view beyond the horizon to the south. This maneuver by the U.S. fleet presented me with some irrefutable evidence: At Pearl Harbor, the fleet made most of its entries and departures very early in the morning or after nightfall.

I needed to find ways that I could surveil the harbor in order to gather information. I needed to know each vessel's name, the total number of vessels in its class, and the number of troops aboard. Having done that, I needed to take the information obtained from my surveillance and record it on a chart. However, finding a way to conceal this chart was something that required a considerable amount of scheming.

Although the vault at the consulate-general was secure, it wasn't convenient for the carrying out of late-night analysis and investigation. Meanwhile, carrying the chart on my person was a very risky proposition. I was thus obliged to conceal it somewhere in my residence, even though I wasn't usually at home, and that meant that it could perhaps be discovered during a search.

I racked my brains to come up with every possible means of concealing it there: under the carpet, attached to the back of a wardrobe drawer, within a flower vase, or inside the wastepaper bin. Yet because I was responsible for the symbols and codes used in the chart, nobody apart from myself could read and understand its signs and notations. Even if someone were to discover the chart, it wouldn't provide them with any means of interpretation. This was something that I could feel confident about.

As a place to while away the time while looking down on Pearl Harbor in the morning or evening, the Shunchoro Teahouse was second to none. Consequently, I began to chum around with the geishas and waitresses there. What's more, I always played the part of a tipsy yet somewhat posh dandy.

16

The Decision to Make War

Right around the time that I was making use of the Shunchoro Teahouse to closely monitor Pearl Harbor, the Japanese government convened a special conference on 2 July at which the Emperor was present. At that meeting, major decisions were taken to have our troops "enter French Indochina" and to "prepare for war against Britain and the United States." Although Japan's plan to move into the South was made official policy on that day, America and Britain were determined to stop any Japanese move into the South. As a result, war had become unavoidable.

By then, Imperial Japanese Army troops were entering Saigon for stationing at a base there. Meanwhile, the Imperial Japanese Navy had entered Cam Ranh Bay where it was beginning to build an airfield. In Western Europe, France had already surrendered to Germany and General Petain had become prime minister of the Vichy government. Hence Japan and Germany, East and West, began to work in concert to put pressure on the Governor-General of French Indochina, Jean Decoux. They ultimately persuaded him to agree to invite Japanese forces to be peacefully stationed in that territory for the purpose of mutual defense.

The Americans considered Japan's decision to make its move into the South official government policy sufficient proof that the statements it made during peace negotiations were entirely without merit. By way of retaliation, on 26 July, the U.S. government initiated an embargo on petroleum exports to Japan and it froze all Japanese bank accounts and investments in the United States. At the same time, further policies aimed at keeping Japan contained within the ABCD line were put into place.[1]

During this period, the Japanese Consulate-General in Honolulu was entrusted with all of the belongings that Sweden's honorary consul-general would need when he arrived to take up his office there (in addition to a complete record of those items). The belongings were given to him soon enough, but we brought out and displayed every article before handing it over, even the day-to-day tableware.

The difficult conditions brought on by the economic blockade meant

16. The Decision to Make War

that the Imperial Japanese Navy was facing the most serious of threats, since its stocks of petroleum were sufficient for just one year's naval operations. By then, since neither the United States nor Holland would sell a drop of oil to Japan, the navy was becoming increasingly agitated as the Japan-U.S. peace negotiations headed towards deadlock. If our nation were to take a laissez-faire approach to this situation, it would be just a matter of time before Japan was strangled to death.

Faced with such a situation, it seemed preferable to take the decision to enter the South and grab hold of its natural resources as soon as possible instead of sitting down to await one's death. Thus, in a very short time, support for this policy had spread from the navy to the army, where it soon received widespread support. Thereafter, the public largely approved of the policy and support for it spread right across the nation.

While public support for the policy was on the rise, on 6 September the Imperial General Headquarters-Government Liaison Conference and members of the cabinet held yet another meeting in the presence of the Emperor. During that meeting the decision was taken to go to war if the peace negotiations between Japan and the U.S. had not produced any agreement by 10 October.

Meanwhile, the navy and its air fleet had already begun preparing for a surprise attack on Hawaii. Their preparations were based upon the plans that Admiral Isoroku Yamamoto, Commander-in-chief of the Combined Fleet, had developed. After carrying out repeated practice bombing missions on vessels anchored at port, they had attained very high levels of technical proficiency. Then, beginning on 10 September, a series of war games meant to simulate an attack on Pearl Harbor were carried out at the Meguro Naval College, with military advisors from both the navy and the Navy General Staff present.

At that time, I obviously knew nothing about these events taking place in Japan. In this respect I was no different from the average Japanese civilian, who understood little of matters concerning our national defense. Near the end of September, I suddenly received the following telegram:

24 September 1941
From: The Minister for Foreign Affairs, Tokyo
To: Consul-General Kita, Honolulu

Top Secret
It is hoped that you will henceforth do your best to send a report about the following items concerning the fleet:

1.
Pearl Harbor's water surface area can be divided into five sections. (You might as well adopt the following schema to be concise in your reports.)
Water Zone A—This designates the stretch of water extending from Ford Island to the navy's industrial zone.

Water Zone B—This designates the stretch of water running from the southern tip of Ford Island and along its western flank. Its total area is similar in size to Water Zone A, but it runs along the other side of Ford Island.

Water Zone C—This designates the eastern portion of the bay.

Water Zone D—This designates the central portion of the bay.

Water Zone E—This designates the western portion of the bay as well as the navigable channel that runs between the sea and the bay.

2.

Concerning battleships and aircraft carriers, it is hoped that you will first list those at anchor, then those moored to the docks or to buoys, and then those that have just entered the docks. Ships of these last varieties are of no great importance. Just provide a brief sketch. That will suffice.

3.

It is hoped that you will include simple notes about each ship's class and type.

4.

When two vessels are moored alongside one another at the same dock, do your best to indicate this clearly.

While I wasn't immediately able to determine the reasons behind the sender's message, the meaning of the cable was clear. Its main points were that the harbor should be divided into five distinct zones and that my reports should include details about the zone in which each ship was moored.

However, I had my doubts about the sender of the telegram or whoever it was that had actually drafted it. If it was a staff officer from the Navy General Staff, they would have been familiar with the situation within the harbor. So why did they need to know whether there were any ships anchored in the shallow waters of Zone E? Furthermore, what had they meant when they described the ships that had entered the docks or were moored to buoys as "not very important"? The fourth section of the telegram was similarly enigmatic and I was at a loss as to how to judge its meaning.

I believed that the Navy General Staff would have had a very clear understanding about all of these points and thus would have had no need to give me orders to include them in my reports. It then occurred to me that the telegram might have come from an official at the Foreign Ministry who had no understanding of military matters and had taken on the task of drafting the cable himself, after receiving a verbal command from the Navy General Staff. If that were the case, it wouldn't be necessary to follow the confusing orders detailed by the telegram when proceeding with my reports.

This telegram had certainly been drafted by a layman, but after I had read it several times I hazily stumbled upon a revelation of sorts: The telegram was trying to hint at the fact that Japan was going to attack Pearl Harbor. However, this underlying message was one that I half believed and half doubted.

16. The Decision to Make War

While investigating this matter after the war, I eventually confirmed that the cable was extremely important. Staff officers at Navy General Staff and other navy staff officers had formulated it so as to prepare us for an attack on Pearl Harbor. It concerned "the selection of targets" and the task of researching "how best to attack them." In other words, it was a telegram that communicated the resolve to attack. Nevertheless, I still haven't been able to determine who drafted it.

As far as I can tell, the author of the cable may have been Commander Muchaku, a senior staff officer from Section 5 at the Navy General Staff (who died during active service). He may have sent that quizzical telegram because he was involved in the war game exercises at the Meguro Naval College and was having some doubts about the methods used to attack naval vessels.

The section of the cable that stated "When two vessels are moored alongside one another at the same dock…" may have been inspired by the fact that the ship positioned on the inside would not be susceptible to attack by submarine. Furthermore, the text concerning those vessels moored or docked that were "of no great importance" suggested that those ships were likely to be leaving port within a short time.

Although I had my doubts about the meaning of the cable, I nevertheless followed the instructions it contained when sending my next two reports. In both reports, I divided Pearl Harbor into several distinct zones in order to carefully describe the positioning of the vessels moored in each area:

29 September 1941
From: Consul-General Kita, Honolulu
To: The Minister for Foreign Affairs, Tokyo

Top Secret
 Concerning the instructions received in cable #83 about providing notations for the docks, anchorage zones, and berthing areas. It has been decided that the following notations shall be used henceforth.
 1. KS—The docks at the navy shipyards
 2. KT—Wharfs #10 and #11
 3. FV—The mooring and anchoring zones near Ford Island
 4. FG—The docks at Ford Island (the Eastern docks will be "A" and the Western docks "B")

I only sent two telegrams to Tokyo in accordance with its ambiguous requests. If the style of my reports were to become more important than the substance, I believed that it would constrain the reporting of my reconnaissance work and compel me to provide verbal reports of the activities within the harbor.

As I recall these matters today, I think that Tokyo may have feared that because my telegrams were so detailed and complex, the Americans might have been able to decipher them. Consequently, they had given me those new instructions.

At that time, however, I was fueled by my youthful enthusiasm and I didn't bother to distinguish between large and small when I was writing up reports about my reconnaissance work. In this respect, I was very much like a child who doesn't know his parent's heart. It was for this reason that I had been reprimanded and given the order: "Reports concerning naval vessels are to be sent once a week. That will suffice."

Despite this, I felt that my work shouldn't be limited to reporting about vessels docked, berthed, and at anchor. There were a great many other tasks that still needed to be completed and that work needed to be done right across the Hawaiian Archipelago.

All of the following items (and more besides) needed to be thoroughly investigated: Hawaii's climate and atmospheric conditions; its airports and airstrips; troop numbers and the deployment of troops; various other everyday military matters; merchant shipping; commercial air transport; and so on.

17

The Hawaiian Climate

Everybody knows that the weather can play a significant role in a combat zone. There have been numerous historic battles where, through carelessness or neglect, the weather has helped to bring about the most improbable of defeats. I hadn't initially received any orders to help prepare for an attack on Pearl Harbor by investigating the climate, nor had I received any cables asking me to report on Hawaii's climate, but I was extremely keen to thoroughly investigate Hawaii's weather patterns nonetheless. It was an idea I wouldn't let go of, though I'm hard-pressed to say why this was so.

For reasons of national security, newspapers in both Japan and the United States were prohibited from publishing detailed weather forecasts and maps.[1] Consequently, outsiders were unable to understand much about the local climate. In order to do some research on this matter, I went to the University of Hawaii, public libraries, and elsewhere. None of my efforts produced any satisfactory results, however. All I managed to find was a bit of information about the amount of rainfall required by sugarcane crops.

Through my research I also learned that the local authorities were at their wits' end trying to understand how best to protect their freshwater resources, which formed part of an important freshwater supply line that reached into the South Pacific. They had apparently decided to dig new caves in the mountains, halfway up, to serve as reservoirs.

In September, I heard about a Japanese amateur astronomer in Honolulu who had been studying meteors for a long time. So, I took advantage of a splendidly starry night to pay him a visit at the plain little house in which he lived. He happened to be at home and he invited me, an unexpected visitor, inside.

He then took me to see the small telescope that he had mounted on his roof. I'm not exactly sure why he had taken up this sort of research, but he had evidently been carrying out his studies for more than 30 years. Although I couldn't help but feel surprised by this, I had nothing but admiration for any man with the stamina to spend 30 years in the same corner of the Pacific Ocean compiling statistics about the meteors he'd observed falling through the skies. Sadly, the Astronomical Society had decided to stop subsidizing his activities and he was obviously not very pleased about it. I felt that the aged and eccentric astronomer deserved to be pitied.

I took up his telescope and began surveying the skies. In the eastern sector of the night sky, I actually caught sight of a meteor and it was quite nice to watch. Even so, shooting starts didn't really hold all that much interest for me.

He proceeded to talk to me at great length about his astronomical knowledge. Whenever he began to discuss a topic that had been discussed at the Naval Academy, such as which stars are useful when trying to predict the weather, winds, and tides, I did my best to pretend to be listening intently. But then he also spoke about some quite important observations he had made:

"In 30 years, Hawaii has not experienced a single major tempest. Furthermore, it is always overcast on the north side of the longest mountain chain that runs across Oahu. Meanwhile, it is always clear and sunny to the south of that mountain chain."

When I heard him say those few words, I was wildly happy. It felt as if I had found a most precious treasure. I didn't want astronomical statistics, what I needed were empirical facts such as these.

It is widely-known that the main Hawaiian Islands, which are located at roughly 23 degrees latitude north, enjoy a pleasant semi-tropical, maritime climate. Yet few people know that tempests are frequent events within the Inner South Seas region at the same latitude.[2] Powerful tempests there can become typhoons and these make air travel impossible. The absence of such tempests in Hawaii makes it a very special place because aircraft can fly there throughout the year without ever suffering any disruptions brought on by the weather. This meant that the timing of an attack there would not be subject to change due to the effects of dramatic weather conditions.

When I said goodbye to the old stargazer I told him that I was deeply grateful. And yet, I felt ashamed of myself. I had taken advantage of that specialist astronomer's kind-hearted and decent nature to make use of his knowledge for the evil purpose of waging war. As a result of my feeling that I had taken advantage of the scientist's kindness, I did not discuss his observations with anyone else. Nor did I report the matter to Tokyo by telegram. I just kept it all to myself, deep within my heart.

Afterwards, when I was flying in an aircraft with a geisha I had brought along with me for a tour around Oahu, I made a point of checking out the old astronomer's observations. Sure enough, it was just as he had said. The southern flank of the mountain chain was under clear skies and not a cloud was in sight. Meanwhile, its northern face was covered by layers of white and black cloud and it suddenly began to rain there. In addition, there were "air pockets" (turbulence-causing air traps) over Nu'uanu Pali and Kahuku Point during that flight. As these occurred repeatedly, I was able to experience that phenomenon first-hand too.

17. The Hawaiian Climate

Halfway through that flight, while I was doing reconnaissance work from my seat, my mind began to fix on the idea of a war and I began to ask myself which point of entry to Pearl Harbor would be best once an attack had been launched. But whenever the aircraft entered an air pocket, I immediately felt my female companion's lithe limbs pulling me closer to her. My gaze nevertheless remained fixed on the battle front, as if I were lost in a daydream (one that would subsequently come true).

Not long after that, the Navy General Staff sent an emissary to Honolulu aboard the ship *Taiyo Maru*. He gave me a handwritten document that contained 90 questions. One of those handwritten questions asked "What are the climatic conditions in Hawaii?"

As the situation had come to this, it was no longer possible for me to keep quiet. Consequently, I made the following reply without hesitation: "Hawaii has not experienced a single typhoon in the past 30 years. As it is usually overcast along the northern end of Oahu, you can enter from the north and begin the descent to bomb after passing over Nu'uanu Pali."

Well, the facts on the ground later proved that my prediction was absolutely correct. Should I see that as fortunate, or should I feel grieved about it? As I still have no answer to this question, I leave it to my good readers to decide.

18

A Coral Sea

Kaneʻohe Bay is a small bay on Oahu's windward coast where the navy had an air base for seaplanes. Atop Nuʻuanu Pali, looking down toward the north, you could observe the activities that were taking place at that base. The bay was sheltered from the ocean by a cape that jutted out to the left and then curved inward. The seaplane air base that I wanted to scout out was located at the end of the cape. Yet because civilian vehicles were not permitted to pass beyond the entrance to the cape, it was basically impossible to assess the situation at the base.

I once tried to convince a taxi driver to drive to the base, but he said that we could not go there as visiting it was prohibited. When I came up with the pretext of our having entered the zone by mistake after taking the wrong road, the driver would have none of it.

On several occasions, I went on tours around the island "to enjoy the fresh air." Whenever we were driving down the road that passed Kaneʻohe Bay, I took advantage of the opportunity to scout things out there. However, not once did this give me a good idea of the situation at the base. Although I tried to think of every possible means of getting past all the obstacles there, I never managed to come up with a sound strategy for doing so.

At that time, the U.S. Navy was strengthening the fortifications at the Kaneʻohe air base and it had a big budget to carry out work there. While construction had not yet been completed at the site, there were signs that made it obvious the work was progressing rapidly. When I arrived in Oahu, there was no sign of aircraft taking off or landing there. However, by the month of August there were slowly increasing numbers of orange-colored aircraft taking off from the airport with the lettering "PBY" under their wings.

One Saturday afternoon, I was speaking with a Japanese-American attendant after having my lunch when I learned that she worked half-days every Saturday. She was preparing to tidy things up and return home once the lunch service had ended, such was her weekly routine.

"Tomorrow is Sunday," I said to her jokingly. "Where are you and your boyfriend going to go for fun?"

18. A Coral Sea

Her boyfriend apparently worked as an usher at a local cinema and she went to help prepare his meals every day after finishing work.

"Oh, tomorrow I'm going with Kimiko on a tour of the coral sea!" (Kimiko was an attendant who worked at the consulate-general's employee residence.)

"Huh? Is that some kind of excursion?"

"Yes, exactly."

"This coral sea, where is it?"

"It's really far away. Don't you know about it? It is a really beautiful sea, over there!"

"A beautiful sea? Where is this place anyway?"

She was speaking English very quickly, so I hurried to get a map to show her. The place that she pointed out was in fact Kaneʻohe Bay. She told me that there was a coral reef in the middle of Kaneʻohe Bay and that the sightseeing boats there were fitted with some glass on their underside, which made it possible to look through a "window" and admire the seabed. She called this sort of boat a "glass boat."

I felt pleasantly surprised as I listened to her description, but I did my utmost to keep calm and act as if nothing had happened.

"That sounds like such an amazing place, I would really like to go and see it too!" I said quite deliberately, hoping to feel her out by listening closely to the tone of her reply.

"Well, let's all go together then!"

I hadn't expected that she would reply in such a relaxed manner. Yet in the end it seemed that neither of the two really objected to having me along on the tour with them, which made me feel relaxed about the whole idea.

After some discussion, we agreed that they would prepare a box lunch for me and that I would cover the cost of the taxi. Although I was more than willing to spend as much as one or two hundred dollars to scout out Kaneʻohe Bay, it would have made them suspicious if I appeared to be too generous. I had all the more reason to be cautious when I considered the possibility of their finding themselves in the custody of the FBI after being implicated in my activities. Consequently, each of us paid our own way on this group excursion in the end.

That evening, I prepared for our departure by familiarizing myself with all the available information on Kaneʻohe Bay. After that, I got into bed for the night. However, after my thoughts moved from the importance of Kaneʻohe Bay to its significance in a future war, I began tossing and turning and I couldn't get a wink of sleep.

The U.S. Navy was apparently in the process of blasting the coral reefs in Kaneʻohe Bay with explosives in order to increase the depth of the water there, which would make takeoffs and landings by seaplanes possible. The navy also seemed to be preparing to transform the bay into a base that could provide a safe berth to its vessels.

The long-distance patrol flights that the PBY seaplanes made around the Hawaiian Islands without refueling, especially those flights to the north, plainly revealed that some considerable planning had gone into all of the activities there. Its significance was all the more apparent when I thought of Kaneʻohe Bay as the central hub around which Dutch Harbor, Midway Island, and Guam marked the outer ring. I soon felt that Kaneʻohe Bay was of real strategic importance and could not be ignored. Thus, I quietly made a vow to myself. "Tomorrow, I shall take the fight to Kaneʻohe Bay!"

Shortly after the car turned up at nine o'clock the next morning, the others arrived wearing rather magnificent Japanese clothing made of rayon. Although I felt that they would not be easily fished out of the water while wearing such novel costumes, I forced myself to wear a broad smile and showed them into the car.

After reaching Nu'uanu Pali, we got out of the car. There were large numbers of tourists around, as it was a Sunday, and the Japanese clothes that the two were wearing soon attracted the attention of the foreign visitors. Several tourists so enjoyed the freshness of their outfits that they asked them to stand in front of the rocky backdrop and took lots of pictures of them.

My head was raised upward as I basked in the distinctive maritime wind that was blowing around us, "sah-sah." Yet my eyes were spying on the activities inside the zone below, Kaneʻohe Bay. Once that fierce northerly wind had crossed the far reaches of the Pacific Ocean and arrived in Oahu, it passed over perilously steep slopes and was transformed into a whistling, gale force wind that could sweep you off your feet.

After buying our tickets for the boat excursion, we waited with some other passengers for the tour to begin. There weren't many other passengers that day, just two foreign couples. The tour boat was very crudely made and could hold 20 people at most. Soon after we had boarded, the boat's horn sounded its ear-splitting signal and we set off.

Just before we reached the middle of the bay, we began to enjoy the scenery that the site was famous for. One after another, the other passengers took turns looking through the boat's glass window bottom to admire the coral reefs. Yet for reasons of my own, I was by turns studying the facial expressions of the foreign tourists aboard and setting my gaze upon the distant Kaneʻohe military base.

I used the binoculars that I had brought with me to carefully survey the site and I was actually able to make note of the numbers painted on the fuselages of the aircraft. Although I couldn't tell whether one of the FBI's special agents was following us, I craned my body forward and brazenly carried out my inspection of the site.

18. A Coral Sea

After 30 minutes or so of pleasure-boating, I felt that I had gathered a lot of information. I discovered that the construction of the Kaneʻohe base had progressed enormously and that the number of troops garrisoned there was slowly increasing. The pace of development at the site greatly exceeded my expectations.

By the end of August, I had basically completed my survey of the base at Pearl Harbor and the other military installations across Oahu. It was now time for me to do the necessary groundwork to scout out the other major Hawaiian Islands and I began to fret about how best to proceed with this. I eventually decided to begin with Hawaii, the largest of the islands in the archipelago.

Yet before I did this, I felt that it was necessary to convince Consul-General Kita (who was always very discreet in his dealings with me) about the suitability of my plans. Once I had received his approval, I could begin putting things into motion. When I approached him and explained my ideas, he was initially somewhat reluctant to lend me his support. In the end he supported my plans, on the condition that they only involve travel at the weekend and that I not do anything to invite any suspicions. He also asked me to take along a young second-generation Japanese-American who was an employee at the consulate-general as well.

I decided to travel by airplane to Hawaii and Maui. The main objective of this trip was to carry out aerial reconnaissance at Pearl Harbor and Hickam Field and to check if there were any naval vessels anchored along the Lahaina Roads.[1] After I'd bought a plane ticket and a travel guide at a travel agency, where I also picked up some travel brochures, I went to Honolulu Airport.

While waiting in the passenger lounge before boarding the airplane, I cautiously scanned the areas around me for any sign of suspicious activity. As it didn't appear that there were any FBI agents tailing me, I felt quite relieved.

It was a fine, clear day and as soon as our airplane had taken off from Honolulu Airport I saw Pearl Harbor sitting immediately below us, as well as the entire Hickam Field air base. Hickam Field was a very large base with two intersecting runways. A big B-17 bomber was stationed on the tarmac, soaking in the sun's rays.

I held my breath as I studied the situation on the ground. Just then, the stewardess reminded me that I needed to fasten my seatbelt as she handed me a package of chewing gum to help with the variations in cabin pressure. While chewing on the gum, and enjoying its satisfying flavor, I told myself that this trip was going to be a success.

After I scanned the rest of the cabin, it still appeared that there were no agents following me. Despite this, I reminded myself of the need to proceed very cautiously. As I did so, I tried my best to put on an ordinary "nothing to see here" expression.

Soon afterwards, the aircraft entered the zone above the Lahaina Roads. There our flight path was riddled with "air pockets" and the plane bounced up, down, and sideways quite a bit. I discovered that there were as yet no ships anchored along the gently tossing waters of the Lahaina Roads, nor was there any sign of sea buoys used for mooring vessels. Despite this, I was sure that this sea lane would be used for such a purpose in the future. Just then, I saw a San Francisco-class heavy cruiser navigating towards Pearl Harbor.

As I looked down from the aircraft to the left, I saw a thin covering of cloud over Maui's Haleakala volcano. To the right, tiny-looking Molokai Island sat covered by a lush green layer of forest. The very well-known leprosy settlement was located on that island.[2]

The aircraft made its scheduled stopover at Maui's Puunene Airport before taking off again for Hawaii. Checking out that airport was yet another objective of this trip because the U.S. government's budget report noted that Puunene Airport was eventually going to serve as a commercial airport and as a military air base. I hadn't heard much at all about this airport before then, so I felt especially happy about having the chance to scout out the site on this trip.

19

Airfields and Army Bases

The U.S. air troops stationed in Hawaii had a total of about 350 aircraft between them, approximately 50 of which were B-17 "Flying Fortress" bombers. The aircraft were generally stationed according to their type at one of several air bases: bombers were stationed at Hickam Field; training aircraft were stationed at Ewa Airfield; fighter planes were stationed at Wheeler Airfield; carrier-borne aircraft were stationed at Ford Island and at the Maui air base; and reconnaissance aircraft were stationed at the Kaneʻohe air base.

Ever more small aircraft were being sent to Hawaii aboard aircraft carriers at that time, and increasing numbers of large aircraft were being flown over to Hawaii from the mainland. This made it very difficult to determine the true number of aircraft stationed there. The only way to deduce the actual quantity of aircraft was to collect information that provided clues, such as the number aircraft hangars and their size, the number of daily practice flights, the number of pilots, and the length of the runways.

The key questions to be answered about these U.S. air troops concerned the number of aircraft at their disposal, the skill of the pilots, and the technical capabilities of the aircraft. Of these, the greatest unknown was the skill of the pilots.

For their part, the Imperial Japanese Navy's air troops had become somewhat overconfident about their technical skills. This was due to the fact that Japan had almost invariably used air troops to wage war against China, whose air power was considerably weaker than Japan's, following the Marco Polo Bridge Incident.

One day, I had the opportunity to watch an air show that was being held at Wheeler Field. As I took in the spectacle, sitting on the grass and smoking cigarettes, I found myself right in the middle of a group of the air troops' family members.

Judging from what we saw that day, the pilots' technical proficiency with their fighter aircraft was quite impressive. For example, the pilots were skilled at flying their aircraft right through a dome-shaped aircraft hangar that was left wide-open. Another one of their excellent tricks was to swoop down until they were only ten meters or so above the ground and then roll the aircraft and rise up again. Apparently, only ten percent of pilots were able to perform such acts of derring-do.

While I watched the air show I was also making note of the various installations at the base, the types of aircraft there, and their total numbers. Even though the U.S. Army Air Corps had put up wrought iron fencing around the base and had posted notices saying that entry to the base was prohibited, there were some quite significant lapses in security at the site.

Through news reports, I learned that the U.S. military was using aircraft carriers to transport increasing numbers of aircraft from Hawaii to the advance base at Midway Island. However, I still hadn't obtained precise intelligence information about this. Nevertheless, the U.S. air troops stationed in Hawaii had at their disposal a total of about 300 aircraft (older and newer planes combined). Furthermore, there were additional aircraft aboard the three aircraft carriers based in Hawaii. With these added, I reckoned that there were approximately 500 aircraft there in total. The composition of the air fleet was slowly changing as new B-17s, P-36s, and PBY seaplanes were brought in.

Although I arrived at this assessment of their air power in the summer of 1941, my figures scarcely differed from the actual numbers of U.S. aircraft in Hawaii at the start of the war.

Ewa Airfield was located just west of Pearl Harbor within an area of dense vegetation. I had never been able to get near that air base to check it out because it was within a restricted military zone. Right around the time that I was trying to think of some way to scout out the base, I heard that some young people in the area were beginning to take part in a new sort of fad called "going on a moonlit stroll." Taking advantage of a moonlit night to get to the seaside and have fun there until the break of dawn was what this was all about. So I decided that I would take two or three female friends along with me and make it a "family-style" outing, in order to dupe any FBI agents who might be in pursuit. I also decided it would be best to let them choose Barbers Point, the site for our outing, all on their own. I would just put on a face to give the impression that I was going along with whatever they had chosen. Had the choice been mine, it would have looked suspicious.

At the appointed time, I loaded my fishing gear and some prepared food into the car that Miss A's father then drove to our destination. Although I didn't manage to find out about the activities within the inner areas of the base, I was able to scout out my objectives in the end.

The situation of the U.S. air troops stationed in Hawaii was more or less as I have described above and I didn't think it was necessary to monitor this closely. However, I was concerned about the PBY seaplanes at the Kaneʻohe air base. That was because those long-distance reconnaissance planes were

19. Airfields and Army Bases

beginning to fly to the air base at Dutch Harbor and back again, which meant that they were patrolling the North Pacific non-stop. What's more, there were ever growing numbers of those orange-colored PBY aircraft, which resembled large dragonflies, every time I went to check them out.

The distribution of the U.S. Army's ground forces in Hawaii also needed to be checked out. There was an entire division of its soldiers stationed across Hawaii. The U.S. Army's Hawaiian Headquarters was at Fort Shafter, while the Schofield Barracks was its most important base. Special army units were located within the City of Honolulu and on Hawaii. I was never stopped for questioning around any of these bases when traveling by taxi to do my reconnaissance work.

When the Japan-U.S. peace talks seemed to be on the verge of failure, it seemed to me that war probably was going to break out between Japan and America. If that were to happen, Japanese forces would probably invade Hawaii soon after the war had started. This made it imperative that I thoroughly check out those sites where Japanese troops could land.

Consequently, I brought a female friend with me on swimming outings at Waikiki, Barbers Point, the west coast of Oahu, and at some other sites with sandy beaches along which I carried out "on site" topographical surveys. While carrying out these inspections, I managed to discover many significant details. For example, I found out that there were breakwaters just one meter below the water's surface sitting roughly a kilometer from the shoreline at Waikiki. In addition, at a beach on the west coast of Oahu, I discovered that the sandy gradient dropped away very sharply just beyond the shoreline and that there were very large rocks lying off the coast that were pummeled by the tidal waters. This made landing there extremely dangerous.

At some of the beaches I chose to visit, my female travel companion tried to warn me against swimming by saying there were large sharks around that made going into the water too risky. Despite her warnings, I decided to take the risk and swim at a number of such sites to fully investigate the terrain along the seashore.

It occurred to me that after Japanese forces had invaded Oahu, it would be necessary to seize every boat if the locals were to be kept apart from the white residents on the other islands. Thus, I thoroughly checked out all the local marinas and docks as well as the weight classes of the vessels that could dock at each.

If anyone had asked for my strategic advice, I would have said that repeated attacks were going to be necessary to make a success of any initial surprise attack. After that, ground troops would have to be landed at Pearl Harbor to occupy the island so that Hawaii's 300,000 American residents could be taken hostage and used as a shield. Had things unfolded in this way, there would have been a dramatic turn of events in the subsequent war for the Pacific. In reality, however, the United States was to use Hawaii as its base while waging war against Japan. The U.S. military would adopt the tactic of "island-hopping" (using individual islands in the Pacific as stepping stones) to carry out the large-scale bombing of Japan.

From the middle of October onwards, the instructions sent by cable from Tokyo to Honolulu seemed to be flying down like snowflakes in winter. Almost all of the cables asked questions about the location of the navy's vessels and about its mooring sites. What's more, these questions were asked so frequently that they tested the limits of my patience.

Very early on, I had written several well-versed reports about the anchorage zones used by the fleet, the sites where the fleet was present, and its activities. After carefully reading my reports they ought to have been able to get a clear picture of the U.S. Pacific Fleet's anchorage zones, its usual deployment patterns, and activities. Yet they were now asking me the same questions again and again, which left me feeling quite displeased. It was at this time that I received another such telegram:

> Concerning the enemy fleet anchored in Water Zone A, we have a full understanding of the situation thanks to your cables. You should now focus on investigating the battleships at anchor or moored to buoys there. Hoping for a fast report.

Soon afterwards, in early November, I received yet another incredible telegram that gave rise to further doubts in me. Were there new staff officers at the Navy General Staff without any understanding of the situation at Pearl Harbor? Or had some official from the Foreign Ministry who lacked any knowledge of military matters been responsible for drafting the cable?

The text of that cable was as follows:

8 November 1941
From: The Minister for Foreign Affairs, Tokyo
To: Consul-General Kita, Honolulu

Cable # 113
   Hope that you can cable information about ships at anchor in the following water zones:
   Lahaina Roads, Pearl Harbor Water Zone N and the Water Zones that neighbor it. (Hope investigation of this will be treated as top secret.)

After studying its contents, I considered this telegram superfluous. When I worked at the Navy General Staff, it was possible to study a map of strategic military zones around Oahu and determine right away that Pearl Harbor's Water Zone N was located on the west side of the bay and that the water was very shallow in that area. Not only would ships not anchor there, commercial ships would not even enter that zone. So there was basically no point in asking such a question.

What's more, I had sent many telegrams concerning the situation at the

Lahaina Roads and I had recently said that there was no sign of any ships anchored there. Yet now they were cabling instructions asking me to investigate this, while treating it as "top secret."

In light of all of this, I asked myself: (1) Whether or not they believed the intelligence reports that I had been sending all along. (2) Whether or not the cables I had been sending had actually reached the Navy General Staff. (Or had they been kept under lock and key at the Foreign Ministry?) Although I thought about these questions a great deal, I was unable to come up with any sort of answer.

But then I came up with a guess. Perhaps the true meaning behind this message was that the Navy General Staff wanted to confirm that the only anchorage zones were those at Pearl Harbor and that none were to be found elsewhere? If so, that would explain why they had attached such importance to this cable.

I had to use my own brainpower to collect information for my reports and devise any sort of strategy or artifice that I could come up with to go out and study a situation. In every case, as I had nobody else to rely on, I had to check things out for myself. As a result, whether I was dreaming or wide awake, my brain was always turning over questions about the ways and means that would be best for me to use.

The Shunchoro Teahouse remained the place that I frequented most often, as I had become very chummy with the geishas who worked there. "I hear that you can go sightseeing on a small plane here," I said to them in jest while we were chatting together one day. "Is that true? If any one of you wants to go on one, and if you're willing to 'die for love' with me, why don't we go together and see? What do you say?"

I had said this initially just to sound them out about my idea. I hadn't expected that they would vie with one another to see who would accompany me.

"Well, let's say this Sunday then. Which one of you will accompany me?"

They continued to dispute the matter until I finally asked my three lady friends to draw lots to decide who would be my companion on each one of my next few outings.

Every time I began planning a new activity, I always had to think about the worst possible outcome and prepare for it. When I asked my female friends to draw lots, I did so fully aware that they would quite happily testify that the destination for our date hadn't been decided by me alone if they were taken into custody for questioning.

On the agreed date, I arrived at the airport first. Not long afterwards, "H" (the female friend who had been selected to accompany me) came running up to me. She was wearing a red top, a white western-style skirt, sunglasses and a scarf on her head. She looked really beautiful in her outfit.

The lightweight tourist airplane that we boarded was a small "pay when you board" sightseeing aircraft. There were two of these aircraft and both of them were either taking off or landing on the hour. It took the airplane roughly 50 minutes to do the tour around Oahu.

The aloha-shirt-wearing pilot for our flight showed us to our seats in the aircraft, which was an old-style two-seater. Then the airplane started with a thunderous roar, floated forward, and went up into the air. It was convenient for looking out on both the left and right sides. My main objective on this reconnaissance mission was to check out the situation within Pearl Harbor and inside Hickam Field, since neither site could be scouted out internally from ground level.

In the end, I obtained information that was very useful for the purpose of identifying those sites from the air. I also noted a variety of targets that could be selected at the time of an air attack and I gained a better understanding of the prevailing air currents above those sites.

20

The Secret Envoy

During the meeting of the Imperial General Headquarters-Government Liaison Conference on 6 September, at which the Emperor was present, Japan resolved to prepare for both "war" and "peace." Meanwhile, the concurrent Japan-U.S. peace talks were not progressing smoothly. In fact, those talks had already reached the stage where there was little, if any, hope of success.

Various countries had begun to evacuate their citizens from Japan by then, although their diplomatic personnel remained, because the severing of diplomatic relations between Japan and the U.S. seemed imminent. Meanwhile, in order to conceal its plans for war, the Japanese government had decided to allow those passenger ships that regularly set off from Yokohama to leave port as scheduled, despite the risk that the authorities might impound them upon their arrival at U.S. ports.

When the *Tatsuta Maru*, the passenger ship carrying the final group of expatriate evacuees, set off from Yokohama on 15 October, the Navy General Staff had two officers aboard under new identities. Lieutenant-Commander Minato Nakashima from Section 5 of Bureau 3 was disguised as the ship's purser, while a midget submarine officer, Sub-Lieutenant Keiu Matsuo, was disguised as one of the ship's stewards.

On 20 October, the passenger ship *Hikawa Maru* set off from Japan. Once again, the Navy General Staff had selected an officer from Bureau 3 and placed him aboard ship in the role of purser. Lieutenant-Commander Eikichi Fukushima was the officer who had assumed this disguise.

Lieutenant-Commander Minato Nakashima had been charged with the task of reconnaissance at Pearl Harbor, while Lieutenant-Commander Eikichi Fukushima was made responsible for scouting out the U.S. Navy on the mainland.

While Lieutenant-Commander Nakashima and Sub-Lieutenant Matsuo were aboard the *Tatsuta Maru* as it sailed into the port at Honolulu on 23 October, neither of the two participated in the attack on Pearl Harbor. However, both were killed during the Battle of Sydney Harbor in Australia on 31 May of the following year.

The day they arrived, Consul-General Kita told me to meet him in the gardens of the consulate-general.

"Mr. Morimura," he said. "Do you know Lieutenant-Commander Nakashima?"

"Yes, I know him."

"Well, I must tell you that he has arrived. Do you want to meet with him?"

"I think it is best that I don't," I replied, after thinking about that question for a moment. "I'm afraid of someone tailing me, or having a bug listen in on what I'm saying."

"Fine! I agree that it's best that you do not see him. Well then, I'll go to the ship and make contact!"

After he had said that, a smile appeared on Consul-General Kita's ruddy face. Yet his bright, eagle-eyes revealed his great courage. He had already concluded that the secret emissary had been charged with handling an intelligence report of no small importance.

Consul-General Kita was a tolerant and open-minded man who didn't trouble himself over trivial matters. Whatever the situation, he always faced it with a smile. Basically, he didn't fit the mold of a diplomat at all. He was both audacious and careful and he dealt with things very thoroughly. Yet he also enjoyed study and learning.

I often recall a few words he once had for me after he had downed a third glass of whiskey and was feeling slightly tipsy:

"Mr. Morimura, the studies that someone does… We ought to say that they don't truly begin until he has reached the age of 50. After Ambassador Shiratori was sent to Northern Europe to take up a post, he once again threw all his energy into his studies. He apparently mastered seven foreign languages and he had to study Geography, Astronomy, Geology as well as some other sciences in those languages. We too have to start from scratch, and study."

After that, he said:

"The understanding that Japanese people have of China is insufficient! We still need to investigate it and study it well, especially those areas in which the Chinese are more advanced, because our understanding is simply not good enough. And we really ought to study their moral character, which is both resolute and flexible."

He also said:

"Since the Marco-Polo Bridge Incident, some people in Japan have taken it upon themselves to write a new 'literature of warfare' and have published a few things. But I have yet to read any work that compares to Tolstoy's *War and Peace*."

It feels a bit strange saying this. Whenever I start to lose faith or feel fed up while thinking about Japan's future, or about my own work, for some reason I simply call to mind the words Consul-General Kita said to me.

Now let's turn our attention back to the topic at hand by examining some U.S. intelligence reports about the movement of the transport vessels that had set off from Japan at that time:

1. The *Tatsuta Maru* (with Lieutenant-Commander Nakashima and Sub-Lieutenant Matsuo aboard) set off from Yokohama Harbor on 15 October 1941 and arrived at Honolulu on 23 October. On 30 October, it reached San Francisco. On 2 November, it left San Francisco on its return journey. On 14 November, it reached Yokohama once again.
2. The ship *Hikawa Maru* (with Lieutenant-Commander Fukushima Eikichi from the Navy General Staff's Intelligence Bureau aboard) departed Yokohama harbor on 20 October 1941. It called at Vancouver on 31 October, and at Seattle on 1 November, before departing on its return journey to Yokahama on 4 November. It reached Yokahama on 18 November.
3. The ship *Taiyo Maru* (with Commander Maejima and Lieutenant-Commander Suzuki aboard) set off from Yokohama on 20 October 1941 and arrived at Honolulu on 1 November. It departed Honolulu for Yokohama on 5 November and got back to Yokohama on 17 November.

Through all of this, one can see that Japan had begun to intensify its surveillance of developments in the Mid-Pacific region and on the West Coast of the U.S.

In a feint designed to deceive the enemy, on 2 December the *Tatsuta Maru* set off from Yokohama for Panama under the pretext that it was making a second journey to evacuate Japanese nationals. Yet after war broke out midway through its journey, the ship reversed course and returned to Yokohama.

Now let's return to Consul-General Kita. Once he had come back from the ship, he showed me something that Lieutenant-Commander Nakashima had given to him. I examined it carefully. It was actually a paper spill, a long piece of paper that had been rolled up so as to be used as a firelighter.

Consul-General Kita then said:

"The two of us met in a cabin aboard ship. Although he was disguised as a purser, he was in fact Lieutenant-Commander Nakashima. He asked after your health and said it had 'always caused you troubles' and that he was 'truly sorry about that.'

"He also said that relations between Japan and the U.S. were going from bad to worse and that his main task was to make contact with you. Then he told me to give you this paper roll and asked me to ensure that you reply before his ship leaves port tomorrow."

After saying that, he quietly passed the "firelighter" to me under the table.

I carefully unrolled the paper and had a look at it. I was surprised to see that it was completely covered with small words that had been written in pencil. This was the list of 97 questions that I have already described. It instructed me to answer the following questions on the basis of the intelligence information that I had been able to gather thus far:

1. How many naval vessels are docked or at anchor?
2. How many different classes of vessel are there? How many of each type? What are their names?
3. Where are the battleships and aircraft carriers anchored?
4. What is the situation of the battleships now moored or at anchor?
5. What are the current patterns of deployment for battleships and aircraft carriers (port entries/exits)?
6. How long does it take a battleship at anchor to leave the harbor?
7. On what day of the week do you reckon that the number of ships at anchor reaches its maximum?
8. When the battleships are at anchor, are they protected by anti-torpedo netting?
9. The average number of days that battleships stay at the docks and their position?
10. You frequently state that battleships are moored, or at anchor, side by side. Is this an exception or is it the rule?
11. Are there large aircraft on patrol at dawn or at dusk? If so, how many set out each time?
12. Where are the air bases on the Hawaiian Archipelago? What is the troop strength at each?
13. When the aircraft carriers have left the harbor, do the aircraft aboard take to the skies?
14. How many aircraft are stationed on Ford Island?
15. Are there any obstruction balloons positioned around Pearl Harbor?
16. Apart from Pearl Harbor, are there any other anchorage zones?
17. Have the Lahaina Roads been used as a temporary anchorage zone on any occasion?
18. Do navy servicemen commonly go ashore?
19. Are there any signs that the number of defensive troops deployed by the Army is increasing?

20. The Secret Envoy

20. What is the status of the fuel depots (above or below ground)? Are any under construction?
21. Are the oil storage containers around the port actually filled with oil, or are they decoys?
22. When the fleet leaves port, where does it go to? In which direction does it set off? To do what?
23. If there are any signs of unusual shipments of fuel or food, please report immediately.
24. Which possible landing zones could be used to confront the enemy?
25. Please do your best to report on the activities of the submarine fleet.
26. Is any anti-submarine netting used around the harbor? If so, please reply quickly with details.
27. Provide information on any increase in air traffic to Kiska Island, Dutch Harbor and the mid–Pacific zone.
28. Has there been any unexpected change in anti-espionage activity?

I felt very happy that the Navy General Staff had asked these questions of me. "This finally looks like something from the War Operations Bureau," I told myself.

That evening, I had to make use of all of the intelligence information that I had exhausted my energy collecting day after day and I must have looked like a student answering exam questions. I was up all night answering the 97 questions.

The next morning, I handed over my answer sheet to Consul-General Kita. Kita then hid it under his belt and patted it down on his belly with a slap. "Pah."

"Make sure you hand it over to him yourself!" I said.

Please allow me to provide some idea of how I dealt with those questions.

Question: "On what day of the week do you reckon that the number of ships at anchor reaches its maximum?"

Although I was initially somewhat unsure about the answer to this, after reviewing the statistics provided by my notes I answered without hesitation. "Sunday."

Among those questions were some to which I could provide only provisional answers and nothing more, because they required additional investigation. For example, "Is any anti-submarine netting used around the harbor?"

Even though I had done underwater reconnaissance many times, I still hadn't managed to gather sufficient information on this matter. In any case, after reading these questions, I sensed that the Navy General Staff was using seemingly theoretical military questions to hint at its focal points and thus at the direction that my investigation of Pearl Harbor should take.

At the same time, these questions made me understand that from now on my activities were of "most pressing" importance. Consequently, I quietly resolved that I would rouse all of my energy, summon all of my abilities, and pour all that I had into my reconnaissance work.

21

Activity in November

Japan-U.S. relations had begun to worsen with every passing day by the time I received the following cable from Tokyo in mid–November.

15 November 1941
From: The Minister for Foreign Affairs, Tokyo
To: Consul-General Kita, Honolulu
Cable # 111

> Due to rapidly worsening relations between Japan and the United States, we ask that you send two weekly reports on the vessels berthed or at anchor in the harbor. Don't concern yourself about the timing of those reports. Naturally you are very careful, but you must take all necessary precautions to maintain secrecy.

After reading the telegram, I truly didn't know what to do. Had they been concerned about maintaining secrecy, they ought not to have sent the cable at all. And why had they requested that two reports be sent each week while also instructing me that I was not to concern myself about the timing of my reports? Didn't Tokyo realize that I only wrote up my reports about the vessels at anchor, as well as the accompanying analysis, after many reconnaissance missions and thorough research had been completed?

I chose just the right words for my reports so that Tokyo would receive the most effective material upon which to base its decisions, even though that meant I had to pour every last ounce of my energy into my work. I didn't believe that anyone could be a good undercover agent by simply sending in lists of things that they had seen.

"Never mind," I told myself. "It's only the death penalty if you get caught, isn't it?"

I vowed that I would further intensify my reconnaissance work, no matter what. And I swore that I wouldn't give myself cause for any regrets about this exceptional opportunity.

As Consul-General Kita was an experienced diplomat, he sought to keep an eye on me (and prevent me from acting impetuously) by regularly inviting me out to the cinema or to eat American food. I nonetheless continued my reckless activities, just as I always had done.

"He's just a wimpy little diplomat," I used to say to myself at the time, "so what does he know about anything? Even if they do catch me, I will never confess. And if I don't act now, I will regret it for the rest of my life."

As I write this book, I am the same age that Kita was then. I feel deeply ashamed when I think back to that time and compare Kita (with his ability to carefully think things through and come up with good plans) to my younger, arrogant self.

On 17 November, in order to scout out the activities of the U.S. forces at Pearl Harbor, I moved into the Shunchoro Teahouse. From there I spied on the activities of the Pacific Fleet non-stop, day and night.

As Tokyo had ordered me to report once every three days, I sent the following cable on 18 November:

> From: Consul-General Kita, Honolulu
> To: The Minister for Foreign Affairs, Tokyo
> 18 November 1941
> Cable # 222
>
> 1.
> On 15 November, the naval vessels anchored in the harbor were the same as those mentioned in cable # 219, which was sent on 14 November. In Zone AD, the battleship *Oklahoma* had entered the harbor and an oil tanker had exited the harbor. In Zone CC, there were 3 heavy cruisers at anchor.
>
> 2.
> On 17 November the aircraft carrier *Saratoga* was not inside the harbor. The aircraft carrier *Enterprise* was in Water Zone C. There were 2 Chicago-class heavy cruisers and 1 Pensacola-class landing vessel moored in Water Zone KS. There were 4 merchant ships at anchor in Water Zone DD.
>
> 3.
> At 10 a.m. on 17 November, 8 destroyers were seen entering the harbor. They used a single column formation while entering the harbor and there was a distance of 1,000 meters between each ship. Their speed was 3 nautical miles per hour when entering the harbor. Once inside the harbor, the ships changed direction five times before they anchored. Every change of direction was a turn of approximately 30 degrees. It took each ship roughly an hour to anchor. One of those ships passed through the waters on the east side of the harbor to enter Water Zone A.

I then decided to take as much time as was needed to get a complete picture of the situation on the ground. So I went to Pearl Harbor, Hickam Field, Wheeler Field, Kaneʻohe, and Ewa Airfield every day to check on the activities at each site. After doing that, I had to draft and then encrypt my telegrams. Of course, I regularly asked the cryptographer at the consulate-general to encrypt them for me, but he was often too busy working on the coding of the consulate-general's official diplomatic messages. In any case, it wasn't a good idea to give too much extra work to anyone else.

21. Activity in November

On 20 November I received yet another encrypted cable from Tokyo, the gist of which was as follows:

> Hoping for a wide-ranging investigation of naval vessels in the waters off Hawaii and in the neighboring water zones.

It was difficult for me to decide how I should interpret this cable's compound adjective, "wide-ranging." Was the cable referring to the entire Hawaiian Archipelago? If so, that archipelago was over 1,500 nautical miles in breadth. What's more, the total surface area of its "Big Eight" islands alone equaled that of Japan's Shikoku.

In addition to this, it was difficult to understand the meaning of the so-called "neighboring water zones" mentioned in the cable. Which areas were being referred to? Was that a reference to the waters around the archipelago itself? Or did it describe the area that ran west to Midway Island and as far south as Johnston Atoll? If so, the distance represented by the radius of such a zone was so great that the fleet would require two or three days to traverse it. Whatever the case, one question remained: How could you possibly reconnoiter such a vast area?

Whenever a group of vessels left the harbor, the navy made a practice of including at least one cruiser capable of carrying a reconnaissance aircraft on its deck. Those aircraft, known as "attics," were scout planes that conducted aerial searches. After I had noticed them, I decided to take a leaf from the navy's book and make use of aircraft to carry out my reconnaissance tasks.

There were regular flights from Honolulu to the islands of Hawaii, Maui, and Kauai in those days. Flights to the most remote of the islands only took about two hours. I had noticed these scheduled flights quite early on and I'd visited the ticket office to learn all about them: how many passengers they carried, the flight schedules, and so on.

Wanting to take one of these flights wasn't really a problem in itself, the trick was knowing how I should justify my interest in such an itinerary. Initially, I had simply used sightseeing as a pretext to get on board a flight. Yet after having used that excuse repeatedly, it was bound to start looking suspicious. As a result, I asked one of the Japanese-American employees at the consulate-general to buy a plane ticket in his name and then hand it over to me. I then disguised myself as him before boarding the flight. Fortunately, the journey was without incident and I managed to achieve all of my goals. Not only had I managed to collect military intelligence at Pearl Harbor, I'd gathered it on all of the main islands.

Toward the end of November, I was busier than ever. On 24 November, I sent two long telegrams to Tokyo in rapid succession:

24 November 1941
From: Consul-General Kita, Honolulu
To: The Minister for Foreign Affairs, Tokyo
RE: Cable # 114
Top Secret

1.
As per its usual practice, the fleet is departing from Pearl Harbor to conduct its exercises and then returning to Pearl Harbor for the night.

2.
The fleet has seldom stopped at the Lahaina Roads recently, nor has it conducted any exercises in that area. From time to time there are destroyers, submarines, or other smaller vessels at anchor in that area.

3.
There are no naval vessels entering port at Hilo, Lahaina, or Kaneʻohe or at the other ports of similar size.

4.
The main elements of the deployments made by the fleet are roughly as follows:
Battleships always travel in a small flotilla, alongside 2 to 4 merchant vessels, to the southwest corner of Hawaii Island. This exercise at sea takes roughly one week to complete.
Aircraft Carriers always conduct their practice exercises alone.
The seaplane flagship carries out practice exercises with other vessels of similar type.

5.
Firing and bombing exercises are carried out by aircraft near the southern end of Kahoʻolawe Island.

I sent yet another telegram concerning the activities of the fleet on the same day:

> A unit of 6 heavy cruisers will soon go to the Samoan Islands to carry out exercises over a period of 2 or 3 weeks. But first they will spend around 4 or 5 days at anchor or moored to the docks in Pearl Harbor.
>
> Apparently, a unit of 5 light cruisers will soon go to the seas near Panama to carry out exercises lasting 1 or 2 weeks.
>
> The submarines go out to sea every Monday, Wednesday and Friday for 24 hours of practice exercises.
>
> The destroyers, minus their usual complement of accompanying vessels, conduct practice exercises in the waters off Hawaii.
>
> Minelayers that form part of the 'O' fleet are conducting exercises around Manila for more than three weeks. For 23 days and nights, 5 minelayers will be laying anti-submarine mines outside Manila Harbor.

As I have said, I was simply being run off my feet gathering information on the activities of the fleet. It wasn't clear to me what Tokyo's objectives were in requesting these sorts of intelligence reports, though. In fact, I couldn't have guessed what their true intentions were. I could only comply

21. Activity in November

with my orders and do everything in my power to carry out my activities. That was all.

It was at this time that I received the following two cables in quick succession:

28 November 1941
From: The Minister for Foreign Affairs, Tokyo
To: Consul-General Kita, Honolulu
Classified to other Departments

Concerning intelligence information of the utmost importance. It is hoped that you can report on the following points:

1.
On those occasions when the battleships leave port, please report if you believe their departure is not per their regular schedule. During this period the fleet may sometimes leave Hawaii altogether and travel to a distant location, at which point contact with the target is lost for a time. On the basis of your judgment, please report freely on this sort of activity.

2.
Hope to receive a report on the port entries and exits of the fleet's capital ships and their time at dock or at anchor.

29 November 1941
From: The Minister for Foreign Affairs, Tokyo
To: Consul-General Kita, Honolulu

We have received a steady succession of reports concerning the operations carried out by the fleet. Henceforth, please report even if there is no activity.

After reading those telegrams, I sensed that Tokyo was keen to closely follow the activities of the principal ships in the fleet. Comments such as "please report even if there is no activity" and "we have received a steady succession of reports concerning the operations carried out by the fleet" made it clear that Tokyo placed great stock in my reports. This left me feeling greatly relieved.

Then again, other phrases were quite ambiguous and it was difficult to guess at their significance:

"The fleet may sometimes leave Hawaii altogether and travel to a distant location, at which point contact with the target is lost for a time…"

"On the basis of your judgment, please report freely on this sort of activity."

First of all, how was I to know if ships leaving the harbor were going to return within a week or within some other time period? At the same time, did I know anything about Tokyo's present thinking or planning?

In fact, it's an understatement to say that I was uncertain about these things. The aircraft carrier-based mobile strike force, the *Kidō Butai*, which was to launch the surprise attack on Hawaii, had secretly set off from Hitokappu Bay and was already on the first phase of its operation by then. As I was no clairvoyant, I had no way of foreseeing such a development.

One can imagine this made Tokyo most uneasy at that moment! How they must have hoped that my eyes, the only pair of "navy eyes" they had in position to scout out the situation at Pearl Harbor, would provide them with the most accurate and reliable intelligence reports possible!

"The fate of crown and country depends entirely upon those two eyes!" Supreme Command might have been grumbling at that time, as a result of their inability to tell me the truth about what was going on.

After all, who could guarantee that our coded telegrams wouldn't be deciphered by the enemy? Who would communicate our nation's biggest secret to a diplomatic post abroad beforehand, anyway? Would they send such a message abroad to someone, such as myself, who seemed likely to be detained by the enemy at any time? How exactly would they have told me of their true intentions? Consequently, they hedged their bets by sending me those telegrams that beat around the bush.

Had Tokyo been able to send the following sort of cable, the situation would have been absolutely clear:

The mobile force sent to launch a surprise attack on Hawaii left Etorofu Island on 20 November. It is expected to launch its attack on Pearl Harbor on 8 December. Hope for a detailed report concerning the activities of the Pacific Fleet.

In reality, this was basically impossible. Consequently, expressions such as "on the basis of your judgment" had to be used instead. These seemed all right at first, but didn't seem so upon closer examination.

As Kita and I were unable to make out what Tokyo's true intent was, the two of us began speaking about it.

"Something really seems a bit strange. Doesn't Japan want to attack the South? So, uh, they probably won't come here?"

"No, they might be coming."

"Hmm, they might come."

"The cables that have arrived recently really are a bit strange. It's getting harder and harder to make them out!"

"Oh, do you find so too? They definitely are a bit strange."

"Hmm. The orders coming from Tokyo are getting increasingly fierce. You have to be careful. You absolutely cannot allow yourself to get caught at this critical time!"

"Yes. I will definitely go about my work cautiously."

The two of us talked and talked, yet we didn't discuss the whys and wherefores of the situation. Our discussions always found us restating the same observations: "How strange!" and "It's strange…" We remained, as always, half

21. Activity in November

doubting and half believing. Diplomatic personnel stationed abroad are truly childlike because of this inability to understand their "parent's" heart.

Despite this, I sent Tokyo the following casual but composed telegram.

28 November 1941
From: Consul-General Kita, Honolulu
To: The Minister for Foreign Affairs, Tokyo

1.
The aircraft carrier *Midway Island* has eight B-17s aboard. Its anti-aircraft guns are capable of reaching 5 kilometers in altitude.

2.
On Sand Island they are currently carrying out firing practice with live ammunition. Twelve shells have been fired. Shells are airborne for 13 seconds. Shots are fired at two-minute intervals. None of the shells has hit a target.

3.
It was recently estimated that the total number of marines here will reach 12,000.

4.
There is a cruiser stationed 1,500 meters outside the harbor and 2 destroyers are always deployed at the harbor entrance.

22

Cash for an Undercover Agent

I have some very unhappy memories of Lanikai Beach. Since these memories are difficult for me to write about, I feel compelled to get right to the point. My comments about this matter will not be especially detailed, however, because it is not appropriate for me to reveal all of the facts here.

At the end of November 1941, Tokyo realized that those of us in Honolulu would likely be arrested and imprisoned when war broke out. Tokyo was nonetheless counting on maintaining an undercover agent in Hawaii to ensure that someone would continue to supply intelligence reports. Otto Kühn, the candidate selected for this task, had been an officer in the German military and he lived near Lanikai Beach. A sum of cash had to be delivered to him. However, it would have been very difficult for Consul-General Kita to do so personally. Making such a delivery was so dangerous that each and every one of us would have been taken away if word of it had got out.

Although Consul-General Kita may have tried to find someone suitable for the mission among the other employees at the consulate, in the end he called on me.

"Mr. Morimura. There is a very important matter to be dealt with and I would like to ask you to deal with it. Some money must be delivered to undercover agent Kühn."

"Undercover agent? This is the first I've heard of him. Please tell me what this is all about, will you?"

"No. Don't ask me what this is all about. And don't ask how much money is inside this paper bag. Naturally, I don't want you to look inside it either!"

"Well, when you put it like that, this sounds like a simple matter of sending me out to deliver some money. But you want to keep me from knowing more about this mission… Since the job was arranged by someone else, it's best that I stay out of it. It's too risky. Let the person who planned it ask somebody else to deliver the money and all will be well."

"…" (Silence)

"Consul-General, sir. Didn't you once say, 'Undercover agents should work alone, do their own work, and they should not make any unexpected contacts'?"

22. Cash for an Undercover Agent

"Hmm. Yes, that's right. However, Mr. Morimura, all of our work is done for the benefit of our ancestral land. And actually, apart from you, I can't find anyone suitable to deal with this. Please. I am asking you to go and do this, no matter what. Don't ask me anything more about it. I'll ask you again. Please!"

Shiny beads of sweat were stuck to the consul-general's face. For a very long time, the two of us remained silent beside the table.

"Consul-General! I'll, uh, go then," I finally blurted out in the end.

He took hold of my hand and held it very tightly. I believed this was going to be the last time the two of us would shake hands.

I then thought about the many times I had wracked my brains trying to determine how to carry out my undercover work over the previous eight months. Fortunately for me, I hadn't been detected by the FBI. Yet this task was almost certain to put an end to that state of affairs. The place that I was now obliged to go to had undoubtedly been under FBI surveillance for some time and was probably being watched from all sides.

The consul-general casually picked up half a piece of paper and then handed it to me.

"Your counterpart has the other half of this piece of paper. When you meet, put the pieces of paper together. If the letters on them join up and form a word, give him the money. I wish you success."

He then explained to me that the name "Kalama" had been written across the whole piece of paper, which meant that Kalama would be fully visible when the two pieces of paper were placed together again.

I left the consulate-general wearing casual trousers and an aloha shirt. In my left hand I was carrying a parcel of money wrapped in newspaper. I got into a taxi and went to Lanikai Beach. After I had arrived there, I got out of the taxi, sent it away, and began to walk.

I found the address I was supposed to get to. It was a fine-looking house. I walked right around the house and had a good look on all sides of it. I didn't discover any sign of an FBI presence.

I walked up to the main door, opened it, and went straight on inside. I called out "hi" and "hello" several times, but the house was silent. Yet while nobody inside was responding, my sixth-sense told me that someone was definitely there. I then decided that since I had come this far, there was no point in turning back. After walking over to the porch that was just outside the large dining room, I looked around in every direction. "Hi," I shouted. "Is anyone here? I'd like to speak with you."

Just then, a stupid-looking man with shifty little eyes suddenly appeared out of nowhere.

"Hello! Please, can you tell me if there is a 'King' family living in this area…? Uh, actually, it seems that's the name on the nameplate … of your house."

While I was rambling on, I took out the piece of paper and began to fan it back and forth. I studied his expression and noticed that it had changed somewhat. I then concluded that he was the very man I was looking for. As a result, I quickly moved beside him and displayed the paper right under his eyes. He reacted immediately with an expression of horror, but then he pulled out a similar piece of paper from the right pocket of his suit jacket and opened it on the table. I took both pieces of paper and put them together. The name Kalama then appeared. In spite of this, both his hands were trembling.

"Let's talk over there."

He used a finger to point to the pavilion that stood off to one side at the back of the very spacious garden. It was a Japanese-style pavilion with a few stools inside. From the outside you could only see the upper bodies of any people within. He seemed more than a little scared as he scanned his surroundings with his shifty eyes.

"I am sure you are a reliable man," he said. "Did you happen to have any difficulties on your way here? Did anyone follow you here?"

As he spoke English with a very heavy German accent, I asked him to repeat his words three times before I finally understood him.

"Nothing happened, it was without incident. Don't worry," I told him.

After that, I gave him the parcel of money. Without a word, and without bothering to open it up to look inside, he took the parcel and stuffed it into his pocket.

"Now that you have received this, what are you going to do?"

He responded to my demand with a most cowardly expression. "In the present circumstances, it's too dangerous," he stammered. "We must ... use a signal ... to do it. From my house, from a car ... agree on ... a signal. On another day, we..."

It seemed to take him forever to get his words out and I couldn't get the gist of what he was trying to say. It was imperative that I get a clear reply from him, but his English was far from easy to understand.

"Go and write a reply, and be quick about it. I will wait for you. I don't plan to come here a second time. It's much safer for both of us that way!" I told him.

"Well then, let's do it like this. I will contact you within one week. I'll provide you with the day and time and location in an appropriate way," he declared confidently after hearing me out.

"Okay. I will be waiting for you to contact me."

I was looking straight into his blue eye as I waited for him to finish speaking. And then I left Lanikai Beach, just as it was beginning to get dark. I can still remember the tall eucalyptus trees reflecting what remained of the light of the setting sun.

As for Kühn's subsequent activities, I knew nothing of them. However,

22. Cash for an Undercover Agent

the following is more or less what I came to learn about him after the war ended.

Otto Kühn was a German-American who had arrived in Hawaii quite some time earlier. To the casual observer, he would have seemed an ordinary manager at a sugarcane plantation. In fact, he was secretly providing intelligence reports to Japan. Two or three days after I met with him, he came up with a plan as agreed. He had decided to provide reports on U.S. Navy vessels in the region by using both house lights and car headlights to signal to Japanese submarines hiding nearby.

He accepted this work after someone had entreated him to take it on, while offering him $20,000 to do so. Not long after receiving the money, he gave someone a book of numeric signals as agreed. Someone then used Consul-General Kita's name and title and secretly reported to Tokyo.

The following cable was sent at that time. It contained a detailed list of those signals.

> From: Consul-General Kita, Honolulu
> To: The Minister for Foreign Affairs, Tokyo
>
> From now on we plan to use the numbers 1–8 to signal the following messages. Please keep for future reference.
>
> 1. Indicates that enemy battle forces (including scout ships) are gathering and about to leave port
> 2. Indicates that several aircraft carriers are about to leave port
> 3. Indicates that all enemy battle forces have left port (within the past 1–3 days)
> 4. Indicates that several aircraft carriers have left port (within the past 1–3 days)
> 5. Indicates that all aircraft carriers have left port (within the past 1–3 days)
> 6. Indicates that all battle forces have left port (within the past 4–6 days)
> 7. Indicates that several aircraft carriers have left port (within the past 4–6 days)
> 8. Indicates that all aircraft carriers have left port (within the past 4–6 days)
>
> Signals
>
> 1. At night, we will use lights in the beach house at Lanikai to communicate the above-listed signals.
> 2. On the Lanikai coast during the morning from eight o'clock until noon, one cloth sheet indicates 1, 2, 3 or 4 (according to the hour), while two sheets of cloth mean 5, 6, 7, or 8
> 3. A star on the sail of the sampan in the harbor during the morning will indicate 1, 2, 3, or 4, while a star with the symbol 'III' will indicate 5, 6, 7, or 8 (according to the same hours)
> 4. If there are lights on above the dormer window of Kalama House between 7 pm and 1 am, they will indicate signal 3, 4, 5, 6, 7, or 8 (according to the hour)
>
> (The remaining information has been omitted)

The cable containing these numeric signals was intercepted, however. And then, on 11 December, that cable was decoded by the U.S. Navy.

Early on, the FBI had become very suspicious about the sources of Kühn's income. Apparently, the authorities had secretly checked out his savings account and discovered that it contained $70,000. Once his secret codes had been deciphered, they arrested him right away. During questioning, Kühn confessed. What's more, he confessed that he had received money from a man that he did not know (i.e., me). He was locked up during the war, after having been sentenced to 20 years in prison.

After the war broke out, the FBI put me through harsh interrogations about this matter while I was under house arrest in Arizona. There, a furious middle-aged FBI agent kept trying to put the blame on me. "Were the clothes that you wore at that time as I've described? Who else among the employees at the consulate was young, apart from you? Your counterpart has already provided a full confession. We will take you to San Francisco and torture you if you keep talking nonsense and fail to tell us the truth."

I was subjected to lengthy interrogations day after day and this went on for an entire week. I wasn't really up to the challenge and Consul-General Kita begged me to give in: "Mr. Morimura, I am truly sorry for you. I hope that you can take the blame for this."

But I had secretly promised myself that I would not spill the beans before the war came to an end, no matter what sort of pressure they put me under. So, I persisted in refusing to accept any responsibility for the situation.

"I don't know. My work kept me so busy. Did I have time to go and do that sort of thing? I basically have no memory of that at all."

In the end, the FBI didn't seem to have any grounds to hold me. Consequently, the agent admitted defeat with a smile. "We've never really had any evidence that we could use against you," he told me. And then he took out some loose tobacco that ranchers in the West use. After showing me how to roll it well, he gave me a light.

Apparently, Otto Kühn was deported after the war and he left the country with $20,000 in savings. Today, he and his wife live in Argentina. I'm afraid that he's not yet 70 years of age!

The number of instances where undercover agents have been successful are greatly outnumbered by those instances where undercover agents have failed. This is because the majority of undercover agents are undermined by one or more of the following shortcomings: the desire for money; the lure of women; physical weakness; and weakness of purpose.

I have read countless books and novels about undercover agents. Of those agents, Lawrence of Arabia with his great physical strength and unwavering resolve has earned my greatest admiration. I don't possess superhuman strength, however, and I lack willpower. It was because of this that my father once said that if I went net fishing for three days, I would spend two of those days roasting in the sun. As for the charms of women? I do have a keen interest in them, perhaps because I was born in the Year of the Rat. And as for money? I am quite indifferent to it. This may be because I grew accustomed to life in the navy.

All in all, I am an ordinary man. Although my morals were suited to the circles that I moved in at the time, I was very young. Nevertheless, I did take my duties seriously and I always completed my work on my own. Anyway, when I was in Honolulu I didn't lead a life filled with song, wine, and a gorgeous woman on each arm (as some people seem to imagine it). That's sheer and utter nonsense.

Of course, for the purposes of my work, I really did get into taxis and go out on the town, or sightseeing out of town, with a lot of women. Yet no serious relationship ever developed between myself and any woman there. When I saw those women after the war while I was visiting Hawaii, I could speak freely and honestly with them and not feel the least bit ashamed. Today, Miss "S" is a married mother of two children. Miss "T" still hasn't married and works in a beauty salon. And though Miss "Y" lost her common-law husband on the frontlines in Italy, she perseveres in her work with great determination. Back then, none of them knew anything about the work that I was doing.

At that time, my monthly salary was $150 U.S. plus an allowance of $100. I spent all $250 on my work. During that period, I did not send a penny back home to my family. Nor did I buy anything for myself, apart from an RCA shortwave radio. I returned home empty-handed, without a penny. This is my "accountant's report."

Back in those days, I did sometimes imagine what it would be like to lead the ideal life of a secret agent and spend money like there was no tomorrow, enjoy the company of as many beautiful women as my heart desired, and do the most interesting of work (despite having to take risks from time to time). Yet as I now recall those past times, it all seems like a dream.

I am currently doing some research on the subject of "human weaknesses." Even though I am leading a settled life at present, and residing temporarily near the Sengaku-ji temple in Takanawa, I continue to study the question of man's weaknesses. I frequently think of characters from the play *The Treasury of the Loyal Retainers* in this regard.[1] When we analyze the essence of human weakness, it turns out to be human ability taken to an extreme.

Since Asano Naganori stabs Kira Yoshinaka, after the latter insults him, he is compelled to commit hara-kiri at the beginning of March. Before long, his death leads to the confiscation of his estate and the various members of his household are scattered to the four winds. A senior official then petitions to become the new lord of Akō Castle. Time marches on and after a year the head servant, Oishi Yoshio, resolves to gather the *rōnin* to take revenge for their late master.

Yet during the very short half-year that follows, from the moment Oishi Yoshio takes his decision to the night of their attack at the official's residence, those fearless and resolute *rōnin* who are preparing to meet their deaths must experience changes of mood.

The face of each *rōnin* reveals his impoverishment, while feelings of love and worry also intermingle in his expression. It is said that this sort of emotional instability is extremely dangerous in any collective enterprise. Taking things to the very limit is what causes this.

Seen from this perspective, I fear that the maximum amount of time that people can remain in a state of extreme nervousness cannot exceed one year! Although my period of service in Honolulu was nine months in duration, I had already begun to feel that I was about to reach my limit. If I had been obliged to continue for another two or three years, a leak would no doubt have occurred due to "human weakness" at some point and then my cover would have been blown.

Let me provide some further examples of this. If someone selected for pilot training with a "special commando unit" of *kamikaze* pilots was expected to continue training in a state of perpetual nervousness for two or three years, that person would surely not become a special commando in the end.

Space flight also requires specially trained units. However, neither the U.S. nor the Soviet Union will permit the members of these special units to return to space on successive missions.

And, as the saying goes, "Once a man has experienced relations with a woman, he can contain his desire for nine months but he won't be able to contain it for five years."

All of which is to say that human beings can never go beyond certain limits. I was fortunate that my experiences happened to take place in the United States, a civilized country in which I was never subjected to torture. Yet if I had been tortured at some point, I don't know how much of it I would have been able to bear. When a mere man is faced with a difficult choice, death can end all his troubles in an instant. Moreover, I'm afraid that no one can stand pain, suffering, and torment for very long!

PART THREE

The Fateful Day

23

Activities in December

On what day would the war begin? This was something that I could not predict. And yet, in light of the unusual nature of the most recent instructions sent by Tokyo and their incessant requests for reports on the activities of the U.S. fleet, I had taken the hint and was beginning to feel that the start of the war was imminent.

Thus, I began to intensify my reconnaissance work. Apart from the time that I spent in the morning or afternoon drafting telegrams at the consulate-general, I passed my days out in the field conducting my activities.

In order to monitor the morning and evening maneuvers of the fleet as much as possible, I kept watch over Pearl Harbor from various vantage points: a nearby hill; from my seat on the buses that sped past it; and from the fields of sugarcane that overlooked it. In order to monitor the air patrols that were carried out at nighttime or at dawn, I sometimes slept out on the mountainside or inside a flower garden. I barely slept at all then, apart from getting a bit of kip at three or four o'clock in the morning. As I didn't have an assistant, I dearly wanted to cut myself in two so that I might better do the work of two people.

When I was sleeping rough on the mountainside, getting soaked by the dew and freezing in the cold, I began to curse my fate and my work, which did nothing but bring me trouble. Yet when I realized that not doing my job would prevent me from thoroughly exposing the secrets of that old enemy, the U.S. Navy, I swore to myself that I would go on right to the very end and my spirits were instantly bolstered.

It was at just this time that Tokyo sent another telegram (At present there is no material available on the original cable.) It read more or less as follows:

> According to the many cables that you have sent, the port entries and exits of the enemy's capital ships are quite clear. But where is the fleet positioned at present? The activities it is conducting at present are not clear. Hope you can send an urgent report on the basis of your judgment.

It goes without saying that information concerning the activities of a naval

23. Activities in December

fleet is kept the most secret of secrets, regardless of the country. Thinking that an outsider could possibly obtain such information about the fleet's activities was nothing but a technicolor dream. In fact, officers weren't allowed to know the full extent of their own fleet's activities. The only people able to understand all of the fleet's activities were the commanding officers and a small group of high-level advisors. Asking an ordinary young man like me to verify the activities of the enemy's fleet, and to have me rely entirely upon my own abilities to do so, was without doubt simply ridiculous.

If you really wanted to know the situation of the enemy's fleet, you need only have paid a visit to the Commander of the U.S. Pacific Fleet Admiral Kimmel. Apart from that, there really was no way to find out.

Despite this, I was a specially appointed undercover agent and that meant I never wanted to send in a reply that read "I don't know." Well then, could I have replied with a report that gave an approximate idea of the situation? No. That would only have harmed my reputation and definitely wouldn't have worked.

It was a tight spot to be in, but I was not prepared to give up without a fight. I hurried over to the busy streets downtown that evening to invite some of those sailors in white uniforms to have a drink, in the hopes that I could extract a little information from them. However, they were immediately on their guard when they saw that I was Japanese. And they were all talking nonsense anyway. Moreover, it would have been inappropriate for me to ask them "What battleship?" or "What aircraft carrier are you with?" Consequently, nothing came of my efforts.

At that extremely nerve-wracking juncture, the only thing that I could do to scout out the activities of the enemy fleet was to spend day and night lying low in the hills, squat in sugarcane fields, and take taxis time and again. The following telegram is the report that I sent after having spent many sleepless nights up in the hills gathering intelligence.

1 December 1941

From: Consul-General Kita, Honolulu
To: The Minister for Foreign Affairs, Tokyo
RE: cable #119

1.
   The site where the enemy fleet's capital ships carry out their training exercises is about 500 nautical miles southeast of the harbor. The reasons for inferring that this is their direction of travel are as follows:
   i. When the fleet leaves port, it is always traveling toward the southeast and always disappears beyond the horizon in that direction.
   ii. The fleet has never been observed traveling toward the west or along the Kauai shipping channel to the north.
   iii. The sea to the west of the Hawaiian Archipelago is riddled with reefs and islands, so it is unsuitable for maritime training exercises.

    iv. Training maneuvers probably need to be carried out as far away as possible from merchant shipping routes.

The reasons for inferring the distance traveled are as follows:
1. With a full supply of fuel, it is possible to carry out activities at high speeds over long distances.
2. The sound of cannon fire is never heard around the port here, which means that long distances are involved.
3. In a seven-day period, the actual time spent on training maneuvers is four days (or 96 hours).

If we calculate that 50% of this time is spent on the exercises, and we take the hourly speed of travel to be 12–16 nautical miles, we can determine the distance traveled out and back again during the exercises. That distance is roughly 500 nautical miles.

2.
    The schedule for battleships leaving port and then returning to port is as follows:

    i. (i) Leave port on Tuesday, return to port on Friday

    Or

    ii. (ii) Leave port on Friday, return to port on Sunday

After a battleship returns to port it will remain at anchor for about one week, regardless of the day of its return.

I sent this telegram reply at a time when I was throwing every last ounce of my energy into my work.

    At this point, I would like to add a few comments about the telegrams presented in this book. All of the telegrams presented here directly quote the cables that were intercepted and deciphered by the Americans, which have been kept in an archive to this day. The telegrams are presented here in their original form and I have not added or removed a single word. Furthermore, all of these original telegrams have been preserved thanks to a book published by Japan's National Institute for Defense Studies.

    The deductions that I made in the above telegram were, by some stroke of luck, quite accurate. Japan's strike force entered Hawaii from the north and did not encounter any U.S. Navy vessels on its approach. Furthermore, the enemy fleet's capital ships were in fact anchored in the harbor that Sunday. Today I have no wish to boast or to give myself any special credit, but I still can't help but feel amazed about the surprising accuracy of my report.

    I received yet another cable soon after that, which read as follows:

From: The Minister for Foreign Affairs, Tokyo
To: Consul-General Kita, Honolulu
Confidential

Cable #123

    In light of present circumstances, it is of the greatest importance that we have a clear idea about the battleships, aircraft carriers and cruisers anchored within the harbor. From now on, do your utmost to report once per day.

23. Activities in December

> Have any obstruction balloons been sent up into the air around Pearl Harbor? Or is there any sign that preparations are underway to send up such balloons? Please report.
> In addition, please cable information on whether the Americans have installed anti-torpedo netting to protect their battleships.

After reading through the cable I was completely stunned. I stopped breathing and stood dumbstruck beside Kita. "Maybe they really are treating Pearl Harbor as their target!" I blurted out a few moments later. In an instant, I was calling to mind all of the activities that I had carried out up until then and thinking about whether or not I had made any mistakes. I felt some comfort when I thought about all those activities into which I had put the greatest amount of effort, but I felt enormous regret about the activities that I had carried out without adequate preparation.

After a time, Consul-General Kita pointed to the telegram.

"Mr. Morimura. These obstruction balloons that they mention, what sort of things are they exactly?" he asked in a deep, steady voice.

"Ah, they put a lot of those balloons in the air overhead to prevent enemy planes from flying in at low altitudes. They were first used in battle in Europe, but apparently they really aren't very effective."

"And the anti-torpedo netting?"

"It is the wire netting that is installed on both sides of a battleship to defend against torpedo attacks. Most countries' navies don't make great use of it because it invariably reduces the speed at which a ship can travel. However, it is a protective device that's sometimes installed on older battleships."

In order to calm my nerves, I had deliberately taken my time and provided him with a relatively detailed explanation.

"Ah!" Kita said with a nod of his head.

He then lifted his head and looked directly at me with a knowing smile.

"It looks like there's work to do!" he mumbled to himself.

I immediately returned to my room in the dormitory and began to organize my belongings. I got hold of all of the notes on the fleet's activities that I had hidden away, which I had exhausted so much energy in creating, and burned them. Those materials were the fruit of over half a year's work that had cost me so much effort and energy. I really couldn't bear to see them committed to the flames.

As for the photos that I had taken with my friends, I burned them too as I feared that keeping them would only sow the seeds of future troubles. Even the contents of my wastepaper basket and drawer contained possible pieces of evidence for the enemy, so I burned those things along with a tourist map of the Hawaiian Archipelago.

Yet inwardly, I was unwavering. Now that I had burned all of those materials to eliminate the threat of any possible reprisals, all that I had left was my determination. Henceforth, I would put everything I had into providing intelligence reports. And I would fight to the death to do so.

Since I was certain that I would be arrested by the U.S. authorities, there was no longer any need to act furtively around the other employees at the consulate-general. Naturally, there wasn't any reason to behave with an excess of caution around my superiors either. If the attack on Pearl Harbor were a success, I would die a contented man.

I sent the next report about naval vessels on 5 December. I have just noticed that the number of the cable that I sent on 1 December was # 241 and that the cable sent on 5 December was # 252. This means that I sent out a total of 12 cables between 1 and 5 December.

From: Consul-General Kita, Honolulu
To: The Minister for Foreign Affairs, Tokyo
5 December 1941

Cable# 252

1.
The three battleships I mentioned in cable# 239 returned to port in the morning on the 5th (Friday). They were conducting exercises at sea for 8 days in total.

2.
On this same day, the aircraft carrier *Lexington* left port along with 5 heavy cruisers.

3.
Ships at anchor and berthed in Pearl Harbor on Friday afternoon were as follows:
8 Battleships
3 Light Cruisers
16 Destroyers
4 Brooklyn-class Cruisers
2 Omaha-class Cruisers were moored at the docks

By that time, the Imperial Japanese Navy's mobile strike force had already received the order "Climb to the top of Mount Nikita! 1208." They were now rushing in for the kill at Pearl Harbor.

Just then, Tokyo again sent another urgent telegram:

Regarding the reports about vessels at Pearl Harbor. You must report twice every day, once in the morning and once in the evening.

Oh my! And Tokyo already had me nailed to a cross at Pearl Harbor! Despite that, there would never have been enough of me for them. Not even if they'd had me chopped up into pieces!

The next day, 6 December, I received yet another cable that read as follows:

From: The Minister for Foreign Affairs, Tokyo
To: Consul-General Kita, Honolulu

Please report on the second half of cable# 123, which was sent to you the other day. (Note: obstruction balloons and anti-torpedo netting)

23. Activities in December

On the morning of 6 December, I made the following reply:

From: Consul-General Kita, Honolulu
To: The Minister for Foreign Affairs, Tokyo
6 December 1941
RE: The latter section of cable# 123

   i. In November, the U.S. Army began training its obstruction balloon team at Camp Davis in North Carolina, USA.
      They have apparently placed orders for 400–500 balloons and are planning to use them for the defense of Hawaii and Panama. After scouting out Pearl Harbor it does not appear that that any obstruction balloon equipment has been put into place, nor have any troops been trained on how to deploy them yet. What's more, it is hard to imagine that they have any such equipment in stock here.
      If they were to try to use such obstruction balloons to control the airspace over the ocean and Pearl Harbor, as well as in the skies over the runways at Hickam Field, Ford Island, and Ewa Airfield, they would only be of limited practical use.
      I believe that a surprise attack carried out on these sites is almost certain to be successful.
  ii. I don't believe that anti-torpedo netting has been installed on the battleships. However, the precise situation is still not clear. I will report again after further investigation.

That morning, after I had sent the preceding telegram, I immediately went by car to Pearl Harbor. It was a quiet Saturday and the usual roar of aircraft flying above Pearl Harbor wasn't to be heard, nor could you hear any other sounds for that matter. After the car had passed Hickam Field, I immediately noticed the scene unfolding in the harbor.

"Hey! They're all there! They're all there!"

I was overcome with excitement and my heart was pounding. It was the first time that I had ever seen the entire fleet gathered together: 8 battleships, 2 aircraft carriers, 10 heavy cruisers, 3 light cruisers, and 17 destroyers. In addition, there were numerous other vessels. There was no noise, nor was there any smoke. All of the vessels were quietly floating on the water as it gave off dazzling flashes of light.

As I sat in the car, my mind suddenly took me back to the days when I had gone out to hunt while convalescing in my family village. I often carried my rifle to a pond by the mountainside to shoot ducks and I still remembered the time I was lying flat on the earth, in the middle of some tall grass, taking aim with the rifle. The ducks that were swimming on the pond suspected nothing and went paddling along without a care in the world. There wasn't a noise to be heard anywhere around me. All I could hear was the sound of my heart beating. "Pinngg," went the sound from the gun. And I actually killed seven ducks.

The scene before me was very much like the one I had seen when hunting those ducks. In my mind, I was shouting "I've found a flock of ducks!" non-stop.

I went to the docks at very end of the peninsula that divided Pearl Harbor, as was my usual practice, and I scouted out the situation of the enemy ships. What my intuition told me then led me to a conclusion: It must be done. Now.

Thus, I sent yet another cable that same day.

From: Consul-General Kita, Honolulu
To: The Minister for Foreign Affairs, Tokyo
6 December 1941

1.

In the late morning on the 6th, the following naval vessels were berthed or at anchor in Pearl Harbor:

8 battleships moored side by side in Water Zone A, 2 aircraft carriers anchored in Water Zone B, 10 heavy cruisers at anchor in Water Zone C, 3 light cruisers and 17 destroyers anchored in Water Zone C. 4 light cruisers and 2 destroyers were moored to the docks.

2.

Nothing unusual about the fleet's appearance has been discovered, nor is there any sign the fleet is preparing for battle.

3.

There are no obstruction balloons in the skies above.

As that day was a Saturday, the secretary in charge of the secret coding of messages had long since finished work. Therefore, I got right down to work in the code room and encrypted the cable myself. After that, I made use of my rudimentary typing skills to type up the coded text. Immediately after that, I asked Ozaki (the Consul-General's driver) to deliver the text to the cable office.

It was already two o'clock by the time I had finished lunch. I dragged my weary body back to my room on the second floor of the residence and climbed onto my bed with my clothes on.

I woke up after barely managing to get 20 minutes' sleep, rolled over, stood up and began to think about going to Pearl Harbor that evening to scout out the situation there.

I was soon reconsidering the idea.

"Oh! That's unlucky! Today is Saturday, isn't it? I'm sure the fleet isn't going to leave. It's best to forget about doing any reconnaissance work this evening. That's too bad!

"No, no! That's no good! I don't know what changes might occur, so I ought to go out and carry on with my duties. The surprise attack could begin at any moment now and I would regret my failure to act for the rest of my life!

"That may be true, but isn't it possible that the surprise attack may not be planned for today or tomorrow? Tokyo still hasn't sent out the date of the attack on Pearl Harbor, has it? And hasn't everyone else gone home? It's only me here and I'm the only one who's out risking life and limb on the job. This is ridiculous, isn't it?"

A battle had broken out within my innermost self. Yet before long, I heard my inner voice deliver what seemed to be a warning from God. "You need to stay true to your calling!"

All of a sudden, this had me standing up straight.

24

The Final Telegram

I lived on the second floor of the consulate's employee residence and the nearest telephone was on a landing halfway down the stairs. It may have been placed there because the Americans made a practice of having telephones installed midway between floors. I seldom made use of the telephone at my quarters since I knew that it had quite likely been fitted with a listening device.

In any case Miss Yoshie, the dormitory attendant, and her boyfriend practically had a monopoly on the use of the telephone nearest to my quarters. They used it for their love talk, or to make dates, and I was frequently relaying messages to her. "The local FBI bureau is eavesdropping," I told myself. "So why don't I let them listen in on the cooing of those two over the telephone? After all, it is quite interesting." As a result, I didn't oppose their telephone conversations. I rather welcomed them.

However, when that telephone rang in the middle of the night it was usually Consul-General Kita calling me.

"Hi. You're at home," he might say. "It doesn't matter how much I try, I can't seem to get to sleep. Come over for a drink, will you?"

"Hello, Mr. Morimura? I think the two of us bachelors have had enough! Come on, let's go somewhere for a drink." he would say on other occasions.

I never once refused his invitations because I enjoyed drinking too. I was always happy to go out with him, although FBI agents would invariably follow us to the tavern whenever we went out together. However, Kita only needed to have three drinks before he began to get tipsy and then his tougher, more audacious side would appear. "FBI," he frequently shouted at such times. "Beat it, will you!" And a gale of laughter would immediately ensue.

As I have just explained, I seldom used the telephone at my quarters. Yet on this day, perhaps because I was excessively tired, I just went down the stairs, picked up the phone and gave my taxi driver, Mikami, a call. "Hello, is that Mikami? This is Morimura. I want to go out for a ride. Can you come over soon?"

I never took taxis from the consulate-general to Pearl Harbor. Each time I made the trip I would either catch a taxi out on the street somewhere, ride a

24. The Final Telegram

bus and then switch to a taxi further down the road, or catch a bus and simply walk on from wherever I had disembarked. Yet when I wanted to go for an excursion somewhere further afield, or do a tour around the island, I would call Mikami and ask him to meet me with his taxi since I had come to know him well.

Mikami had gone through some Japanese military training. What's more, he had frequently served as an intermediary for the consulate-general in various business transactions over the years. He was a fairly trustworthy man.

From my first day in Honolulu onwards, he had taken me to and brought me back from places all over the island. Furthermore, he had explained many American customs and practices to me. For example:

"When you're walking, you must walk on the right side."

"Don't just go and piss anywhere."

"Hey! Don't spit whenever you like!" And so on…

What's more, he seemed to understand just what sort of places I was interested in seeing without my telling him. For example, he didn't need me to tell him to take me to the very end of the peninsula that served as an ideal observation point. He even took me into the Schofield Barracks on one occasion. Once inside, he was turning this way and that way so often that we lost our way. However, he then very cleverly took the initiative and asked a sentry where the exit was.

His only shortcoming was in fact his car. It was just a little too noticeable since it was old and its very high roof was painted black. Yet he offered a benefit that saved me considerable worry and a lot of money. Once the cost of the taxi ride and extras had been agreed, it was up to him to go to the accountant at the consulate-general to receive payment. However, very soon after the war began, he was arrested by the FBI and interrogated about this. "You frequently went to the Japanese Consulate-General. Who were you driving? Where did you go?"

After the war ended, he was kept in detention until he was deported to Japan. Although Mikami apparently lives somewhere or other in Chiba Prefecture now, I still have not had the opportunity to meet with him to thank him for looking after me all those years ago.

I will now stop this digression and return to my discussion of that Saturday.

Perhaps it was because I was so tired, I'm not sure why it was, but I had a premonition of sorts that told me the next two days would be my last in Honolulu. As a result of this, I decided that I would go to the grocery store and to the Shunchoro Teahouse on my way back from scouting out Pearl Harbor to pay off my tabs.

Just as I was figuring out that day's activities, I suddenly heard Mikami calling upstairs from the ground floor. "Mr. Morimura! Hello!" During our telephone conversation he had promised to arrive in about ten minutes. Sure enough, he was there right on time.

As we walked out the main doors, I looked around but couldn't see a car.

"And the car?" I asked.

"It's over there."

Without a word, Mikami went walking off. As it turned out, he had decided that his car would have been too conspicuous had he left it in front of the consulate. He had hidden it under a lush mangrove instead.

I was extremely satisfied by the high degree of vigilance he had shown. Nonetheless, I quite deliberately took no notice of it. "Today I intend to go to a few places to pay off the money I owe," I said.

The car then followed Nu'uanu Avenue downhill before reaching the busy streets downtown. There I gave some money to Mikami, along with my tabs, and I asked him to settle some debts for me.

"This time, on our way back, I'd like to go to the Shunchoro Teahouse. Do you think we could stop off there and stretch our legs?"

"Sure we could. Hey, there's an unusually large number of sailors on shore leave today. Look how poorly behaved they are! Okay, let's go and see Pearl!" (He meant Pearl Harbor.)

Mikami forcefully clapped his hands onto the steering wheel, promptly negotiated his way through the heavy traffic on the main road, and then began driving west.

After we had been driving for 15 minutes or so, the twinkling lights of Pearl Harbor were before us. In the middle of the harbor there appeared to be a battleship; its mast was standing tall like a tree. It was, without doubt, a warship.

"It was right to come here after all!" I thought to myself while looking in the other direction and scanning the verdant green mountains that could be made out in the distance.

Just then, Mikami used a finger to gesture towards the harbor. "Look sir! There are ships moving off in the distance!" he said.

He was looking left and right while driving the car. It was his way of showing me that although he was driving, he was still able to spot a group of ships at sea. He evidently wanted to make a display of his abilities.

"Hmm," was the only sound I made in reply.

It was difficult to tell what type they were, because the vessels were so far out to sea. I quickly ordered him to follow our previous itinerary, along the ring road past Pearl Harbor and then over to the tea shop right at the end of the peninsula.

From the ring road it was only possible to see the east side of Ford Island, its west side wasn't visible. The west side of the island was where the

24. The Final Telegram

aircraft carriers and heavy destroyers anchored, and those were the ships that I had to see. After the car had reached the end of the peninsula, I had a very careful look around.

How strange! With my own eyes I had seen the heavy cruisers and aircraft carriers anchored there in the morning on that very day. How was it that they were now nowhere to be seen?

It went without saying that those ships had swaggered out of the harbor after noon that same day, without my having known anything of their activity. As things had already reached such a pass, all that I could do was carefully survey the scene to see if any other ships were leaving the harbor.

Naturally, I had no control over vessels that needed to leave the harbor. Nor did I have any control over those wanting to enter. My remit was to seize the moment and provide Tokyo with factual and timely reports.

Once we reached the Shunchoro Teahouse, I invited Mikami to join me for dinner. I considered this a suitable reward for his efforts. I then said to the landlady, "I must owe you a lot of money by now!" I was left with only two dollars and 50 cents after my debts there were paid off.

I hurried back to the consulate-general after dinner and quickly went to work in the code room to draft a report for Tokyo. I then gave the draft to the code clerk to encrypt and send off. The cable was as follows:

From: Consul-General Kita, Honolulu
To: The Minister for Foreign Affairs, Tokyo
6 December 1941

Cable# 254

1.
The 2 aircraft carriers and 10 heavy cruisers that entered the harbor on 5 December had all left the harbor by the afternoon on 6 December.

2.
At nightfall on 6 December, the following vessels were anchored or berthed in Pearl Harbor:

9 Battleships (this includes the *Utah*, a vessel used for training purposes)
3 Light Cruisers (four other such vessels are in the shipyard)
17 Destroyers (two others are in the shipyard)
3 Submarine Flagships
And many other assorted vessels

3.
There are no signs that the fleet's aircraft are about to carry out reconnaissance missions.

This telegram arrived in Tokyo 6 hours before the start of the war. It was the very last cable that I, or the consulate-general, would send to Tokyo. At 8 a.m. the next day, that enormous fleet, nearly a hundred vessels strong, would undergo its baptism of (bomb) fire.

If the two aircraft carriers that had been anchored in the harbor hadn't left port, they definitely would not have been spared. Had this been the case, Japan would not have suffered such a terrible defeat at Midway Island in the days that followed. Instead, those two aircraft carriers went on to serve as the shield that protected the U.S. Navy during the naval battle for Midway Island.

It's little wonder that the Commander of the Combined Fleet, Isoroku Yamamoto, stamped his foot in a rage when received this last cable of mine.

Had the fates decided to forsake Japan from that day onward?

Fortunately, eight battleships were anchored in the harbor that day and they were the Pacific Fleet's main force. During my nine months in Honolulu this was the first time that I had seen eight battleships gathered together. Nevertheless, because greediness knows no limits, I rued the absence of the two aircraft carriers.

As I recall, the Japanese Consulate-General in Honolulu sent Tokyo a total of 254 telegrams between 1 January and 7 December 1941. The vast majority of those cables were military intelligence reports. The fact that our consulate-general was sending intelligence reports had long been a poorly-kept secret. Intelligence reports were being sent out from our consulate-general long before I took up my post. Furthermore, all the other consulates in Honolulu were doing exactly the same thing. Their intelligence reporting was by no means equal in scope, though. As one might expect, all of Japan's naval ports were equally prone to scrutiny from the ever-watchful eyes of the various foreign embassies and legations there.

Anyway, there is no denying the fact that from 12 May (the day I sent out my first cable) onwards, the number of military intelligence cables that were either drafted by me, or based upon my views, began to rise sharply. The first cable that I drafted was the 78th cable that Japan's Consulate-General in Honolulu had sent that year. The final telegram to be sent out, #254, was the 177th cable sent in 210 days.

This total includes telegrams sent by the consulate-general for its own purposes, of course. These were routine cables that concerned overseas Japanese citizens, business interests, and trade. Yet more than 80 percent of the cables sent out directly or indirectly reported about military intelligence matters. Furthermore, I had painstakingly drafted more that 100 of those cables myself.

I am by no means trying to flaunt my work here, nor do I want to suggest that it was possible to achieve great success on the basis of the work of a single undercover agent (regardless of what anyone else might care to say or think). I have never thought of myself as someone without fault. I was a resentful 30-year-old infant, still wet behind the ears at that time. Consequently, I have no wish to overlook the effective guidance and help that I received from the Navy General Staff, nor the gracious favors shown me by Consul-General Kita.

24. The Final Telegram

The only thing that I'm trying to explain here is this: I went out and did my work, regardless of everything, because I was completely dominated by an invisible yet mighty force known as "*sokoku*" (the land of our ancestors).

I would also like to add that all official documents and coded telegrams sent from the Consulate-General in Honolulu, which naturally included the cables I had drafted, were sent off to the Foreign Ministry in Consul-General Kita's name. Each and every one of these dispatches had to receive Consul-General Kita's prior approval and signature.

Since my status was actually that of an assistant to Consul-General Kita, I did not possess any power to act on my own authority where official documents were concerned. Thus, the old saying "the military controls diplomacy" does not in any way describe my situation at the time. On the contrary, I was actually under the care of the entire staff at the Japanese Consulate-General in Honolulu. It was because of their efforts that I was able to follow the path mapped out for me by government policy and thereby make my small contribution.

25

Pearl Harbor's Last Day

By the time I had finished encrypting the cable and returned to my lodgings, it was already past nine o'clock in the evening and I was feeling completely exhausted after countless days of rushing around. Once I'd had two or three glasses of whiskey, I looked across the consulate-general's extensive grounds towards the consul-general's residence. I was hoping to determine whether or not Consul-General Kita was asleep. When I noticed the weak light that was coming through his window and shining on the leaves of the nearby mango tree, I decided that he was almost certainly listening to Tokyo on a shortwave radio. I was too sleepy to do likewise, though. Once I had climbed into my bed, I was going to sleep and not get up until well past sunrise.

Little did I suspect that Japan's Carrier Striking Task Force was at that very moment pressing towards Hawaii at the greatest of speeds, covered by a jumble of clouds that barely allowed the light of the moon to reflect on the ocean's surface. At about four o'clock the next morning, all the officers and troops in the strike force began to make ready for the attack. By around six o'clock, almost 200 carrier-borne bombers and fighter aircraft had begun closing in on Pearl Harbor!

Meanwhile, I was stretched out and fast asleep.

"Hey sir! Get up and have some breakfast!"

I was awakened suddenly by a high-pitched call from Miss Yoshie, a Japanese-American attendant. As I was still sleepy, I was very slow to get up. She then called out to me again.

"At eight o'clock I have other things to do! Hurry up and eat breakfast, sir!" she said.

"Going on another date, huh? Oh, that's right, it's Sunday today!"

I was joking playfully with the fit and pretty 18-year-old attendant, while staying put beneath my duvet. She came in for her work at the consulate-general and arrived very early on Sundays. After Sunday's breakfast service had ended at eight o'clock, she left for the day. As I feared that her departure would oblige me to wash up the tableware, I reluctantly got up.

25. Pearl Harbor's Last Day

Washing my face and putting on my clothes took about ten minutes. When I got downstairs and had a look at the dining room table, there was almost nothing appetizing to speak of.

As usual there was rock-hard toast, coffee, eggs and papaya. Put simply, there was nothing whatsoever that appealed to me. It seems strange that I have just said all this. I don't know why I still remember the breakfast that was served that morning.

"Well now," Miss Yoshie said upon seeing me arrive for my meal. "Please take your time and enjoy your food. I'll be back in a little while to tidy up."

Yet she kept checking her wristwatch, which meant that she really wanted to leave.

"You may leave, it's all right!" I replied.

While I was putting one or two teaspoons of sugar into my coffee, just after having put some papaya into my mouth, I suddenly heard a terrible, ear-splitting crash. I looked at my watch; it was 7:55. As luck would have it, Miss Yoshie's date had caused her to wake me up and that allowed me to properly witness the explosion of the first bomb.

When the explosion went off, I mistook it for an earthquake! Then, in less time than it took me to bite into the fruit I was eating, there were two or three loud noises. Following that were the sounds of an explosion and intense artillery fire.

"Perhaps they are carrying out some large-scale training exercises," I thought to myself. "Well that's fine, I'll go outside and have a look!"

I ran outside and looked up in the air. I was surprised to see that the skies above Pearl Harbor were shrouded in billowing smoke. One column of dark smoke drifting towards the south was particularly conspicuous.

There was an airplane flying over Hickam Field, about 1,000 meters above the coast. Its wings pierced through the pale morning mist as it drew nearer and then I was quite able to make out the "Rising Sun" symbol it bore on its wing.

It was a Japanese aircraft! War had definitely broken out!

I ran across the grounds to the consul-general's official residence because I wanted to inform Consul-General Kita about this critical situation. Just then, Kita was making his way outdoors.

"Consul-General, war has broken out!"

"You're not mistaken about this, are you?"

"No. I'm definitely not mistaken! We ought to dispose of the ciphers, no?"

"Please call Mr. Tsukikawa here, right away! Mr. Morimura, they have begun to strike at last! I was just listening to the shortwave radio broadcast and I heard the words 'East wind, rain.' That's the code to let us know we must burn the cipher books. Although there was a lot of interference during the broadcast, I am certain that I heard it."

"Look! That's a Japanese plane! They've done it! They've done it! Ah, look at all that thick smoke! Listen! A public announcer is shouting, 'Air raid! Air raid! This is not a drill! All military personnel return to your posts!' And his voice is trembling a little."

The two of us stood still and looked up at the sky while calling out our support to the Japanese aircraft. Tears welled up in Consul-General Kita's eyes as he gave me a firm handshake. "Mr. Morimura, they're striking at last!" he said.

"Oh yes! They're striking! They're striking!"

I was still looking up into the sky, with tears streaming from my eyes, as I firmly shook Consul-General Kita's hand.

Since the sound of the bombing at Pearl Harbor and Hickam Field was especially fierce, we were not particularly surprised by the sound of bombs falling in our vicinity. One such bomb was said to have fallen quite near to the consulate-general and it killed several people, even though it hadn't hit a specific target.

By that time, the gates of the consulate-general had already been firmly shut by the armed members of our special security squad. Yet we could not get into the code room because our cryptographer, Tsukikawa, had still not arrived. I was extremely worried about this.

Soon afterwards, before the security squad had hurried back into the consulate-general, Tsukikawa arrived. Then the two of us entered the code room and firmly secured the door before we began to burn the code books in a metal basin. We had already burned some in the preceding days, because of the gradually worsening situation, and there were not many left. Yet after the remaining material had been burned, black ash half-filled the basin.

Just after we had shredded the last code book, we threw it onto the bonfire and it made the flames blaze. And then the police came rushing in. This happened because some residents in the area had seen smoke coming out of the consulate-general and, having mistaken it for some sort of "smoke signal," reported it to the FBI.

"Open the door! Open up, quickly!" shouted the policemen as they knocked on the door. We refused to open it, though. And then we began to quarrel for a long time, until five or six policemen knocked the door down and came crashing in. Each of them was holding a pistol or a rifle, which they leveled at us while they yelled "Put your hands up!"

Tsukikawa and I had no choice but to comply.

After discovering the code book that was still giving off smoke, they hastily plucked it from the fire and stamped on it until its flames had been extinguished. While they were flipping through those of its pages that had not been charred, I took advantage of the moment to slip out of the room.

I turned my head and looked behind me, but nobody was in pursuit. I

25. Pearl Harbor's Last Day

then ducked into a corner of the courtyard. I wanted to look into the distance and fully take in the results of the surprise attack by Japanese aircraft at Pearl Harbor. But at that very moment, something happened in the code room that would prove to be a huge problem.

Tsukikawa was an honest and reasonable sort of man. Consequently, when the police asked him to raise his hands, he complied and remained standing there. After that, the police said that they would have to conduct a full body search and they actually compelled him to remove his underpants. The two cipher code books that the cautious young man was carrying under his waistband promptly dropped to the ground because of this.

For the FBI Chief directing the five or six policemen, finding those code books was like finding a rare treasure. After snatching them up, he went away simply brimming with joy.

Tsukikawa had begun to hide those code books on his person some time earlier, after Consul-General Kita had given him the order to do so. Kita had reasoned that the code books could prove to be of further use, since he might be transferred to a neutral state in Central America or in South America. Besides, according to the conventions of international law, the possession of such code books is permitted. Nevertheless, they were unlawfully seized by U.S. authorities.

From that day until the day he returned to Japan, Mr. Tsukikawa took this matter personally and very much believed himself responsible for what had happened. In fact, the person who deserved condemnation was the plunderer, not the victim. Then again, who can be reasoned with in times of war?

There was a high-level cipher code in those books and all cables sent from the consulate-general as of 24 November were encrypted with it. Consequently, those cables were decrypted by the Americans. The majority of the telegram material presented in this book is taken from the cables that were decrypted by the Americans.

The matter of whether or not those cables had been decrypted by then was largely irrelevant of course, since war had already broken out. Yet while that cipher could only be of belated service, the consequences of this episode nevertheless proved to be very serious.

First of all, our last remaining undercover agent, Otto Kühn, was unfortunately arrested because the signals that he was sending out were decrypted. He was apparently sentenced to death, but this was later reduced to 20 years' imprisonment. In the end, he was forced to endure much suffering and expelled from the country.

In addition, when examining the telegrams that had been sent by the consulate-general since November, they discovered that there was someone within the consulate-general who had gone to every corner of the island gathering information. When they began to make inquiries of all of the consulate-general's many employees, they learned that the person who had most frequently gone on walkabouts was none other than Morimura. I was mentally prepared for every possible contingency, though. I had already determined that they were definitely not likely to let me go easily.

By around 9:30 or so, the skies over Pearl Harbor had gone quiet, yet more and more black smoke was coming up on all sides of it. A flash occurred at times, when reddish-black flames suddenly leapt out from the black smoke.

Just then, in the midst of all the excitement, I came to my senses. I had a look all around me and saw that there wasn't anyone else within the grounds. The main building was completely silent too. "If I were to make a run for it, I could definitely slip away from here," I thought to myself. "But where would I run to? It doesn't matter where you might flee to on this island, every place is difficult to move on from."

Had things gone to plan, I would have flown to Mexico as soon as the war had broken out and continued to send intelligence reports from there. I had actually reached an agreement about this with Consul-General Kita. Yet Hawaii had now become a battlefield and it looked as if flying out would not be possible. I mulled it over, but soon I was at my wits' end. All that was left for me to do was to stagger back to the main building. There was no other alternative.

Every one of the male employees at the consulate-general had been arrested. All of them were being detained in the office. In the doorway there were five or six policemen, holding their guns leveled, watching over the men. Everyone was keeping a melancholy silence.

"And who are you?" a policeman who noticed me passing by asked hastily.

"I am an employee at the consulate-general."

"Where did you go, huh?"

"Uh, I was in the grounds watching the air attack. It's still burning!"

"Shut up! Get in there, you!"

The policeman shoved me into the office by the shoulder, so I was confined there as well.

"Consul-General! It's still burning!"

I had hardly finished uttering those words when the same policeman eyed me fiercely. "No talking allowed! Sit down quietly!" he said.

Everyone was forced to sit there without saying a word.

26

Life Under House Arrest

Consul-General Kita was placed under house arrest along with six male members of his staff and we were detained in the consulate-general's office building. Meanwhile, all the family members of the staff were kept under house arrest at their lodgings in the residence building. What's more, no movement between the two areas was permitted. In addition, both newspapers and the radio were prohibited to us. It seemed that they had adopted these measures in order to strictly limit our activity.

One of the attendants who worked in the consul-general's residence, an 18-year-old Japanese-American named Miss Shakura, had not managed to get home and was detained in the employee residence as well. Consequently, she was allowed to take on the duty of serving food and drink to all seven of us men.

On that day, because the chaos had continued right into the afternoon, we did not eat lunch until two o'clock. The surveillance over us was extremely severe and we were constantly followed by the police, even if we wanted to use the washroom. In addition, the small knives we used to peel fruit were actually taken away from us.

Subsequently, due to the curfew that was put into effect, we were invariably obliged to eat an early dinner. After that, we promptly climbed into our makeshift beds in the office and got to sleep at a very early hour.

Not only did Miss Shakura have to assist those employees with family members by going to their lodgings and fetching pajamas and undergarments, she also had to assist Kita, Tsukikawa, and myself by washing our clothing (as all three us were bachelors). This only added to her bothers.

The police confiscated nearly everyone's money during their examination of the goods that we had with us. Those American policemen seemed to be used to treating the confiscated property of the people they had arrested as a source of extra income. By contrast, when someone has been arrested in Japan the police must provide a receipt for any belongings taken and return them when that person is freed. I handed them $2.50, which was the only cash I had, quite gladly. I took the attitude that I had everything that I needed and that I cared not in the least. Yet because some of the others had seen a large chunk of their personal wealth confiscated, the fact that they were on the verge of crying clearly showed.

There was a sudden and violent rainstorm at nightfall. I was sitting in the room made dark because of the curfew, listening to the sound of the rain, and thinking about something that I was hoping would happen: I wanted Japan's air troops to attack a second time. However, my hopes were dashed when I didn't hear any further explosions.

After nightfall, I was hoping that Japanese warships would be able to carry out shelling or that a submarine unit could carry out a night attack. Yet apart from a thunderous explosion that I heard at roughly eight o'clock in the evening, after a short burst of small-caliber gunfire, I did not hear any sounds until daybreak. Although I did not hear the roar of our planes, I didn't hear those of the enemy either.

I really was not sleepy at all, I was simply eager to know the results of the air attack on Pearl Harbor.

"I wonder what has become of the *Pennsylvania*," I said to myself. "And what about the *Arizona*?"

"And was that ship with the large clock installed on the basket around its mast, the *West Virginia*, sunk or not? As for that ship with the three-sided base to its mast, the *Colorado*, was its mast blown off and sent flying?

"Those light cruisers at the docks, were they blown up along with the docks and scattered to the winds?"

My mind kept racing and I couldn't get to sleep.

Successive days of house arrest were truly boring beyond measure. After getting up at daybreak each morning, I just sat in my chair in the office and leafed through old copies of Life magazine to while away the time. Things were no different for my colleagues. Every source of news had been cut off so there really was nothing to talk about.

"Hey, how many of the navy's ships were sunk in Pearl Harbor?" I ventured to ask a policeman who was guarding us one day.

"The *Arizona* was the only one!" he sneeringly replied.

As he had replied that only one ship had been sunk, it seemed to me that they were just trying their best to keep calm.

"Are any newspapers being delivered to the consul-general's residence?" I asked Miss Shakura later on, while she was bringing our meals to us.

"I don't know!" she replied curtly.

Immediately after that she gave vent to her feelings. "Mr. Morimura, you're actually asking me about newspapers! If only you knew how many difficulties I have to face!"

"What's this? Is it because you're not allowed to go home?"

After hearing what I had said, she suddenly began to cry.

26. Life Under House Arrest

"Rice! Rice! People in the street are in an uproar and they won't let anyone sell rice to the Japanese Consulate-General. I am unable to buy any rice!"

I was greatly shocked by her words. "She needs to leave here, but things are bad out there!" I told myself.

I immediately began imploring her to act. "Can't you go and find Ozaki and talk about this with him? Ask him to help you."

Our monotonous life under house arrest continued just like this, day after day.

"Mr. Morimura, please help sir!"

I could hear Miss Shakura calling out while she was setting the table. I quickly ran out into the corridor, but the policeman didn't try to stop me. It seemed he had decided to turn a blind eye to me.

"The warships 'destroy' but did not 'turn over' because of shallow water," she whispered to me. As she was speaking Japanese very quickly, some English unintentionally came out with the other words.

I slapped my thigh happily. "I understand, I understand!" I said. "That means that although the ships didn't sink, it was only because of the shallow waters they were in. Yet they were very badly damaged."

In saying "only the *Arizona*" had sunk, the policeman had chosen his words carefully so as to avoid conceding their losses. I was very happy now that I understood what had happened.

At that point, I never could have imagined that the attitude of the policemen would suddenly change for the better. And yet, just a couple of days later, that was what happened.

When someone asked for permission to go to the washroom, they simply replied "Please do."

And when someone asked for permission to take a one-hour stroll after the meal, they replied: "Yes. If everyone goes together, then you may."

And after someone requested a few more cigarettes, they said "Okay."

When we asked them to escort the attendant so that she could go and buy some groceries, they said "Fine."

And whenever we offered them an apple they said "Thank you."

So I asked a policeman, "What's happening in the war?"

"Japan's armed forces are too powerful!" he replied with a shake of his head.

According to Consul-General Kita, he was strolling within the grounds one day when a policeman approached him. "There are a lot of rumors going around on the outside," he told Kita. "They're saying that Japanese forces are going to land on Hawaii. When that happens, our respective situations will be turned on their heads. If I treat you leniently now, don't forget about me when that day comes!"

"Mr. Morimura, the situation now looks favorable for Japan's forces!" said Kita after telling me about this,

"I'm trying to think of a way to get some newspapers, what do you think?"

"Hmm. It's a critical moment. Oh! You will have to be extremely careful!"

"Ha, ha, ha…"

After a long, long time the two of us were finally laughing again.

27

A Special Submarine

In the previous chapter, I wrote about the "thunderous explosion" I heard at approximately eight o'clock in the evening. This loud noise, I would later learn, involved a special midget submarine.

At the beginning of October 1941, I received a cable from Tokyo that instructed me to "report quickly" on whether or not there was any anti-submarine netting in the harbor. To this I provided quite a simple reply: "There may be, but the precise details are unclear." At the time, I was rather angry about the completely amateurish style of their cables.

According to U.S. Navy regulations, it was absolutely necessary to set up anti-submarine netting in those areas where the fleet usually anchored. This had long since been common knowledge. Despite this, at that late stage, Tokyo still needed to ask whether any anti-submarine netting was in place. Weren't they simply asking a question to which they already knew the answer?

At that critical time, I felt it was necessary to collect information about the activities of the fleet and the deployment of aircraft and I was devoting all of my energy to doing just that. However, Tokyo wanted me to report quickly on whether or not anti-submarine netting was in place. "Isn't this a case of not seeing the forest for the trees?" I wondered.

Moreover, Lieutenant-Commander Suzuki, the officer who reached Honolulu aboard the *Taiyo Maru* on 1 November, had put the same question to me on the list of 97 questions.

And I replied:

> It is certain that there is netting in place. Submarines apparently pass a control device, which has been installed somewhere near the entrance to the harbor, and it causes the underwater netting to either rise up or drop down. When a submarine is entering the harbor, the netting drops down to the seabed. After the submarine has passed the entrance point, the netting is raised again. However, it is still not clear where this installation is located. As the anti-submarine netting is underwater, it is not possible to definitively locate it.

Tokyo sent further instructions by cable not long after that. "Hope that you can do everything possible to provide detailed reports on anti-submarine netting and anti-torpedo nets."

Having receiving this cable, I felt that I couldn't regard the matter as unimportant any longer. As I was certain that Tokyo was trying to plan some sort of operation, I had to get out in the field and investigate things for myself. However, the harbor entrance location at which the anti-submarine netting had been placed was undoubtedly within a "restricted zone." I would need to pass through either Pearl Harbor or Hickam Field if I wanted to get to such a place, and that was extremely dangerous. If I were captured, the secret identity that I had spent so much energy and effort trying to keep hidden would be quickly exposed and all of the intelligence that I had collected bit by bit would suddenly come to naught.

Then it occurred to me that if I went sunbathing and turned my face and body a swarthy color, I could disguise myself as a hardy Filipino worker and go to areas near the harbor without raising any suspicions. Thus, I went to the beach at Waikiki every day to bask in the sun. Back then there really weren't very many people sunbathing there, so I could casually stretch out on the sand and let the sun roast my face, legs, back and belly. I even tried my best to ensure that the soles of my feet were tanned too.

After that, I got my map and began to plan the route for my diving expedition. After much indecision, I finally decided to take the long way around and enter the water near Ewa Airfield. To fully disguise myself as a Filipino-American worker, I wore a red aloha shirt, green trousers, and I set off barefoot. I was also carrying a Japanese fishing rod, which made me look like a young man using his free time at the weekend to go fishing. After taking the Pearl Harbor bus, I went into a small grocery store and drank some Coca-Cola. Once I had calmed my nerves, I continued on my way.

While walking down the road, I looked all around but I didn't see anyone following me. The asphalt road was baking hot and it thoroughly scalded my feet. I had decided to go barefoot after noticing that many disadvantaged Hawaiian youths went about barefoot and that Hawaiian children tended to go to school barefoot. Some long-haired Japanese-American youths also went barefoot, with an arm around their girlfriend's waist, chewing gum as they strolled down the road. Despite this, the young women accompanying them would not actually go barefoot.

At the side of the road there was an extremely eye-catching sign. "Attention! Trespassing Is Strictly Prohibited!" So, I waited for the moment when I was sure that no vehicles or pedestrians were in my vicinity and I darted off the road and into a forest of elm trees.[1] I ran for about 200 meters before stopping to catch my breath. Then I looked at the soles of my feet and saw that they had been cut open and were bleeding in many places.

I checked the ground around me and noticed that there were small vol-

27. A Special Submarine

canic rocks everywhere, which made it really difficult to walk. My surroundings were completely tranquil and only a few small birds were calling. The woods were thick with elm trees that obstructed my view, so I did not have a clear line of sight in any direction. Should I go forward or should I retreat? For a moment, I was feeling fairly uncertain about this question. However, my "mission" (that great, invisible power) promptly spurred me forward once again.

After walking on for a bit, I discovered an underground ammunition depot. After walking further, I saw yet another. I thought that these were perhaps intended for a time when the troops had to scatter.

I resolved to press on toward my objective, Ewa Airfield, which was a U.S. Navy air base. After reaching its easternmost limit, I would dive into the water to get to the harbor entrance. Yet by that point, the soles of my feet were causing me great pain and my arms were scratched all over. It was all so hard to bear that I simply wanted to cry out. Then suddenly, I heard the sound of someone whistling. I stopped and listened carefully. Then, through an opening between the trees, I spied some soldiers a distance away.

I moved closer to take a look. Hanging between two trees was a long clothesline. "I'm quite sure those guys are either off-duty sentinels or ground crew and they don't seem to have spotted me," I told myself.

I then quietly skirted around that area and continued to walk, on a slight angle, toward the place that I reckoned was in the vicinity. Sure enough, I soon saw the open water and that meant I had reached the entrance to the harbor. After checking for any sign of movement, I slinked into the scrub. Everything was completely still. All I could feel was my heart racing, "thump-thump, thump-thump." In order to calm my nerves, I sat on the ground cross-legged and waited for nightfall.

There seemed to be some sort of oil floating on the water and it was shimmering brightly. Not only was this area unfit for swimming, no one could remain standing against the force of the largest waves there either. The exceptionally high mast on a nearby warship was another matter of concern to me. I was certain that someone was up in the crow's nest keeping watch with binoculars that could zoom in 16 times.

Since nothing was floating atop the open water before me, I would immediately be found out if only my head were to pop up above the surface. Under the circumstances, the only thing I could do was to mimic the "underwater escape" technique used by the spies of old. I would only make a success of this mission by plunging deep underwater and making a steady path forward. Consequently, I slowly entered the water and began to breathe through a bamboo pole. I was in fact using the fishing pole that I had handy.

Even though the force of the tide was pulling around me, it didn't matter since I could use the fishing pole that I held in my mouth to breathe. With it,

I could remain deep underwater for 15 to 20 minutes. I prevented my body from coming up to the surface by carefully monitoring the level of the bamboo pole and by holding on to rocks. Where my "periscope" (the fishing pole) poked out above the surface of the water, I covered it up with leaves and seaweed that looked just like some refuse floating on the water.

In the end, despite using both my feet to feel all around the seabed, I wasn't able to detect any sort of anti-submarine netting device.

Just after emerging from the water, I took cover in a concealed spot with the thought that I would have a bit of a rest. All of a sudden, I discovered that a sentinel was approaching. Oh my! At that point where would I run to? In that spot, I could only resign myself to my fate.

There was no alternative, I had to go back underwater and breathe through the bamboo pole. Once there, I was looking up at the surface and waiting for the sentinel's knife to stab me. Three minutes, five minutes...

All I could hear was the sound of the intense pounding of my heart. "At a time like this, you cannot get flustered," I told myself. "If your breathing becomes irregular, or if you take in some water, you will certainly have to go back up to the surface."

I tried my best to stay calm and I kept on using the bamboo pole to breathe. Eight minutes, then ten minutes passed. I couldn't hear the sound of footsteps, but I didn't dare surface. I was like a frog, lying underwater and passing the time away. Fifteen minutes, twenty minutes… Because I was still holding out, I felt as if I had become an amphibian and I was irrepressibly happy. The sentinel had walked away and the crisis had finally passed. I slowly came to the surface and took a deep, deep breath. Ah, such sweet-smelling air! Right at that moment I could tell that we humans don't just use our noses and mouths to breathe. Our skin breathes the air too!

When people go underwater, they find breathing very difficult because their lungs have to bear the increased pressure of the water when they inhale. What's more, breathing becomes more and more difficult the deeper the water gets. On the basis of my latest experience I knew that I would not be able to go any deeper than three meters underwater while continuing to breathe, regardless of the length of the pole I used.

It was well into the night when I finally got back to the consulate-general. I immediately drafted a telegram that I would send off in the morning:

RE: Cable# XX

The precise details are not known.

After risking my life to carry out my most recent on-site investigation, this short cable a few words long was all that had come of it.

All too often, cables sent by diplomats are excessively lengthy and detailed and thus all the easier for enemy intelligence operatives to decipher.

27. A Special Submarine

Yet even if this short cable had been decoded, it would have been for naught. Nevertheless, I fear that Tokyo was quite dispirited because of it.

As I recall this matter now, it seems likely that Tokyo urgently needed information about the location of the anti-submarine netting and its control installations in order to plan a bombing mission that would allow the five special midget submarines to enter Pearl Harbor. At that time, however, I really did not know they intended to attack Hawaii. Nor did I know anything at all about the existence of any special submarines.

As a result of this matter, I have come to a very serious realization. When receiving instructions from his superiors, an employee stationed overseas must understand the unspoken implications of their every word and phrase. Nonetheless, a young person may sometimes overlook the importance of the word or the phrase. "That's common knowledge," he'll say to himself, without doing any serious reflection or drawing the necessary inferences.

Here, I would like to provide some background information about the special midget submarine. It was developed by Commander Iwasa and a few other young officers at the start of June 1941.[2] They used Kurahashi Island as their base and carried out testing in Sankan Bay. This submarine was capable of traveling for ten hours at 6 nautical miles per hour or for one hour at 20 nautical miles per hour.

After Commander Iwasa and the others learned of the attack that was to be carried out in Hawaii, they requested that the special midget submarine be allowed to take part in it. However, Admiral Isoroku Yamamoto said that using this sort of submarine would be "tantamount to suicide" and he refused to allow it.

On three subsequent occasions they again put forward their request and they guaranteed the submarine's technology was good enough to give it the potential for success. In addition, they adopted some measures that made the rescue of its crew members possible, if necessary. This was enough to secure Admiral Isoroku Yamamoto's approval.

In short, it was an armament that had never been tested.

The plan for the attack was as follows: Form a unit of five special submarines and transport each one aboard an "I-series" submarine. On 7 December, an hour before sunrise, arrive at a boundary line five nautical miles outside the harbor. Then, at 30-minute intervals, have each midget submarine leave its transport submarine and motor toward the harbor at six nautical miles per hour. Once there, wait for the air raid to commence and then immediately begin to attack.

However, after the midget submarines were discovered by enemy destroyers guarding the entrance to the harbor, they were attacked by torpedo. Thus, they did not succeed.

Nevertheless, the Japanese firmly believe that:

- Ensign Kazuo Sakamaki's midget submarine was not able to attack because a compass malfunctioned. The vessel was consequently battered by the tide and its crew taken prisoner.
- Another such submarine sank just outside the harbor and was therefore unable to attack. It was subsequently salvaged by U.S. troops on 2 February 1962 and transported to the Naval Academy where it was put on display.
- Fragments from another midget submarine were dragged up from the seabed after they were discovered by a vessel that was sweeping for mines.
- The whereabouts of the fourth midget submarine are not known.
- As for the special midget submarine piloted by Masaharu Yokoyama, its mothership I-16 received a message at 18:10 that said "I have successfully attacked." At 20:00 I-16 again received a message, this time on a weak signal, which said "Unable to navigate...."

Ensign Kazuo Sakamaki's Type-A Kō-hyōteki-class submarine beached on Oahu after the attack on Pearl Harbor (Naval History and Heritage Command).

27. A Special Submarine

Yet according to an investigation made by American authorities, this special midget submarine did not have any success at all in the battle.

In 1960, I received an invitation to visit the War History Office of Japan's National Institute for Defense Studies to provide an account of the surprise attack on Pearl Harbor. There I explained that I had heard a thunderous explosion at around eight o'clock on that evening. Commander Sakamoto, an expert on the history of submarine battles who was seated beside me, responded by strongly affirming that they had received the signal "unable to navigate" at 20:00 on that day. From this we may conclude that at least one of the special submarines was successful.

Although I obviously knew nothing of the signal Yokoyama's submarine sent out at the time, the event I've already described and the signal that his vessel sent out do seem to have coincided.

In summary, the Americans firmly believe to this day that no losses were suffered due to any attacks made by the special midget submarines. Yet the Japanese firmly believe that at least one special midget submarine was successful in battle. This debate centers on the "thunderous explosion" heard that day at eight o'clock in the evening.

28

Remember Pearl Harbor

In the middle of January 1942, our monotonous life under house arrest inside the consulate-general came to an end when Shivers (the chief of the local FBI bureau) paid us an unexpected visit one evening. He had come to make an announcement to all of us.

"Now we must send you to a secure location. Please prepare to depart immediately. All of your luggage and belongings will be sent after you once we have packed them up."

"Where is this so-called secure location?" asked Consul-General Kita.

"Someplace!" was all that Shivers would say before he walked off.

A short time later, six or seven cars drove up to the consul-general's official residence. Then Shivers stood on the stairs to shake hands with each one of us and say goodbye. It was the first time I exchanged a handshake with the FBI chief I'd always considered an enemy. Yet I could not stop myself from saying "Thank you very much!" to him.

My words had two meanings. First of all, I was thanking him because he had set me free in the end. Secondly, I was thanking him for all the trouble we had gone through over that long period of detention.

I repeated his parting expression, "Goodbye!"

He then gave me a forceful handshake, as if to return my salute.

Shivers died of an illness after the war ended. This happened following the breakdown he had suffered during the war due to overwork.

A few years ago, while I was reading a Japanese translation of *The FBI Story*, I came across some of Shivers' recollections that I found very interesting:

> When war was on the verge of breaking out, there were seven official FBI employees on our team.
>
> In preparation for war, we compiled a list of the names of several thousand people who were in league with hostile forces. We were ready to round all of them up within twenty-four hours of a declaration of war.
>
> Otto Kühn had already come under suspicion because he had far too much money in his bank account. Therefore, we had been keeping an eye on him.
>
> As for the citizens of Japanese descent, we weren't able to find any evidence of

wrongdoing after interrogating them despite the fact that we detained some two thousand suspects from the undesirables among this group. In fact, we got a bit carried away.

However, we were unable to find the sender of those frequent telegrams because Morimura was inside the consulate-general. If we had been able to gather any evidence on him before the war, I am certain that we would have arrested him. What a pity.[1]

There was a light drizzle falling that evening and everything was shrouded in darkness. Blue cloth had been placed over each car's headlights, which allowed just a hint of light to come through. This did not seem to bode well for us. The seven cars drove downtown and then turned right. "Isn't this the way to Pearl Harbor?" I wondered to myself.

After a while, as I'd expected, the cars drove through the main gate at Pearl Harbor. Nothing could be seen in the darkness, apart from the flash of the sentinels' bayonets. The wrecked remains of a battleship that had been blown up ought to have been somewhere around there, but it couldn't be seen in the darkness.

As I recall this matter now, their reason for transporting us under cover of night was to prevent us Japanese from seeing the destruction wrought upon Pearl Harbor 40 days after it was bombed. It was utterly silent in the harbor, with not a person in sight. This stillness made it seem as if the port had died.

The cars stopped in front of a destroyer that was moored to the docks and then everyone got out. After that, we promptly got aboard the vessel. There wasn't a sound to be heard on board the ship either.

Not long after that, a U.S. Navy lieutenant in full military dress announced that he needed to check any belongings that we were carrying with us. He spoke extremely softly, as if he had some misgivings about the situation that he found himself in, and I was quite surprised by this. Americans always seemed to be so calm and composed in critical times, whereas Japanese people were always kicking off and causing a fuss when confronted by similar circumstances. I felt that this calmness was so much more powerful than confusion.

At the time, even though America was confronted with enormous difficulties and its situation was extremely unfavorable (Pearl Harbor had met with disaster and been destroyed, the Philippines had been taken by storm, the U.S. Pacific fleet was in retreat, Japan's military successes had defied everyone's expectations, and so on…), the Americans nevertheless kept calm. They followed the curfew rules to the letter and carried on the work to rebuild Pearl Harbor by day and night.

Despite myself, I found that I was completely won over by their calm demeanor.

The lieutenant told everyone to stand in the dimly-lit hallway and then he carefully checked every person's belongings. He was holding a small knife, which he used repeatedly to cut open suit linings in order to take a look inside. He even looked at the soles of our shoes.

He was wearing a protective mask, a lifejacket, and a sidearm. And his face was covered in sweat. "That truly is hard work," I thought to myself.

I did not wait for him to utter a word to me. I just took off my shoes, turned my jacket inside out, and waited for him to inspect them. But he simply felt inside my pockets and said "okay" before letting me go.

After that, he led us to a large and very clean conference room. There the male and female members of our group were put into separate areas. He waited until we were calmly settled in and then the watertight doors were locked, "kuh-cha."

Everyone was finally able to rest, if only for a little while. However, because we were unsure about exactly where we were being sent, we looked at one another in dismay, simply dumbstruck.

Somebody, I'm not sure who it was, timidly put forward a question.

"If the ship starts to sink, will they refuse to let us leave?"

"Even if they let you leave, you wouldn't stand a chance in the middle of the Pacific Ocean!" I quickly retorted.

"We would just have to accept our fate, if we couldn't survive," someone else said.

There was nothing left for us to do, so we all squeezed into our cocoon-like beds.

It didn't feel as if the ship was moving, so I placed a pendant on a thread and left it hanging over the top of my bunk. I hoped this would signal when the ship began to rock and thus enable me to determine when the ship had left the harbor. After that, I intended to figure out where we were actually heading based upon the ship's speed and the duration of our journey. However, I did not detect any movement as we were leaving the harbor.

Any ship, no matter what type, is going to make some noise when it sets out to sea. There is noise from the pulling in of the mooring cables, the noise of an air horn, noises from sailors running on deck, the noise of machinery in motion, and so on. So much noise is made that people in bunks on the lower decks may not even be able to get any rest. Yet there was not the slightest noise to be heard aboard this ship. By the time I felt the ship rocking somewhat, we were already far away on the high seas. Without our even being aware of it, the ship had actually made its way out of zigzag-shaped Pearl Harbor. Through this, it was possible to see how the Americans were able to remain calm.

It occurred to me then that some Japanese submarines might be on the prowl for the enemy. I was sure they had already quit the Hawaiian waters that they had been frequenting. Consequently, our vessel was unlikely to extricate itself from the danger zone until after daybreak. It would have been quite good had a Japanese submarine made a surprise attack on the warship, although that would have spelled great misfortune for those of us aboard.

Some four or five of my fellow recruits had become submarine captains. Were they lying in wait somewhere in the vicinity? Or were they taking advantage of the night to resurface and breathe in the fresh air while recharging their batteries and thus evade aircraft and torpedo attack? Whatever the case, the destroyer that we were aboard specialized in hunting down submarines.

"They absolutely must not be discovered!" This was the short prayer I said for them as I was lying in my bed and feeling the ship rock from side to side. I still had no idea about the ship's direction, though. Was it actually traveling north, east, or south?

The watertight doors opened with a "kuh-cha" sound and then the naval officer from the previous evening walked in. He asked that everyone follow him to the canteen. It was already daytime by then, sunlight was gleaming on the horizon off the ship's bow.

"Japanese devils! Japanese devils!"

About ten shirtless sailors were eyeing our group from a corner of the ship's middle deck. One after the other, they each hatefully chimed in. They were all burly men and they all had tattoos on their upper arms. Although the atmosphere was somewhat tense, there was no indication that they were about to get violent.

After breakfast, we were taken back into custody and led to our hold below deck.

"Consul-General Kita! It seems as if the ship has changed course and is moving toward the southeast instead of the east," I said to Kita.

"If that's the case, it means we must be headed toward the U.S. mainland. Could it be San Francisco?" Kita asked me.

"No, but it could be somewhere further south. Our current speed is around 15 nautical miles per hour, so in four days we will have reached our destination."

"It will be good if they take us to a neutral country in South America."

"Oh yeah. But since we are traveling southeast, I am afraid that we won't get as far as Mexico. We will get to Los Angeles at best!"

"But … if we got to somewhere like that, it surely wouldn't be long before we could go back to Japan."

"No, they might put us on a train from Los Angeles to San Francisco. After that they might send us the long way back, from somewhere further north. What do you think?"

"…"

The wild suppositions and farfetched ideas that formed the basis of our conversation proved to be misguided. If the hopeful predictions that we made were to come to pass, however, they would have to send us to San Francisco and from there on to Japan via the North Pacific. This was because we reckoned that the seas south of Hawaii might no longer be navigable as a result of various war operations.

When our ship had reached the high seas, a signal suddenly rang out from the loudspeakers. It may have been the signal for the crew to take up battle stations. After that, all we could hear was the sound of the sailors running, "Pa-da pa-da," along with the sound of something being dragged.

"Djuh, djuh, djuh…" Two or three times a day, the loudspeakers would broadcast that signal. Every time this alarm sounded, there was a flurry of activity aboard ship. I wondered whether the signal was an order that meant "A submarine has been found. Take up your battle stations!" Yet during those four days at sea, there never was any sort of sea battle and we reached our destination safely.

We disembarked from the warship by making our way down a dark-colored gangplank. On shore we were greeted by a tall man, roughly 40 years of age. He identified himself as "Billy" and said he was an employee of the State Department.

I cast a glance toward the gangway and noticed that the word "Pedro" was written on it in white paint. I understood immediately that this was San Pedro, the American naval port. There were many coconut palms lining the seashore.

We were taken to a very large railway station where there were masses of people on the platform waiting for a train to arrive. For a few moments there were, on all sides of us, men and women embracing and sharing long kisses before reluctantly taking their leave of one another.

In the past, I had mistakenly believed that the Americans' "individualism" would make it impossible for them to willingly go to the battle front when their country found itself at a critical juncture. And yet, during the present war, these previously well-off and carefree Americans were actually ready to rush out to face danger on the battlefield without any fear. They were resolute about joining the struggle and in high-spirits. This was something that I had not expected.

With Billy leading us, we got aboard the train and fell into our seats in a brand-new Pullman sleeper car. However, Billy declined to tell us where we were and he refused to explain where they were sending us. "Each and every one of you can go to the dining car if you want to eat," was all that he would say.

I was the first person to run over to the dining car, but it was already packed with passengers when I got there. Initially, I had hoped to sit and enjoy a sweet, tasty breakfast. Yet when I picked up the menu to look it over, there were some eye-catching words written in large-type on the cover: "Remember Pearl Harbor." I could not help but be taken aback by this. America

28. Remember Pearl Harbor

was quite obviously angered about the Pearl Harbor Incident and was calling out for revenge from its innermost heart.[2]

After hurriedly eating my breakfast I wanted to drink some coffee, so I picked up a packet of sugar and read what was printed on it: "Please save sugar. Help to conserve our nation's resources."

Although the Americans were the world's number one consumers of granulated sugar, they were now conserving it as part of their war effort. As

A U.S. government propaganda poster circa 1943 (U.S. National Archives).

this too was something that I hadn't foreseen, it greatly surprised me. The war had only just broken out, some 40 days earlier, and yet they were able to instate a system of controls on their food supply and take measures to mobilize their citizens to unite against the enemy with great speed. I could not help but admire them.

The train was rushing to the north. "Was I right, or wasn't I? We are heading north and I'm sure that we're going to San Francisco. Well, what do you think Mr. Morimura?" asked Consul-General Kita, who seemed to need to demonstrate the validity of his conjecture.

Our journey aboard the train was very comfortable. The view from the window of our compartment was one of endless orchards and farms. The sky was deep blue, the fields lush and green. The region's vast and gorgeous landscapes, and its southern ambiance, made me feel carefree and happy.

Our passenger car was separated from the rest of the train at Los Angeles. Apparently, we were supposed to spend the night there. However, our car was hitched to another train in the middle of the night and it then began to move. As we were all anxiously waiting to reach our destination, we stopped worrying once the train began moving and every one of us fell fast asleep.

Very late into the night, however, there was something of a disturbance in the women's compartment. This occurred because our men and women had been forced to stay apart ever since the start of the war, nearly 50 days earlier, and that meant the husbands and their wives had not had an opportunity to talk with one another. The same situation continued to prevail in our respective sleeping compartments.

Nothing untoward had occurred during the initial stages of our journey, because we were all filled with a disturbing admixture of excitement and dread. Yet once the atmosphere became more relaxed, romantic feelings between the husbands and wives were revived. Consequently, Mr. K (the chef) secretly made his way into the women's compartment and onto his wife's bunk. As chance would have it, he was found out by the children in the cabin and they began to kick up a fuss. Since the incident concerned public decency, the other women were quick to put forward their views.

Although Consul-General Kita felt that this incident was somewhat difficult to sort out, he knew just how far to take his criticism of the chef while still managing to laugh about it in the end.

Consul-General Kita slept in very late because of that night's mishap. The next morning, he had not yet got up when I ran over to see him. "Consul-General," I said in a soft voice. "This train is headed due east. A big red sun is already up in the sky ahead of the train!"

"What? Heading east? And where would it be heading for? Could we possibly be heading to New York?"

"I really don't know. However, the wide river that we just crossed was the Colorado. And we seem to be running along the Southern Pacific Railway."

"Oh really? This is actually my first time on the U.S. mainland. I'm not familiar with the place and Billy has kept his mouth tightly closed right up to now. Please try to be a bit careful."

The engine was pulling a long convoy of rail cars behind it as we headed due east, crossing endless desert and wide marshlands. The train kept on running for two days and two nights, yet we were still not clear about where we were actually going. After we stopped at two or three stations along the way, I was finally able to determine that we were in fact traveling on the Southern Pacific Railway.

A mountain chain appeared to the right, which might have been the frontier with Mexico. On our left side was the kind of terrain seen in American "Western" movies. There were wondrous rock formations and forests of large cactus all over. When I began to survey this landscape, I felt that it was very fresh and new. However, only a little while later I found it simply dreary and monotonous.

As a result of this, I could not help but think that there were so very many unused lands in America's interior that extended far beyond what the eye could see. The southern, northern, and western regions of the United States all contained such lands. So what need was there for them to keep Japan in one place, or to continue rushing from pillar to post to control territories that were about as big as a handful of sand? Japan had needed to go to the South Seas and to Manchuria in order to get natural resources. How exactly was America hampered by that?

In the final analysis, the U.S. was the underlying cause of this war. Was it not? The war finally broke out because you (Americans) did not understand Japan and because you were jealous of the influence and authority Japan had acquired in East Asia. When the actions of another people are only slightly at odds with your purposes, you label them "aggressors" or "a threat to peace." Is that not just a little bit domineering?

If I may, I'd like to offer a piece of advice to America's leaders. You need to remember that as long as you refuse to give up your dream of world domination, a war will one day break out that you will be unable to stop.

While leaning on the train window, and looking out at continental America for the first time, I mulled over these questions and called on others to account for their actions.

The train finally stopped at a temporary station in the middle of the desert. It was an extremely small station of the sort that the faster trains seemed to bypass altogether. We thought that the train had stopped to take on water, but we soon found that we were totally mistaken.

"All right everybody," Mr. Billy said as he approached us with a smile. "We have arrived!"

We were quite taken aback; this turn of events shocked every one of us. Nevertheless, we made our way off the train one after the other. Once the train had deposited us in the middle of the empty desert, it made off with a toot of its whistle.

Consul-General Kita and I looked at one another in dismay. After a while, Kita finally spoke.

"Oh my, Mr. Morimura. Coming to a place such as this is hardly encouraging."

"I wonder, do they want to execute us by firing squad in this big desert?"

"That is quite possible…"

The two of us quickly fell silent, but our grim expressions remained fixed in place.

Under Billy's direction, a few men who seemed to be police officers divided us into groups and then showed us into five cars.

"Are you police officers?" I asked the officer who was driving our car.

"No. We're not police officers, we're members of the national guard."

Upon hearing this, I began to relax. Those national guardsmen would definitely not be allowed to carry out executions by firing squad.

"Where do you have to take us to?"

"To a ranch over there."

"Is it a nice place?"

"Oh, it's not bad. Quite a few people from the city come out here to sunbathe, right up until summertime. It looks like the rest of us are going to have to live there with you."

By then I was able to stop worrying altogether and relax.

The cars had been speeding along at about 100 kilometers per hour for 30 minutes. Everywhere you looked there were huge rock formations and evergreen trees. There were also some large, dog-like and tea-colored animals running around.

"Is that a wolf?"

"No, it's a lion."

"A lion?"

"It's an animal called a 'mountain lion.' It runs away as soon as it sees people."

We traveled on and on, without seeing any houses where ordinary people lived. The road was a very smooth asphalt carriageway, though. And we did pass some large luxury cars that were painted red or blue.

29

Triangle T Ranch

"Here it is," our young driver told me. I took a careful look at the place. It was a ranch that was enclosed by a simply constructed fence made with planks of wood. Beside the main gate there was a sign painted in white paint that read "Triangle T Ranch."

Now that I am mentioning this, it has occurred to me that similar names are given to farms in Japan. For example, there are many farms in Japan called "ni" or "ka." Triangle T Ranch was yet another farm named in this manner.[1]

The ranch house was made of concrete and shaped in the form of a 'U' (a square that was missing one of its sides). Each of its rooms opened into the adjoining ones. The courtyard was filled with pebbles.

After they informed us that this would be our temporary residence, they left it up to us to decide how to allocate the rooms. After some discussion, it was decided that the bachelors would share one room while those with families would share the other two rooms. Our collective life there began with 21 Japanese people occupying three rooms.

The dining hall and the main living room were not far from our rooms. Mrs. Matthey (our hostess), the young ranch manager and his wife, a black couple, and a few others lived there as well. Billy and five or six national guardsmen lived in another building. That meant that there were around 35 people living on the ranch, which was about 30 kilometers away from the nearest residence.

Billy served as the leader of the team of national guardsmen. It appeared that their principal duties were to keep us in detention, gather information about our reactions and responses, and prevent us from making a run for it.

Billy made this announcement to us:

"Within the walls of this enclosure you can walk around as much as you like and you can play any sports or do any exercises or other activities that you like. (The enclosure was square-shaped and made of wire mesh. Each of its sides was 500 meters in length.)

"As for food and drink, you can speak to the manager if you have any special requests. You just need to tell us if there is anything that you need to buy. We will buy it for you.

"We can find a way to get you some reading materials, but only if you want to read something other than newspapers or magazines. Recent newspapers and magazines are not permitted here.

"Now, I would like you to think about whether there is anything at all that you are not happy with."

"Thank you very much for looking after us. We do not have any opinions," Consul-General Kita replied.

"There is something else that I want to stress. Please do not lean on the metal fence and don't ever try to go a step beyond the metal fence."

After adding this, Billy looked at me and laughed. His words seemed to carry a message that was directed at me: The only one among your group who intends to abscond is you.

I was forced to respond with a bitter smile. Whenever I recalled the mountain ranges to the south that we had gone past, I also remembered they were in Mexico and that made me feel motivated to act.

Twenty-one years after this period of detention, the above-mentioned Mrs. Matthey came to Japan for a visit. Vice-Consul-General Okuda and I called on her at the Tokyo Hilton Hotel. While we were speaking there, she shared some of her memories with us.

"In order to better keep all of you under guard, they installed a searchlight on the roof of the building before installing a machine gun there as well. But when I saw all of you, I really didn't think that you looked like vicious killers.

"And yet they put such strict measures in place to keep you under guard, which made me feel that I didn't understand what was happening. That remained the case right up until last year, when I finally understood the whole story after seeing something on television about Mr. Morimura's deeds.

"Mr. Morimura. No, I mean Mr. Yoshikawa! At that time, you gave me a pair of Japanese clogs! And, just when we were saying our goodbyes, you gave me a rancher's scarf!

"Yes, that's right. I still remember these things. And I've brought a photo from that time with me.

"The reason why I've come to Japan for a visit was because I wanted to see all of you. I live in Houston now and I want you to keep in touch by writing to me often, please…"

As we sat on a plush sofa in the hotel lobby, recalling what we had lived through together, I shuddered at the thought of what might have been. Had I tried to escape, the machine gun's bullets would surely have riddled my body with holes and left it looking like honeycomb. I would have died in that rattlesnake-haunted wilderness.

The place we were living in was near Tucson, Arizona. Both mines and pasture lands were found in that area. The Indians, the local native people, were notoriously cruel. Their men would customarily wear a pistol strapped to their waist when they rode their horses. As soon as any sort of fight broke out, gunfire was sure to follow. They stole cattle, engaged in smuggling, and there was little that they would not do to have their way. It was a truly frightening sort of place.

Now let's stop here for a moment to consider exactly why they had only sent our group to Arizona. Was it because the battleship *Arizona* had been sunk at Pearl Harbor that they hoped to use us as "symbolic" prisoners of war and thereby exact revenge? Or was it because it was a convenient location to keep us in segregation? These questions remain unanswered to this day.

All personnel from the other Japanese diplomatic missions in the United States were apparently sent to Springfield, where they were allowed to read newspapers and listen to radio broadcasts. Those members of Japan's America-based diplomatic corps became worried and heavy-hearted once it was known that the staff from the Japanese Consulate-General in Honolulu had disappeared without a trace.

The cactus flower is the "State Flower" of Arizona. Consequently, that region might be considered the home of the cactus. The biggest were as high as telephone poles and you had to crane your neck to see up to the top of them. They came in a great many shapes and sizes. There were round ones, tall ones, big ones, small ones, and weirdly-shaped ones. Among them were some that could stab a person riding past on horseback. In short, it was a fearsome plant.

The fact that this territory was able to give rise to so many varieties of cactus was ample proof of its aridity. It was evidently impossible to grow crops of any sort there, which meant it was necessary to travel to a town some distance away just to buy a few vegetables. Furthermore, the beef raised there was tough and unpleasant to eat. Yet the air was fresh and the sun shone nicely, so it was the sort of place that was good for your health.

However, it was very cold at night. Every evening, the black workers at the ranch had to light an oil stove in each room. And after the evening meal, we would always gather together in the room beside the dining hall and play bingo along with the children. In that big room was a huge fireplace in which they would burn heavy logs. Large flames would blaze in the fireplace and the warmth from it made us feel very comfortable.

Thanks to Billy and his enthusiastic preparations, we were able to play tennis and hard ball, or take walks and sunbathe. Afterwards, when we were tired and sweaty, we could have a private shower. We could even drink cocktails. As far is life in detention went, there really was not much to nitpick about. Yet any life without liberty, no matter what sort it is, quickly grows tiresome.

I have just mentioned alcohol and I'd like to add a word about that here. I was the only detainee allowed to drink a bottle of whiskey and another bottle of spirits every week. I later learned that our ambassador and special ambassador were both prohibited from drinking alcohol at that time. I was able to drink alcohol because I had once been detained in Hawaii for excessive drinking and that incident was reported to the State Department. As a result, Billy decided to approach me for a chat soon after he had appeared among us.

"Mr. Morimura, I hear that you love to drink. Well, I love to drink too. Anyway, from now on I'll get you two bottles each week. What do you usually like to drink?"

"Well thanks ever so much! I'd like it if you could get me Scotch whiskey and absinthe!"

So, thanks to Billy, I received a weekly supply of spirits. And that supply that was never once interrupted.

I frequently carried a bottle over to Consul-General Kita's room to drink with him. At other times I would hold a cocktail hour for all those who gathered before the evening meal. This allowed them drink to their hearts' content. Yet, unlike Kita and myself, the others really did not make a habit of drinking alcohol. Tsukikawa and Aburashita just needed to drink a little before they suddenly became red in the face, carefree and happy. Vice-Consul-General Okuda only drank a little bit, while Mr. Seki was pretty much incapable of drinking.

I still remember a conversation we had one day after every one of us had downed three glasses of booze.

> KITA: How long is this life in detention going to go on for? I made a suggestion to Billy recently. 'I know we're forbidden from sending letters back to our home country,' I said. 'But we should be allowed to send a letter to our ambassador.' 'No. That won't work,' he said. However, he did agree to contact the State Department for further instructions.
>
> OKUDA: Is that right? Well, that's good news. Although National Day has already come and gone, hasn't it?[2]
>
> ABURASHITA: It seems that we won't be returning home for the time being!
>
> KITA: But Mr. Aburashita, oh that's right, and Mr. Okuda, how are you managing the education of your children over there?
>
> ABURASHITA: My wife looks after them in the morning.
>
> OKUDA: It's the same for me. Over there, this is a very tricky problem.
>
> TSUKIKAWA: In this respect, it's much easier for the bachelors.
>
> SEKI: I asked the guardsmen, 'How long are you going to stay here for?' a few days ago. And they replied, 'We don't actually know how long we're going to be here.'
>
> MORIMURA: I'm afraid they'll never be able to leave as long as we're staying here!
>
> KITA: Hmm. Perhaps we will have to stay here for more than ten years!
>
> MORIMURA: Ayyyy! I'll finally return home when my hair is all white, and then I won't be able to find a woman to marry!
>
> EVERYBODY: Ha, ha, ha.
>
> OKUDA: Ten years? I doubt that things are that serious. However, two or three years is a real possibility!

Kita: In any case, I'm afraid you're going to be the father of an Arizonan child Mr. Seki!

Seki: (…)

Aburashita: That too is an important question. However, it isn't something that only involves those of us here!

Kita: Those of us here who are bachelors don't get to see our female family members. And I wonder how their health is.

Seki: I heard my wife saying that Mr. Kusanagi's wife's health isn't very good…

Tsukikawa: Is it morning sickness, due to her pregnancy?

Everybody: Ha, ha, ha… (Recalling the incident in the sleeping compartment on the train.)

Morimura: At the time, I was a little envious!

Okuda: When they made us leave the train in the middle of the desert before we arrived here, I really was scared out of my wits!

(**Everybody nodding their heads in unison**)

Kita: And when Mr. Morimura said that they were perhaps going to execute us by firing squad, I was scared out of my wits too.

Morimura: … That's absolutely right. By then, I was already expecting it to happen.

(**Everybody seemed to be lost in thought after that was said.**)

Okuda: Yes… If we really are going to be staying here for two or three years, I would like to continue studying English.

Morimura: You really want to study! Well, that's good news.

Okuda: In fact, I've already begun to study. I want to completely memorize the dictionary.

Aburashita: Regardless of whether we are here for five years, or even ten, I want to take my own sweet time doing absolutely nothing. However, I do want to play a lot of tennis.

Kita: Mr. Morimura, what have you planned?

Morimura: I've thought about doing some woodcarving, with wood from the holly tree.

Kita: If you are able to become a first-rate sculptor of wood, the young ladies will be knocking down your door when you get home.

Tsukikawa: I'm an idiot, I can't take up woodcarving like Mr. Morimura. So, I think I'll just polish stones.

Seki: I think I'll read some books, in my muddle-headed sort of way. But anyway, have you made a plan or two Consul-General?

Kita: Well, I would also like to leave some sort of memento… Perhaps I shall follow Mr. Morimura's example and take up carving.

Morimura: I think you ought to give that special lady who is waiting for you at home your own sculpture of *Kannon*, what do you say?[3]

Kita: And if it takes me ten years' time? Ha, ha, ha…

Just then the dinner bell rang, as the cold wind from the Arizona plateau was blowing in.

30

Carving

Some of the grains of sand in that part of Arizona were as big as soybeans because they had been formed by the weathering of granite. Consequently, both shoes and clothing were worn out quite quickly there. This was especially true for those of us bachelors who were always sawing wood or polishing stones, our clothing was worn out in no time at all. Consequently, the three of us (Kita, Tsukikawa, and myself) implored Mr. Billy to buy each of us a set of tough twill work clothes of the type that the locals wore.

All three of us were subsequently wearing clothing that was too long and too wide because there weren't any clothes suitable for the Japanese body type. Consul-General Kita also wore a broad-rimmed, Mexican-style felt hat. Meanwhile, my head was covered by a sports cap and my feet were decked out in running shoes. The two of us could not have been kitted out more disreputably, yet both of us were always coming and going in our work clothes and we did not give a hoot about it. However, some of the men who were there with their wives were unwilling to put on scruffy clothing and would even wear a jacket and tie to dinner. Perhaps each feared looking unattractive in his spouse's eyes.

Consul-General Kita had been born in the countryside and was completely without inhibitions and I was an uncouth and uncultivated sort of person. As a result, we formed a team of bachelors of similar temperament. By contrast, the men with wives and families were completely unlike us in their dress, activities, and their views on things. Furthermore, they wanted to take the rules that governed their family life and impose them on the collective life of our group. Those of us who were bachelors could not have cared less about this, however, so we carried on in our casual and crass manner, even when in the presence of the children. This was not what they wished, of course.

For example, if we sat together with the etiquette-obsessed female family members at meal times, we would feel quite ill at ease. And if we sat with the wives who were picky about the food, we would have to listen to complaints of every description: Such-and-such a dish was poorly prepared, there wasn't

30. Carving

any fruit or any pastry, the meat served up without any garnishes every day was too greasy, and so on.

Then one day, someone (I cannot remember who it was) came looking for the consul-general. "Our wives have a lot of opinions about the meat that is served up without a side dish every day," they said. "And I think that we might ask Billy if they could give us more vegetables and more fruit."

Upon hearing that, the consul-general flew into a rage.

"The treatment that we have received from the American government is already more than sufficiently generous, especially since vegetables are in short supply in this region. You know this perfectly well, but you want to stretch out your hands to ask for fruit and pastry. What exactly do you call that? Just take a look at the mountain lions. They only eat meat every day and yet they are very healthy, aren't they?"

After this outburst from Consul-General Kita, some of the others began to call him "Lion" behind his back.

In fact, Consul-General Kita's view on this matter was entirely correct. Just a bit of thought about our circumstances was sufficient to arrive at the conclusion that we ought to avoid making any excessive demands. However, it was also a bit excessive of Kita to take the lions as an analogy.

The only reason that any of this came about was because the differences in the opinions held by the responsibility-free bachelors and those with families had eventually led to mutual resentment, which boiled over in the end.

I have already mentioned that we wanted to take up carving. However, getting the knives proved to be a problem. That was because we were banned from carrying knives, as a safeguard against murder and suicide. After Consul-General Kita and I discussed this matter, we reached a decision. Since we could not get hold of a knife, we would sharpen a piece of steel instead. Thus, the two of us went over to the tool shed where one of the ranch managers was working.

"Hello, Honneycut! What are you doing?" I said as soon as I saw him.

He was wearing tall boots, overalls, and he had a pistol strapped to his waist. He also wore a cowboy hat and looked very strong. He was working on an iron rod, which was about as wide as a thumb and held in place with a vise.

"Well, you really are strong!" I said, deliberately using an admiring tone to praise him.

He exhaled a burst of air. "Why don't you two give this a try?" he asked.

To give it a try means just that, thought the two of us. And what good would that do?

Nevertheless, each one of us gave it a try soon after that. We were both sent flying off the rod as a result. Then it was his turn. He smiled a toothy grin before using all his might to bend the iron rod.

"Mr. Honneycut, in that outfit you look like a rancher too!"

"Of course," was his simple reply upon hearing Consul-General Kita's words. "I was born in Arizona and I've been a ranch hand ever since I was 15. I'm already 28 years old now."

"Not only that, you are a very handsome man!" I said to flatter him as I stood alongside.

"No, I'm not that handsome. But I do go to Hollywood often, to work as an extra."

"In order to play roles that require you to throw a lasso or fire a pistol quickly?"

"Yeah, we can't play those love scenes. I'm very bashful… Remember that rattlesnake that I showed you a few days ago? I was the one who shot it dead. If you let that guy bite you, you're a goner. It won't matter if you go to the hospital, or anywhere else, nobody will be able to save you."

"Where do those things hide?"

"They are all over the place in the tall grass."

"And where is the herd of cattle?"

"They're in the hills over there… Why are you asking me that anyway?"

"Uhh, we just want to hear some ranch stories told by a rancher."

"Oh yeah?" …

Just then, when he was beginning to look as if he wanted to leave, I discovered a few steel saw blades that had been broken and tossed below the vise.

"You don't need those, do you?" I asked him with an imploring look.

"Those things? They're no good anymore. If you want them, you can have them."

He then picked up the iron rod he had bent and hurried off.

Meanwhile, I selected five or six of the saw blades that had been discarded.

"These are strips of steel. I'll look for some sandstone so we can sharpen them and quickly turn them into carving knives."

"So, the next step is to think of a way to get some sandstone."

Kita and I were both very happy. We hurried over to the wire fencing and began to look for sandstone just inside the fence.

"Morimura!"

"Hmm?"

"We must now make the leap from the stone age to the bronze age! What we call the hallmarks of a civilization are simply things brought about by luck, which then leap forward. That is to say mankind's great advancements occur through accidental discoveries or through long periods of continuous effort, which then takes off. How else would you explain our getting hold of these saw blades?"

"You might say they represent our move into cultural objects."

"That is absolutely right."

"When Japanese people first began to use iron, was it actually the Japanese people who discovered it or did some other people get into it first?"

30. Carving

"I really don't know. It's very likely that iron and the method to process it were discovered elsewhere, though. Anyway, has any Japanese person ever made an independent discovery or invented something of universal importance?"

"Shinto?"[1]

"That is not something of universal importance. What about medical science?"

"We can't call that an independent discovery. And Bushido came from followers of Confucius. It seems that there aren't any!"[2]

"You might say that there aren't any discoveries that have encompassed the whole world."

While picking stones up from the ground, the two of us chatted away casually.

Two or three days later, I finally finished sharpening an extremely sharp knife for carving. After dinner, I heard a rhythmic rubbing sound coming from Consul-General Kita's room. I took a quick glance into his room and saw that he was carefully sharpening a knife.

"Mr. Morimura, you could actually shave off a beard with the knife that I have just sharpened!" said Consul-General Kita, as happy as a child.

After getting the knives that we needed ready, we began looking for some wood from the holly tree to use for carving. It is a variety of wood that is very similar to that of the Eucalyptus. The tree itself is covered in very small berries. Holly trees were found all around the surrounding areas and the largest were wide enough to only just allow two people to link arms around them. Hollywood, America's famous film city, was apparently named after this "sacred" tree.

As this type of tree grows taller, its resin seeps into its core. This turns the wood black and hardens it so much that it has been called "ironwood." I have heard that the Indians used to use this wood to make spearheads.

Once we had got our wood and cutting tools ready, we began to spend all of our time sawing wood or carving. Consul-General Kita's ambitions were considerable, as he was planning to carve a statue of *Kannon* around one meter in height. As for me, I had come up with a design for the cigarette box and lid that I was going to carve. A leaf from the "sacred" holly tree was to be carved on the lid, while the sides of the box were to be carved in the shape of its berries. Taken together, these images would signify "ironwood."

As soon as we began carving, we were completely absorbed in our work. We spent the entire day sitting in a spot that faced the sun, putting all our energy into carefully wielding our small blades. As a result, we forgot about our concerns and everything else besides.

It was at this time that the wives put forward a suggestion. "From now on we are all going to celebrate everyone's birthday, no matter what," they said. After some investigation, it turned out that my thirtieth birthday on 7 March was coming up next. Everyone then agreed that, from Morimura onwards, we would follow the calendar and each of us would have a turn. We planned to celebrate the birthdays of 21 people, or to at least continue doing so until the time came to return home.

I recall that Mrs. Matthey came forward that evening to give a speech of congratulations. Then Sam, the black man, sang a song while dancing. I remember that I too added an extemporaneous performance to that evening's program, but I cannot recall what it was.

I got along very well with the black couple, Sam and Millie. Their responsibilities included sweeping the rooms, doing the laundry, and stoking the stoves. I sometimes invited Sam to drink a glass of whiskey, and he would happily drain his glass in a single gulp before imploring me to keep it a secret because black people were prohibited from drinking spirits.

Although Millie was a plump woman, everybody loved her. "Morimura is a hard name to say," she once said to me. "So, I'm going to give you a name that's easy on the ears."

"I'll just call you Tom," she told me, after giving it some thought.

"Isn't that name almost the same as your husband's?" I quipped.

"Apart from Sam, I just like you," she replied. Having said that, she winked and sent me a knowing glance before bursting into laughter.

All of her children apparently worked elsewhere, and they seldom had the opportunity to see her. I had hoped to get to know both of them better and learn something more about the experiences and ideas of black people, but I never got the chance to do so.

Using the need to clean up some heavy oil that had been spilt on the floor as an excuse, I asked Sam to give me a few old newspapers. "Don't worry about it," he replied. "You can easily use the mop instead."

"It's a bit of a nuisance when you're not here," I said by way of further explanation. "It really would be better if you could bring us a few newspapers."

From then on, he regularly brought us old newspapers. For those of us in detention, these were our only sources of information. Some of the newspapers were from before the war, while others were entirely given over to cartoons. Naturally, some of them contained information that was positive enough to give us encouragement.

On one occasion, I went right over to Consul-General Kita's room after I had read some good news.

"Japan has already begun moving troops into the South and we are in a very advantageous position," I said to him.

"Really?"

After hearing my words, a broad smile completely covered Consul-General Kita's face while he continued to blink unceasingly. This had long been one of his quirks.

31

Rancher Tobacco

Our monotonous life in detention had been going on for more than a month and the adults were already feeling fed up. Meanwhile, the children had lost their innocent enthusiasm because they no longer had any classmates to play with as they were not at school. It wasn't good for them to be constantly subjected to their parents' calls for hard work and studiousness, especially since the children had received an American-style education in Hawaii and thus had their own opinions. In fact, the parents' teaching methods frequently gave rise to resentment, even outright opposition, from the children.

As I looked on, the youngsters were losing their cheerfulness little by little and I became quite worried about it. This led me to come up with the idea of playing games along with them in order to raise their spirits. I then called them outdoors one day so I could speak with them.

"From now on, Uncle Morimura wants to run a summer camp for you. Every day after lunch we will gather here and I will tell you stories. We will also read books and play games. Would you like that?"

"We would like that," the children unanimously replied.

In total there were five children at the summer camp. The eldest was in grade four and the youngest was five years old. The summer camp ran right up to the beginning of June, which was the month we left that place.

From the first day onwards, I intended to introduce every single game that I knew of and let them play. To begin with, we played games such as tug of war and monkey in the middle. We started with these because the children had played American-style games. For the same reason, they were almost completely unfamiliar with popular Japanese games. It didn't matter whether I talked to them about those games or if I just told them to play, they would not know how to play properly if I did not first demonstrate how the game was played. For example, I once had to get atop a mound and tumble down before they finally learned how to do somersaults.

At first, they were afraid of getting their clothes dirty and some of them held back from joining in. After a week, they didn't care and they all followed me while taking part in the games. I often took them to the back of a mountain to play "adventurer" amidst craggy granite outcrops. There we would collect rock crystals or set up a box trap to catch squirrels.

The children's favorite activity was a war game in which I would play the part of the bad apple. Each of them would carry a piece of yucca, which served as a gun, and they would have to track me down and capture me. After hunting me down, they would arrest me and take me prisoner. Then, after pretending to be shot, I would fall off a cliff and roll down the mountainside. Although the children enthusiastically shouted out their approval of my acting because it was so life-like, the youngest of them would repeatedly ask me to "do one more" until I was dead tired.

Every day, I was doing my carving and then serving as the children's teacher at the summer camp. Although I appeared to be very happy, I was hiding the suffering my innermost heart had been feeling all along. None of the others knew anything about this, however. The fact that many Japanese people had been arrested since the start of the war was part of what pained me, but mainly it was the discovery and confiscation of the code books that had left me feeling this way. I was certain that they now had a clear idea about the extent of the intelligence reporting that I had done. As it was not clear what this was going to bring about, I was never able to rest easy.

My worries had begun on the first day of our house arrest at the consulate-general and continued to play on my mind. I had watched my words and behaved cautiously at all times ever since that day. In addition, I had used every possible means to prevent anyone from discovering that I was a naval officer, even doing my best to duck away whenever a group photograph was taken.

When I thought about all these problems at night, I just could not get to sleep. I imagined that while those days were peacefully unfolding, the FBI was definitely in the midst of gathering evidence against me. Nevertheless, I never let these worries show. I didn't even talk to Consul-General Kita about them. I reasoned that since the two of us were powerless under those circumstances, discussion with him could not change the fact that he was unable to help.

I was determined to rely on my own abilities to find a way out of this predicament. If the worst possible scenario were to come to pass, I would take responsibility for everything myself. I definitely would not allow any of the Foreign Ministry staff to be implicated.

When the high plains of Arizona finally welcomed the intense heat of a blazing sun, the desert sands began to reflect the dazzling sunlight and all the Americans put on sunglasses during the day. This was around the middle of May, which was also when Mr. Billy introduced us to someone he had brought along with him.

"This gentleman is visiting us and has some matters to ask you about. Everybody, please stay in your own rooms and do not leave."

31. Rancher Tobacco

After hearing his words, we could not help but hang our heads. We all went back to our own rooms and began waiting. I told myself that the day that was bound to come had finally arrived. I was certain that the guy was an FBI agent. Since it had come to this, I needed to fight on until the battle had been won.

The interrogation room was set up in the office at the lodgings used by national guardsmen, which wasn't far from where we lived. Billy was responsible for summoning us there.

"Uhh, could Mr. Kita come over here please?"

Consul-General Kita lowered his head and walked out listlessly.

I thought that the order in which we were being called had likely been decided upon and I was sure that I had been put at the very bottom of the list. I concluded that I might as well get into bed and have a nap. I had just removed my trousers and climbed under the duvet when I suddenly heard the sound of footsteps.

"Mr. Morimura!"

This summons from Billy gave me a start.

They were calling me after Kita. Could that mean that they had already detected something? After having this thought, I reminded myself that I could not be careless with my words. Halfway there, I ran into Consul-General Kita. "It wasn't anything out of the ordinary," he told me in a low voice.

The official conducting the questioning was a bit older than me, tall, and fair-skinned. He appeared to be a shrewd, capable man. When he invited me into the room, his demeanor was that of a city dweller.

"I am Morimura."

"Please, sit down… And how are you finding life here?"

"It's very comfortable."

"Well, that's just fine… But there are a few questions I'd like to ask you, if you think you could answer them for us."

"Naturally, if you want to know anything about what I know, anything at all, you can… Are you with the FBI?"

"No, I am from the State Department."

He seemed a bit flustered by my pointed question. Anyway, I was actually well aware of the fact that the FBI was a branch of State Department. I had just wanted to make a point by immediately asking him a question of my own: Since you are questioning me, what Department are you with?

Following that, he had a few routine queries for me. "When did you begin work at the Japanese Consulate-General in Honolulu? What was the precise nature of your work there?" etc.

"Would you like to smoke?" he asked me after that. "This is the tobacco that the ranchers around here smoke when they're riding their horses."

He used his left hand to roll the tobacco, before sealing it up with saliva. He then took a match and lit it by brushing it over his thumb.

"Look, you do it like this because the right hand can't let go of the reins. And that means you need to do it this way."

After showing me the method, he asked me to try. However, the middle section on mine was too fat since I was not able to roll it up well. As soon as I started to puff, the tobacco was scattered everywhere.

He had done all of that deliberately to calm my mood.

"What do you think about the war?" he asked me afterwards.

"It's very unfortunate!"

"Unfortunate? … Isn't Japan fiercely waging war right now?"

"They have cut us off from every source of news, so we know nothing about what's happening."

"You traveled everywhere when you were in Hawaii, didn't you?"

"That's right. That was because it was a very fresh kind of place for me. So, I often went sightseeing."

"Did you also go to Pearl Harbor?"

"I went there. No matter what anyone else might say, that is the world's number one naval port!"

"Are you interested in it?"

"Yes, I am."

"Why?"

"Because, from an economic perspective, Hawaii's economy relies primarily upon the sugarcane industry and the military. Furthermore, the 150,000 members of the Japanese expatriate community all rely on those two pillars of the economy. Umm, have you been to Hawaii?"

I had sensed that the reasoning behind my answer had been a bit overstated, so I decided to ask him a question in order to change the topic. "No," he replied. His face betrayed his displeasure.

"Would you like a cigarette?"

"Yes, please."

After quietly rolling our tobacco, we began to smoke. And then he added just one last phrase, "We'll leave our discussion there for today."

I had earned a reprieve.

Consul-General Kita was waiting for me.

"Mr. Morimura, how did that take so much time? Why was that?"

"Oh, no reason. He was just giving me a lesson on how the ranchers roll their tobacco," I wittily replied.

After that, Billy called Okuda, Aburashita, Tsukikawa and Seki in quick succession. As it appeared that I was their main target, it occurred to me that some sort of unhappiness there was now unavoidable.

In the afternoon on the following day, questioning was carried out in the same order as the previous day. On the third and fourth days we went through exactly the same sort of questioning, in the same order, and we chatted about random subjects in an informal manner. It seemed as if he was in the process of grilling us repeatedly in order to get a complete grasp of some sort of evidence. Although I was speaking a lot of drivel, it was getting harder for all of us to bear up against this by the fourth day or so. Everyone else was looking quite tired and I was unable to sleep because I was so worried.

That evening, Consul-General Kita called me over and told me that there was something he needed to discuss with me. After we had pulled the curtains shut and turned out the light, we sat down facing one another. Kita looked somewhat haggard after being questioned over successive days and his mouth was very dry as he slowly began to speak.

"So, Mr. Morimura, how is everything?"

"What do you mean by 'How is everything?'"

"…As you may already have sensed, everybody is thinking about … whether or not we might ask you to take responsibility for everything. That is to say, as far as this matter goes, you are also a military man. If you alone can take responsibility, everyone else will go free. To be honest, it's very difficult for me to say all of this. But I am the group's leader…"

"I completely understand what you are saying. Please let me think about it…"

After our discussion, I returned to my room and began to think seriously about the situation. Judging from the successive days of questioning that we had gone through, the agent in charge of the interrogations was aiming to reach either one of the following two objectives:

    i. Compel Mr. Morimura to admit that he is a spy.
    ii. Compel the people around Mr. Morimura to reveal his true identity.

As far as the second objective was concerned, only Kita knew the whole truth about my identity. And the only one who would have been able to learn a little about my situation from Kita was Okuda. As long as Kita and Okuda refused to divulge the truth, the others would basically know nothing about it. (Though I feared that XX was the weakest link in this psychological battleground.)

As far as the first objective was concerned, I had already decided that I would never confess. As I saw it, confessing and not confessing amounted to exactly the same thing. If they were to use torture, however, there really would be no help for it. When that time came, the dictums "confession is not beneficial to the country" and "not confessing means loyalty to the nation" would no longer apply.

Of course, it had been my responsibility to guide Japanese air troops to Pearl Harbor so they could drop bombs there. As for what followed, that was entirely out of my hands. Basically, I did not need to be eager to make any stupid sacrifices that would bring about my pointless death. Instead, it was best to keep the "haggling ratio" of interrogation to counter-interrogation at 3:7 and to use the words that Yarihei Amano had persisted in saying: "I don't know. I don't remember."[1]

When the final day of questioning arrived, I obviously didn't know that this was to be the last of it.

"Hello Morimura, did you sleep well last night?"

"No. I did not sleep well."

"Why was that?"

"Because you continue to threaten and intimidate me every day."

"Hah, ha… Shall I intimidate and scare you again today?"

"Do as you please!" (Spoken in Japanese.)

"What? What did you just say?"

"I said, 'Do as you please!'" (Still spoken in Japanese.)

He tried several times to repeat my words but was unable to do so. Then, from a folder, he removed a piece of white paper. It seemed to be a treasure of some sort.

"You drew this!" he said.

I studied it carefully. It turned out to be a map of Pearl Harbor that had been drawn on typing paper. He was apparently hoping to use this to prove my guilt.

"It seems so!"

I had used a defiant tone in reply. "I drew a map, so what?" was its meaning.

"What was your reason for drawing this map?"

"I don't even remember what it was for. Where did you find it?"

"Don't worry about where it was found."

"It was probably from when I was out sightseeing. I was listening to someone explain something and I drew it quickly."

"What? Sightseeing? Did you go sightseeing every day? I hear that you were often out of the office. Is that right?"

"No, that's not true. Who did you hear that from? I was at the office every day."

"And what was your work?"

"My job was to manage all matters having to do with the renouncing of one's nationality."

"Was the work very demanding?"

"No, it wasn't very demanding because I had an assistant. It was a fantastic job."

"And because of that you often went out sightseeing, is that right?"

"Uhh, yes that's right."

"Fine!"

He took out some rancher tobacco and allowed me to smoke. As this had occurred every day, I was already able to roll it very well.

31. Rancher Tobacco

"I'll ask you another question. Do you know Lanikai Beach?"
"I know just about every place."
"Back then, what did you give to Kühn?"
"Kühn? Who's he?"

I was shocked. "That guy must certainly have been arrested," I said to myself. "And that means our undercover agent is done for. At a time like this, I have to stay cool."

In order to stall for time, I just asked him a question. I had used this tactic at every occasion to test my counterpart's reaction.

"…You were the one who delivered a bag of money to him, weren't you?"
"A bag of money? I don't know. I don't remember that anything like that ever happened."

After I said that, his fist landed on the table with a bang.

"You don't know?" he said gruffly. "You don't want to use 'I don't remember' so now you are pretending that you 'don't know.' On that day you went off wearing khaki trousers and a Hawaiian shirt, you were holding a paper parcel that was the money bag."

"It's over," I told myself. "They've actually investigated this thoroughly. If it wasn't Kühn's confession, it was the driver's. But then again, it might have been XX." However, I kept wearing a "nothing has happened" expression.

"I don't remember means I don't remember. To help me recall, please clearly explain once again what this situation involved."

"All right," he said in a steady voice while staring at me aggressively. "When you reach San Francisco, they will explain it again clearly. But they'll only take you there. Won't you regret that?"

"That's not my wish, but there's not much I can do about it!"

"San Francisco is not like this place, people are always coming and going on the streets there. They could stage a traffic accident to eliminate you; they might hang you; they might… (He then provided a long list of torture techniques used when interrogating a suspect, but I did not fully understand what he was saying.) … And when that time comes, will you still say: 'I don't know. I don't remember.'?"

"I don't know means I don't know. I know means I know. I don't remember means I don't remember. Apart from that, what else is there to say?"

It looked then as if he had finally given up. He just kept blinking his eyes without asking any more questions.

After a long moment of silence, his attitude softened. "We have reached the end of our one-week time limit today," he said. "However, I have not arrived at any conclusions. At the very least, I've taught you how to roll tobacco using the ranchers' method. Okay then, we'll stop here."

32

Leaving the Ranch

The whirlwind of interrogations that we had been swept up in finally went away. At long last, everyone could relax. My worries really had not disappeared, though. During my conversations with our interrogator, I learned that a group of suspects had been rounded up in Hawaii and that a very thorough investigation was being carried out there.

Nonetheless, I reasoned that even if my driver Mikami or a young Japanese-American woman had been reported to the authorities, and even if they were able to ascertain that he had driven me all over the island and to Pearl Harbor scores of times, their interrogations would not enable them to find out what my intentions were. That was because I never once revealed my true identity to those people, nor did I ever ask them to help me in any way. One of them had taken me in his car down the highways at high speeds in order to satisfy my requests. The other had accompanied me all over the island simply for the love of having fun while sightseeing.

Although it is not appropriate for me to disclose all the details concerning my dealings with Otto Kühn, that situation was only discovered because they had illegally seized the code books. It did not appear as if the FBI had a conclusive set of facts about the money that I had delivered to Kühn, however. Nor did they know anything about the person who had ordered its delivery. There is no need to reveal the full story to them now.

Despite this, they could certainly have conducted a second and then a third set of interrogations. They could even have decided to force us to confess. A few days after that, they might have received an order to send us to San Francisco.

As there was still no sign that we would be able to return home soon, every day felt like a year by that time. Nevertheless, I had to carry on running the summer camp after the children repeatedly requested that it continue. I devoted the rest of my time to carving. I finished three pieces in the end, one of which was the cigarette case that still sits on my desk.

Our luggage and personal belongings arrived in wooden boxes not long after that. Each of our names was written on the boxes, while the name that

32. Leaving the Ranch

appeared on our luggage was Lourenço Marques. All of it seemed to have been sent from Honolulu. Two of the items shipped were belongings of mine.

"Ah ha! They've carefully wrapped up my radio and shipped it over!"

Although I did not feel that those worn out items were worth shipping, they may have decided that returning them was a matter of national honor since the items belonged to enemy personnel. Thus, they had shipped them over.

The one thing that had really caught my attention was the name that had been written on our luggage, Lourenço Marques.

Kita and Okuda appeared to be having a discussion about this very question:

"I've never heard of that place!"

They reckoned that it was probably a small town in America or Canada.

"Do you know about it, Mr. Morimura?"

"No, I don't. However, there is actually a port in Africa with that name."

"What? Africa?"

"What country's possession is that?" Mr. Okuda had become excited and kept repeating this question.

"Well, that should be a Portuguese territory."

"…Consul-General Kita, perhaps they want to repatriate us!"

"Perhaps…"

The entire staff then gathered together in the Consul-General's room and began discussing this happily. It seemed as if we were now seeing some glimmers of hope for the future.

I knew about this place name because I had carried out a study of all of Britain's overseas bases and other sites of strategic importance when I was working in Section 8 at the Navy General Staff. While I was investigating the harbors at Durban, Cape Town, and elsewhere in South Africa, it occurred to me that the main ports in neutral countries could also be used for repairs and to supply fuel. Consequently, I carried out additional research on a few of the ports on the east coast of Africa and this name was among them.

All in all, the speculation and misgivings aired by our group at that point went roughly as follows:

- The Pacific Ocean had already become a theatre of war and was not suitable for navigation.
- Lourenço Marques, the name that had been written on our bags, was in fact in Africa.
- Therefore, it was possible that they would send us to Africa.
- However, why would the U.S. want to do that?
- Which port would we depart from?
- Which flag would the ship be flying?
- When would our journey begin?

It was difficult for us to make any sense of it all. In short, we all felt quite puzzled due to the lack of any further clues. Despite this, everyone was now feeling hopeful and even had faith that we would be returning home.

There was something we could not understand, though. Why was Billy, the highest-ranking authority at Triangle T Ranch, always silent about any new development? Though we asked him to play tennis with us almost every evening, he would not say a word about these matters. "I have not received any instructions. I do not know anything more," was all he would say.

How exactly did the U.S. State Department plan to deal with our group? The situation we faced in America was increasingly unstable, which made us entirely restless and put us in a state of constant worry.

In the middle of June, Mr. Billy gave all of us word of his instructions:

"The time has finally come when we have to say goodbye. The day after tomorrow, they are going to send you on to New York. I'd like to ask everyone to get ready. If there is anything that you still require for your journey, could you please bring it to my attention? That way I will be able to buy it for you."

As we had been living in Arizona for approximately four months, spending all our days and nights hoping for the day we could return home, this truly was a pleasant surprise. However, we did not show any obvious signs of joy in the end because we had been caught between unease and panic ever since leaving Honolulu. The wives simply began chattering among themselves. This was the only sign that they were happy.

For their part, the children did not want to leave. They said that they were used to life there and that they did not want to go off again to some other strange place. What's more, there were some older couples who had always worked at the consulate-general and were now the parents of Japanese-American children. They too were uneasy at the prospect of returning to Japan. They did not know what their lives would be like in Japan following their return, nor did they seem to have made any plans to that end. There were actually a few people who hoped to return to Arizona to settle down in that peaceful haven before the war came to an end.

As for me? I was so eager to return home that, had it been possible, I would have grown wings to get there. I wanted to continue to play a role in that exceptional war.

Everyone wrote up a list of the articles they needed to buy and then asked Billy to help buy them. Such is the way of the world that as soon as the time comes to return home, people begin to think about buying some local specialties or souvenirs. However, those items were largely disqualified from claiming a place on our shopping lists. Only those items essential for travel were permitted.

I then decided that if they were going to eliminate items from our lists, I would counter this by writing down several items of the same kind.

32. Leaving the Ranch

As a result, I quite cheekily made the following petition to Billy.
"A complete set of clothing."
"A suit? Hmm, so wearing work clothes is a bit uncomfortable. Okay!"
"A leather suitcase."
"Okay!"
"A leather carry bag for travel, of good quality."
"Okay, I'll have a look and see if I can buy one."
"Okay. An Omega brand wristwatch. One."
"No."
"Isn't a watch a necessity for travel too?"
"It's a necessity, but you don't need one that is of such high quality. I can get a dollar watch though."
"All right."
"Is there anything else?"
"No, nothing else."
"Ha, ha, ha… You aren't a very materialistic person. Ha, ha, ha…."

I was filled with remorse as soon as I heard him laugh. I regretted not having added a few more items to my list, but that ship had sailed.

Mr. Billy drove to Tucson to buy everything and spent an entire day running around there. It was late night by the time he finally returned. Apparently, in order to meet everyone's requests, he had not only gone to Tucson but had also hurried off to another town that was at least another 50 kilometers away. We were deeply moved by his kindness.

"This carry bag is the most fashionable there is in New York today," he said with a laugh as he was giving me the items that he had bought for me. "While it was slightly expensive, I hope you will accept it as a token of my regard."

I thanked him again and again for his kindness. While doing so, I decided that his good deed might have contained a message: "I never expected that a guy who has caused as much fuss as you have could actually not be any trouble in the end. For this reason, I would like to give you a small reward!"

I took my work clothes, the items I had carved, rocks, cactus, a flute made out of yucca, and various other souvenirs, and packed them all into my suitcase.

We were overcome with emotion when we had to leave Triangle T Ranch to catch to the train to New York. Mrs. Matthey, Mr. and Mrs. Pennycotton, and Sam and Millie all hated to see us leave.

"After the war is over, please come back to see us. All of you!" Millie called out in a loud voice as they saw us off.

"If it were not for the war, this would be such a good place!" I thought to myself.

33

At a Crossroads

The national guardsmen took us by car to the city of Tucson, where we were once again going to get on board a train. Although there were a few strangers waiting for us at the station, two or three of the guardsmen we had lived alongside for several months remained with us and they moved all of our luggage into our compartments when the time came for us to board the train. After we boarded the train empty-handed, they began waving their hands to say goodbye to us.

Even though those national guardsmen were dutifully following their orders, the fact that they had displayed an attitude of impartiality toward enemy personnel at all times caused me to let out a heartfelt sigh. I then thought about the military police in Japan by way of comparison. Did I know what sort of attitude they would adopt toward Americans living in Japan? That thought made me feel somewhat anxious.

We were now in detention inside a Pullman car, just as we had been before. We could not see any of the other passengers, nor could we speak with them. All we could do was lean on our window and watch the scenery outside the train. After getting tired, we would take a nap. After waking up, we would watch the scenery once again. That was how things continued aboard the train for a day, two days, three days, four days…

At several stations along the way, our carriage was separated from one train and then attached to another running on a different line. After several such transfers, we had passed through Dallas and Chicago. Then finally, at seven o'clock on a mid-June morning, we reached New York.

Tight security was in effect at the train station as the place was filled with police. Everyone clearly had some misgivings about this while we waited for our instructions. Then Billy walked over to give all of us a warning.

"Because of growing public anger, there may be some people within large crowds who are prepared to act in a radical way and they may be violent towards you.

"For this reason, we have adopted these strict precautions. Whatever

33. At a Crossroads

happens, I hope that all of you will stay cool. It is now time to go to the hotel, which is very close by.

"Please move together as a group, all of you. And do not leave the group without permission. There will be a team of police officers walking around you on all sides to escort you there."

His words made me come to a sudden realization and this solved a riddle that had long been puzzling me. At every stage of our journey, from the time we left Hawaii, they had always kept our destination a secret. Now, we finally knew why. It was because of this precaution that we had never been set upon by any journalists seeking an interview and had safely arrived without incident.

New Yorkers were very sensitive, however. They might have decided to take matters into their own hands after somehow finding out that the criminal ringleaders of the Pearl Harbor Incident were coming to New York. Consequently, the authorities hastily dispatched large numbers of police to the scene as soon as they had got word of us.

With four burly policemen leading the way, we set off. We lined up in three rows and followed them closely. I took the lead on the right side, Consul-General Kita was in the middle, and a young Japanese-American was on the left side. The women and children followed us. A column of police officers stood on either side, protecting us as we advanced.

City dwellers were standing on both sides of the road, staring at the unusual spectacle presented by our group on foot. "Japanese devils," we repeatedly heard them say as they chattered away. "Japanese devils." With a respectful demeanor, we quietly made our way forward. The women and children followed us solemnly, their heads lowered. Fortunately, nothing happened along the way. That may have been because the show of force put on by a few hundred police officers was enough to stifle the crowd.

I can still remember a few details about traveling with the police escort over that short-distance:

i. Even though we were walking for less than ten minutes, that walk seemed to take a very, very long time.
ii. New York's streets were nowhere near as clean as I had imagined they would be.
iii. There was an old ashen-faced woman, standing at a corner of the road, who seemed to be lost in thought as she watched us blankly. Perhaps it is only my imagination at work, but that old woman's pitiful expression remains lodged in my memory to this day and I cannot get rid of it. Judging from her expression, it may well have been the case that her son had not returned from Pearl Harbor!

At that juncture, however, I did not have any time to contemplate the hostility and hatred of those city residents. I was kept busy by having to walk ahead.

We were staying at the Statler Hotel. When you looked down at the streets of New York from the top of our hotel building, pedestrians looked like ants and cars looked like matchboxes coming and going. The skyscrapers reaching up into the clouds there weren't suffering at all from the flames of war in Europe and the Pacific, as the streets below were as bustling as ever.

You could just make out the Hudson River in the distance, where countless boats and ships were swarming. I began to consider this sight. If Japan wanted to secure victory against America, which had so much material wealth, it would be no easy matter. Of course, America also had its weak points.

I didn't know why, but I was feeling tremendously impatient. I was itching to return to Japan right away and, whatever the needs of the day, rejoin the war effort.

Yet after staying there for two days, we still did not know when we would actually be able to board a ship. We had heard countless rumors from the hotel staff, though.

"They are not going to authorize the staff from Honolulu's Consulate-General to return home."

"All of Japan's diplomatic personnel in America are going to board a transfer ship that is docked in the Hudson River."

And so on.

After that, I heard some other rumors that were a mixture of truth and falsehood.

"They will just keep Morimura here, while the others will be permitted to return home."

"This matter has already become a contentious issue on Capitol Hill. Those advocating that all of the personnel from Honolulu should be detained have the upper hand. So, the government is working non-stop to make its case to congress."

And so on.

Ahh! The game was up! I had experienced countless hardships to get where I was, but now it had all come to naught. Although I had tried to make it to safety, I was a solitary individual who lacked the power to get back home. There was nothing left to be done now, other than accept the authority of a hostile country.

My worries were compounded, however, by the spiteful remarks coming from my compatriots. I was constantly hearing quite deliberate attacks through innuendo from some of my colleagues.

"Regardless of what he says, everybody resents him for what he did."

33. At a Crossroads

Oh, how I regretted this. Time and again, I witnessed the true character of those people. They were willing to share in the good times, but were not able to share the bad times. Thus, they were truly worthy of the saying that "only women and the small-minded are difficult."

At the hotel, my desolate room had already become a prison cell to me. I was lying on the bed and doing nothing except listening to the footsteps of the people coming and going in the corridor. Oh, what a silly scoundrel I was! I disgusted even my own compatriots and had become an object of scorn for the entire world. Now there wasn't even the tiniest bit of land I could call my own.

And yet, I also felt that I could not blame myself. I was just the unlucky one who drew the short straw that somebody had to draw. That was all. I even consoled myself with the thought that I had actually done outstanding work and finished my mission. Furthermore, I was the only person who had ever defeated both the FBI and the U.S. Navy. After thinking of all this, I calmly entered dreamland.

Just after four o'clock that day, Billy quite unexpectedly called on me in my room.

"Morimura, it's time to board ship!" he said.

"That's strange, they are going to take me off somewhere on my own!" I thought to myself.

Following Billy, I walked outside and into glare of the public eye. As I felt that I definitely could not wear a coward's face at a time such as this, I deliberately kept my head high while walking outdoors. The hotel was not very far from the pier, but I do not have any recollection of the surrounding activity or scenery during our trip to get there. This is sufficient proof that my mood then was extremely uneasy.

Consul-General Kita was waiting for me at the docks. Once there, my intuition then told me that I was going to be allowed to return home. Yet as I had experienced the entire range of human emotions over and over again since my time in Honolulu, my heart was now a tightly sealed shell that was keeping my happiness within me.

We left Manhattan in a motorboat and began heading west across the Hudson River. As the light of the setting sun was so intense that I could not keep my eyes open, I cupped my hand over my brow to block the sun's rays. While looking into the distance just then, I saw the white transfer ship anchored in the Hudson River. I began to focus on the vessel and saw that the ship's stern had the name *Gripsholm* painted on it. A green cross was visible on the ship's bulwark and a Swedish flag was flying atop the ship's mast.

On deck there were a good many evacuees looking our way, their hands holding fast to the railing. The ship had already weighed anchor, the gangway had been raised, and the ocean liner had started to float gently downstream.

The motorboat rushed to get alongside the ship as a rope ladder dangled from the stern.

"Climb up! Hurry!" many people aboard ship were shouting by then. I allowed Consul-General Kita, who was quite hefty, to climb up first and then I used both hands and grabbed hold of the rope ladder. I had just planted one foot on the rope ladder, and my center of gravity was not yet fixed, when the ship's engine began to roar and kicked up violent eddies in the water. The vessel had begun powering ahead.

On the deck I saw our ambassador, who had held his post for two years, an envoy, and various consuls-general.

"Is everyone aboard this ship?" I asked a young consul-general I was acquainted with.

"Yes, everyone's aboard. You were the very last one. We were worrying about you!"

"I'm sorry I caused all of you to worry."

I was truly thankful for everyone's concern.

Then everyone moved closer to Consul-General Kita and me. "Well done! Well done!" they said in unison. As it was inappropriate to speak frivolously, since the ship was from a neutral country, everyone just used their eyes and brows to silently signal their thoughts.

It was the first time that the vessel had served as a transfer ship for the evacuation of foreign personnel. Aboard the *Gripsholm* were the staff members from Japan's diplomatic missions in the U.S. (Ambassador Nomura was the most notable among us), entrepreneurs, and ordinary citizens.

We were proceeding to Rio de Janeiro, where Japanese citizens living in South America would come aboard. From there we would steam right past Cape Town, South Africa and on to Lourenço Marques. Once there, we were going to carry out a transfer with a ship called the *Kamakura Maru*. That ship, which had already left Japan, was transporting American diplomatic personnel and ordinary citizens. After the ship-to-ship transfer of personnel was complete, both vessels were going to return to their initial ports by retracing the routes they had taken.

To this day, there is something that I still cannot understand. Why did the U.S. initially detain me and then reluctantly set me free at the very last moment?

After thinking about this question, I have a few comments to make about it here:

> 1. There were rumors that Ambassador Nomura had adopted an intransigent position, insisting that he would not depart unless all diplomatic personnel were aboard ship. This may have happened because Ambassador Nomura was himself

33. At a Crossroads

   a navy man and he knew all about intelligence work. Moreover, he could not afford to lose any of his personnel. The prestige of our top diplomat abroad depended on the security of all the personnel under his charge.
2. Had the U.S. continued to keep me in detention, it would have provoked retaliation in kind from Japan. U.S. diplomatic staff stationed in Japan would have been detained.
3. Had all the details about intelligence reporting from Hawaii been exposed, the political and military leaders responsible for Hawaii would have been punished for their negligence. It might even have led to the punishment of those responsible in the federal government. In other words, the Pearl Harbor Incident had created so much anger in congress and amongst the public that the U.S. government decided it would be more sensible to stir up the patriotism of the citizens with slogans such as "Remember Pearl Harbor" rather than risk disorder by releasing that information.

As so it was that Morimura, the lifelong spy, had finally succeeded in making his way home alive. Aboard the *Gripsholm* he was stretching out quite peaceably in the corner of a cabin.

34

Navigating the Seas

The crew of the ocean liner *Gripsholm* had been eager to put out to sea, and not without good reason. The ship's itinerary had already been transmitted, via a neutral state, to Germany and Japan's submarines in order to ensure its safe passage.

It was for this reason that the green cross served as its emblem during the daylight hours and a cross-shaped lantern was left hanging at night. Yet if the ship were to miss its scheduled stops, or stray from its route, it was possible that it would be mistaken for a military ship in civilian disguise and attacked. Thus, it was imperative that the itinerary that had been provided in advance be strictly followed. Even so, it was very difficult to guarantee that already battle-hardened Japanese and German submarines would definitely not carry out an attack. As a result, some felt jittery aboard the *Gripsholm* as it powered ahead.

After stopping at Rio de Janeiro, we traveled due south while doing our utmost to avoid all danger zones. We then navigated our way across the lower limits of the South Atlantic. Even though a dark cloud seemed to envelope the entire ship all along the way, the voyage never really seemed all that perilous to me. Compared to the dangers that I had faced previously, it felt like a cultured jaunt through never-never land. At long last, after finding myself liberated from the state of intense nervousness that I had been living in for over a year and a half, I suddenly discovered that peaceful days and nights such as those were a part of life too.

As the ocean liner got further and further away from the coast, I knew that it was no longer possible for them to demand my return. I also knew that there were enemy countries all around the world. As a result, I reminded myself that I had to remain discreet at all times and not get careless. I nevertheless got drunk as often as I liked, overcome with the happiness that came with my being reborn.

In order to while away the dull hours of the ocean journey, I made every effort to go and play ring toss or mini-golf on deck. After I had begun to sweat, I went to the sauna that was a special feature of our Swedish vessel for a shower and a bath. Later, I would enjoy a cocktail.

34. Navigating the Seas

Since some of the people aboard did not enjoy sports, and were bored as a result, there was always some form of entertainment in the evenings. There were vocal and instrumental performances, featuring the harmonica for example, and more. The well-known xylophone musician Yoichi Hiraoka was among the most notable performers. Yet because the mood of the passengers ultimately influenced the spirit of those performances, they always carried a somewhat oppressive, melancholic undertone.

The sky above the South Atlantic was shrouded in thick cloud, the great ocean was itself dark, the billowing waves caused a clamor, and the air felt so cold it seemed to attack you. All of which left you feeling that you had reached the back of beyond. This great ocean had previously inflicted numerous adversities on the sailing ships of the likes of Magellan and Da Gama. As in the past, it was making those of us traveling across it feel ill at ease.

There was no land to be seen anywhere, not even any islets. The only thing you could see were the large numbers of albatrosses flying madly in the vast emptiness of the sky. Those great birds were as white as snow and pursued the ocean liner non-stop right through the night, perhaps because they wanted to provide energetic companionship to a rare visitor from afar. Even after this, they were not at all tired as they circled in the air.

At times, some of them would land on the deck for a short rest. When they looked at you with their clever expressions, it seemed as if they had been magically transported there from an ice-covered mountain in Antarctica. After I came into contact with those wild creatures, which were fearful of humans, it suddenly occurred to me that I was the one who belonged in a strange land far away.

Once we had bypassed Cape Town, the temperature increased as the latitude decreased and the albatrosses gradually went away. By then, the ocean liner had entered the Indian Ocean and was heading north along the east coast of Africa. The *Kamakura Maru*, the ship that had come from Japan, was the first to arrive at Lourenço Marques.

At the time of the transfer, the Japanese and American passengers each formed a single line and then took to the pair of gangplanks that had been placed side by side between the two ships. Each group boarded the other's transfer ship by walking across to the opposite side.

While going to the other side, I noticed that the Japanese passengers possessed much better quality belongings than did the Americans. Judging from the poor quality of the Americans' belongings, you could see clearly that Japan's economic power had already slipped quite a bit. Their belongings were packed in crude leather bags or in carry bags made of cloth, while we were all towing lovely leather suitcases and wearing clothes of the highest quality. You could tell from the great disparity in the quality of the two groups' belongings that Japan had already begun rationing and that it did not produce top quality goods. Nobody could buy top of the line gear there.

Although carrying fine quality goods is not necessarily something to boast about, from those goods you could clearly recognize the relative strength of each of the two countries. Japan was nevertheless in the midst of challenging the rich and powerful USA. It was then obvious to me that Japan's attack on Pearl Harbor would not prove sufficient to allow it to subdue that huge country. In which case, how should the war be fought? I was so worried about this question that I wished I could fly straight back to Japan and learn everything there was to know about the war.

As it had already been eight months since I last listened to the radio or read Japanese newspapers, I did not know anything about Japan's occupation of Manila and Singapore. Nor did I know that Japan had suffered defeat at Midway Island in June. Once aboard the *Kamakura Maru*, I finally read the Emperor's declaration of war in a newspaper. Braving a prohibition, I sat on the upper deck where no other people were to be found. There I carefully read the Imperial edict that declared war. I then reread it two or three times. Without my being aware of it, it moved me to the point that tears filled my eyes. When I could bear this no longer, I turned to the east and said a prayer for the prosperity and success of our ancestral land.

And yet, to be perfectly honest, I didn't feel as if I understood the situation. I would like to speak frankly about this here.

I was a member of the younger generation at that time, with only a limited amount of experience, and I did not fully understand the military mindset. Consequently, the Imperial declaration of war failed to inspire any sense of absolute loyalty within me. Moreover, reading the edict actually left me with the futile need to criticize it.

I believe that the following three points sum up the whole of the edict:

1. The Emperor was always concerned about world peace.
2. America and Britain had thrown East Asia into a state of disorder and done away with peace there.
3. As a result, it was necessary to declare war against America and Britain to liberate East Asia.

As far as the first point was concerned, I truly believed that this was the case. As for the second point, it was an established fact that the U.S. was delivering assistance to Chiang Kai-Shek's regime. And because of this, Japan had no other option but to resort to the use of arms described by the third point.

Even so, I had always felt that our reasons for declaring war were forced and that our military objectives were vague. I was particularly uneasy about Japan's military strategy. The rush to attack Pearl Harbor, before our country's long-term policies had been established, was quite reckless.

34. Navigating the Seas

While the transfer ship was docked in the port, we were given a few hours of shore leave. Lourenço Marques was situated at 20 degrees latitude south, had a warm climate, and actually seemed a nice place. The flowers everywhere to be seen were delightfully fragrant and lush green trees provided cool shade.[1]

Yet the original inhabitants had been forced out and sent to live in the interior, while all of the good lands were occupied by white people. If the spectacle provided by their enthusiastic strokes of the ball on the tennis court was anything to go by, you had to feel this was a heavenly sort of place. Nevertheless, I was angered by the thought that even Portugal, a small, weak country, had recklessly invaded other countries all over the world and then turned them into its permanent colonies. Was that in any way fair?

Now that Japan was making use of its armed forces to try and solve the problem of injustice in the world, was there any way to prove that such actions were correct? In any event, Japan was projecting its military might over an ever-widening area.

While the *Kamakura Maru* was crossing the Indian Ocean, I devoured every available newspaper. When the ship reached Singapore, I saw bare-backed prisoners of war at work in the ruined harbor with my own eyes. Only then did I believe that Japan's policy of moving into the South had actually borne fruit.

From there the *Kamakura Maru* hurried straight on toward our homeland. Things became quite tense midway, as we might have been the target of a submarine attack while we were passing through the Bashi Channel on 15 August 1942. In the end, nothing actually came of this and we arrived at the port of Yokohama without incident.

Part Four

Returning

35

The Welcome

On 19 August the *Kamakura Maru* began to reduce its speed and finally drew in to dock at Yokohama. I was lying inside my cocoon-like bed, listening attentively to the cheers coming from the docks, when the roar of the ship's engine petered out and then fell silent. I was overcome by a feeling of calm and then I heaved a great long sigh of relief. I had finally made it back!

"Today, without doubt, I am going to set foot in my ancestral land once again and I will no longer be faced with the threat of persecution!"

During my 17 months inside enemy territory, whether I was getting into or out of cars or traveling aboard ships and airplanes, there was not a moment that I wasn't neurotically trying to guard myself against shadowy police officers, the FBI, customs agents, the national guard, or other enemies. At long last, I no longer had to worry about any of those people.

The docks were chock-a-block with people who had come to welcome the ship.

"Mister, I am right here!"

"Hey! Over here!"

The sound of wives, sons, daughters and friends calling out, one after another, fused together and formed one great commotion. That sound seemed as if it was being made by family members who had waited through years of difficulties and had feared the worst about their loved ones. It also seemed to be a kind of blessing for the *Kamakura Maru*, which had navigated thousands of nautical miles and traversed the flames of war before finally making its fortunate return.

Some people aboard ship were stretching their bodies over the railings, vigorously waving their arms back and forth. It must have appeared as if countless pieces of fruit were dangling from the side of the vessel.

I was standing behind those people and watching the crowds on the docks. There obviously wouldn't be anyone there to welcome someone such as me, an early participant in the war who had not had any contact with his family. If I was going to be welcomed at all, my native land would be providing the greeting. I felt gloomy as a result, just like that day's rainy weather. In

35. The Welcome

fact, I was worried by my homeland. How were my compatriots going to treat someone who had lit the fuse that set off the war? Were they honestly going to welcome me?

What made me feel even worse was that I had immediately begun to question Japan's position in the modern world now that I was back inside home territory, although I couldn't say what compelled me to do so. After I had taken in the sights and cultures of 27 countries, it was simply impossible for me to maintain that Japan was a country capable of conquering the world, try though I might.

What exactly was going to come of this grey-colored Japan? I wondered. I was like the man who sets fire to his own house before beginning to wonder what good it will be after burning down. My frame of mind was inspiring similarly nonsensical ideas. In fact, my concerns were merely those of a garden-variety secret agent. If I could scout out information on the enemy, I was able to complete my mission. Questions about the nation's future were weighty matters for the nation's leaders to think about. An undercover agent who was scarcely worth mentioning basically had no authority to get involved in such affairs. Nevertheless, this contrarian has long had feelings of concern for his country and people.

When I turned my gaze toward the ship's bow for a moment, my heart jumped briefly. Ah ha! Wasn't that Commander Muchaku, the staff officer from Section 5 at the Navy General Staff, standing right next to the bow? Hadn't he just taken off his raincoat? He was unaccompanied as he stood on the drizzle-covered dock. His head was raised and he was looking in my direction.

I quickly walked up to the ship's bow and greeted him with a sign. I felt so grateful to him that I almost wanted to cry. Receiving a personal welcome from this special staff officer, who had a thorough grasp of U.S. intelligence matters, made me happier than cries of acclaim from thousands of people could have done. This was the paramount reward for me. Once again, I came to appreciate the true meaning behind the adage that "a gentleman is always willing to die for his friends." It was for this instant of gratitude that I had gone about my work without giving a second thought to my well-being.

Sadly, just after the war ended, Commander Muchaku committed hara-kiri because of the shame he felt at being taken prisoner.

We got aboard a sweltering, radish-odor-filled train carriage and headed to Tokyo. Once we arrived there, however, nobody was able to put us up. So, Consul-General Kita and I were obliged to stay temporarily at a hotel near Shimbashi Station while we thought about finding more permanent accommodation. It was August, the summer season, and my hotel room was small, narrow, and exceedingly hot. Despite this, it seemed wonderful to me. It was my own cozy little den.

I went to report for duty at the Navy General Staff the following day. I never imagined that the security protocols would have changed since my time there, but the rules and regulations had become extremely strict. Since my identity had been changed to that of an ordinary citizen, I was no longer an employee at the Navy General Staff. Thus, all I could do was fill in a visitor's form at the security gate and quietly wait for my instructions.

The security was so tight there because our navy had suffered defeat at Midway Island in June. Although navy officials had done their utmost to suppress this news, the Navy General Staff was quite obviously shrouded in gloom.

The Imperial Japanese Navy had mistakenly believed that its plans concerning Midway Island would not be leaked, yet they were picked up by the enemy beforehand. As the Navy General Staff came to suspect that it had been infiltrated by an enemy agent, they subsequently carried out a thorough investigation of all personnel working in that headquarters. The investigation came to focus on all the people who had any contact with the typists and even led to searches of the homes of the typists' family members. In the end, their searches and inquiries proved fruitless and they were unable to find any evidence of wrongdoing.

Meanwhile, the very same practice was also imposed on visitors. All regular visitors to the Navy General Staff became surveillance targets as well. Now that I am discussing this matter, it does seem ridiculous. However, this truly was the situation there at that time.

As for our defeat at Midway? It wasn't until I was conducting interrogations of prisoners of war the following year that I finally figured out that Japan's battle operations had actually been detected by radar, which was a new armament deployed by the enemy. You will remember that I had sent a cable to Tokyo (in October) before the war broke out to report that the masts of the enemy's battleships and heavy cruisers had been kitted out with a rack that appeared to be some new form of weaponry. I never realized it then, but that was radar!

The Chief Deputy Staff Officer, Commander Nakashima, called me over to a table that was located in a corner of the corridor. I sat opposite him and gave a simple report. He then told me that the battle front had already moved to the South and that Japan's naval strength was no longer sufficient to reach as far as Hawaii.

I not only lacked any new information to report upon this return visit, I actually wanted to listen to Staff Officer Nakashima speak about the aftermath of the attack on Pearl Harbor since I had been cut off from all sources of news following my detention. However, it did not appear as if Nakashima had a complete grasp of the matter.

I then quite presumptuously put the following question to him:

35. The Welcome

"Back then, why didn't they carry out repeated attacks and strike it thoroughly? At the time, I was hoping that a landing would be made by our army following the attack. After invading Hawaii, we could have used 300,000 Americans as hostages and waged a war of resistance. If we had deployed our forces in that way, it would have turned Hawaii into a special zone that I'm afraid not even the mighty U.S. military would have been able to recapture. It was for this reason that I had investigated the transport capacity of ships and boats in the region, and the like."

"No! It's best if we don't speak about the past," he said.

After advising me thus, Staff Officer Nakashima then added:

"…At the time, there might have been an opportunity to launch repeated attacks, but that was a question for our commanders to consider. Some people subsequently reviewed that very question, about the deployment of our attack forces, and they decided that repeated attacks would not have been appropriate.

"As for the view that you have just expressed, it was simply not practicable. Where would Japan get the petroleum from? How would we manage to feed 300,000 people? And how would the transport of the ground troops be carried out? In a word, Japan did not have the capability!

"Furthermore, to carry out such an invasion, we would certainly have needed at least two or three 10,000-ton oil tankers. Yet we didn't have any. One could only have wished that this wasn't so.

"You helped prepare a glorious exploit and you did your work in an exemplary fashion. As a survivor they ought to promote you specially, by at least two ranks.

"However, there have already been so many killed in action within the navy that all matters concerning survivors have to be put off. I am afraid that you are quite able to understand this…

"To conclude, you worked extremely hard and did a remarkable job. But anyway, what plans do you have now?"

"Sir, if it is at all possible, I would like to return."

"Yes, there are still many things I must speak about with you… But first, you need to rest for a while. When you've got a fixed address, let me know. All right, we'll leave it there for today."

After our conversation, Staff Officer Nakashima went back to his office. My "old haunt" was now refusing me entry.

As for the Pearl Harbor of that day, what was it like?

Apparently, it had already returned to its initial state and was serving as the staging post for the U.S. Navy's counterattack. It had become a place that no enemy could step inside, an impregnable fortress.

36

Longing for the Past

One day, I went with Consul-General Kita to a restaurant in the Ueno district that Kita was "very familiar" with. No, it is perhaps best to say he was "intimately connected" with it. As soon as the beautifully dressed and gently perfumed landlady saw our car drive up, she hastily ran over to greet us.

"Oh, welcome back! I have been waiting so long to see you!"

After the landlady had finished welcoming us, she led us to a guest room on the second floor. I remember that the stairs were rather steep and that it was somewhat dark.

"Landlady," said Kita in his typically forthright manner, without bothering to wait until he was seated, "I have brought one of our nation's best here today, someone who prepared the way for a marvelous exploit. So, you should give us some really good food. Isn't that so, Mr. Morimura? No! That's not right… Mr. Yoshikawa. What I want to say is, give us a bit of wine. But not the same as last time. Just give us two bottles."

"Of course. I'll get that ready for you right away. But, this gentleman?"

"This gentleman is Mr. Morimura. He did top secret work at Pearl Harbor and he survived it, earning himself a special promotion by two ranks! Landlady, you can learn something from this. Don't get involved in illegal management practices."

"You've lost the right to speak! You sir, are you not the one involved in illegal management practices?" After rebuffing Consul-General Kita, the landlady again faced me.

"It's the first time we've met," she said. "Welcome to our establishment. Congratulations on your safe return. Did you return with Mr. Kita as well?"

"Yes, that's right. I returned safely in Mr. Kita's protective arms."

Not long after the landlady walked off, she returned carrying our wine, sushi, chicken, meat, and other dishes. Japan's food supply was growing tighter by the day and this was the first time I had been able to eat an extravagant meal since my return. "These things are still available in certain special places," I noted to myself.

36. Longing for the Past

"Consul-General. The female statue that you carved in Arizona wasn't her, was it?" I asked Consul-General Kita after our third round of drinks.

"Ha, ha, ha… That was only a bit of nostalgia for Japanese women, nothing more."

"You were wearing denim trousers and a Mexican hat at that time, single-mindedly carving the 'sacred wood.'"

Upon hearing that, Consul-General Kita half-laughed and half-sighed. "I believed that we would have to live there for more than ten years," he said. "I never imagined that we would be able to return so soon."

"Even I felt as if I wasn't going to hold out at that time," I blurted out in reply, "during the FBI interrogations."

"You and me both!" said Kita. He then quickly added, "I invited you here today because there is something that I want to discuss with you."

He took his glass, which had been filled with some cool wine, and drained it. Then he poured some for me, refilled his own glass, and looked me in the eye.

"Are you thinking about returning to the Navy General Staff? Or are you going into the Foreign Ministry? There's a chance I might be going to China or Manchuria to take up a post. If you joined the Foreign Ministry, we could go over there together. What do you say? I think, at a time like the present, it's a good idea to take a moment from the sidelines and examine how the war is shaping up. It would be quite a suitable move for you, both from your standpoint and from that of others."

"No. I still wish to return to the Navy General Staff. I hope to once again lend a hand in this war and keep doing so until the day I die," I stated firmly.

"Oh, really?" was all the consul-general said after hearing my words. And, for a split-second, his expression grew somber. He recovered his hearty mien just as quickly, though. "Landlady!" he shouted. "There's no more wine! Landlady!"

Oh my! As I remember this now, I see that I hadn't fully understood the meaning of the indirect language that Kita had used when speaking to me. I was so young and naive.

There was something I still hadn't recognized at that time. Our military authorities were almost entirely unwilling to trust any war survivor who returned home. However, this was not because they wanted to punish us for not shouldering our responsibilities during the war. Instead, it was because the authorities suspected that the enemy's espionage services may have used every possible method to turn our survivors into double agents.

Survivors were not relieved of their important duties as a result of this; they were simply sent off to remote territories and exiled abroad. Thus, in order to "protect the king," those people in charge of the nation's affairs would willingly "give up a pawn." And they would not stint on any brutal tactics necessary to do so.

After my many discussions about this topic, I can safely say that there were no more than three paths open to me at that time:

1. Banishment overseas as a staff member of a Foreign Ministry legation
2. Going off to New Guinea in the South Seas to serve as an administrator in an overseas territory and losing my life in the process so that the leaking of our national secrets might be prevented
3. Working as a technician at the Navy General Staff (i.e., doing work for others that they couldn't do themselves)

As I was so young, naive, and lacking in worldly knowledge at that time, I selected the third path in the end. For better or for worse I returned to the Navy General Staff, my old haunt, where I continued to compile various materials and estimate the strength of the enemy's forces.

Not long after I returned to work, some of my belongings were delivered to the lobby of my hotel. They had been shipped right around the world. It looked as if the American military police had thoroughly searched my room in Hawaii and had wrapped up a few quite unimportant everyday items before shipping them off.

When I took a closer look at them, I saw there was a shortwave radio, a gramophone, cooking utensils, bedding, and the flowery clothing that I had worn when in disguise, which was basically of no use to me in Japan. Before shipping, all of this had been packed in a wooden box that was fastened by loops of steel ribbon. "Ship to Tokyo. For Morimura," had been written on the box in English.

Even though all of those things were somewhat worn out, for me they were "historic" and therefore worth cherishing. I did not feel like tidying up the boxes, though. As there was no pressing need to do so, I just kept them to one side.

I did not have the means to live in a hotel for long, so I frequently went out and wandered the streets with the hopes of finding an apartment. People often have the peculiar habit of yearning for the past, as long as it isn't anything particularly taboo, and I was thinking of living where I had lived previously or somewhere nearby.

After boarding the Keiō line tramcar at Shibuya one day, I was carefully looking out for a suitable place to live along the route when I noticed a thicket of pine trees in the Setagaya district. It was a quiet and tasteful area and there happened to be a vacant flat in a building that faced the woods. The landlord had once lived in America and he was extremely fed up with

36. Longing for the Past

all the emergency measures Japan was implementing (such as air-raid drills, curfews, and all the rest). Since he welcomed bachelors as residents, I did not waste another minute and quickly rented the flat. After that, I moved into my residence on the second floor of the building.

In my wildest dreams I could never have imagined what I later discovered. The woman with whom I had spoken about love just two or three years earlier, and for whom my heart yearned endlessly, had previously lived quite nearby.

In September 1942, Japan was still filled with hopes of victory. The war had not yet reached its most brutal stage and Japan's assault forces were making steady progress in the South. Over the music of the martial hymn "The Warship March," radio broadcasters provided citizens with continuous reports about Japan's glorious battle victories on each and every front.[1]

One day around this time, I decided to visit the posh restaurant in Akasaka that was run by the family of the two sisters I had known. The restaurant was a very quiet place as I had a look through the trees that surrounded its courtyard before lunchtime. Within the restaurant, I could see a young female worker in uncomfortable work clothes. She was using a long bamboo pole to channel water while diligently cleaning the doors of the booths. She might have been preparing for a special banquet that evening.

Lightly treading on my tiptoes atop the freshly washed stone pathway in the courtyard, I walked over to have a word with her.

"Good morning!"

The woman turned her head upon hearing this and looked at me, someone who did not appear to be a customer. After sizing me up for a moment, her expression revealed her surprise. She nodded her head slightly.

"Excuse me. Mr. Tokioka's family is here, right?"

"Yes, yes that's right. And you are?"

"I … I wish to see the young ladies for a moment…"

"Oh, really? Well then, please wait."

After saying that, the woman went inside.

Just then my resolve began to waver. "No … Don't trouble yourself!" I said hastily.

But the sound of a shout from the woman who had just gone inside was soon heard.

"Madam!"

Now I was having second thoughts because I did not know what I was supposed to say to their mother on our first meeting. However, as it was not proper to leave without saying a word, I stood like a fool outside the door.

The woman I had just spoken to came outside again.

"Please do come in," she said to me.

I gathered up my courage and followed her inside. I was surprised to see a woman, around 50 years old, wearing a Kimono and sitting quite naturally on a bed board inside a room that was spotlessly clean.

This was evidently their mother. I made a bow of respect toward her.

"I am the girls' mother," the woman began. "For what reason are you looking for them?"

"This is the first time we have met. My name is Yoshikawa. Some time ago, there was a period during which I shared the company of your two daughters. If the young ladies are present, I wish to see them… For this reason, I have come here and troubled you."

This mother was listening to my words with a smile and nodding her head in response.

"At what time, and in what place, were you in contact with my daughters?" she then asked.

"It was three years ago, at Nagata Manor."

"Oh… It was then!"

She had evidently been reminded of something.

If her expression were any guide, it looked as if she wanted to take her elder daughter's opposition to a marriage arranged by her parents, as well as her decision to march out along with her younger sister, and then pin the responsibility for all of that on me.

I was on tenterhooks and thinking of speaking a few words in my defense, but I did not have a chance to do so. I simply heard the mother utter a single phrase.

"That daughter has already married—"

I could not bear to hear any more regarding her elder daughter's situation, so I hurriedly cut her off.

"Actually," I explained, "the one I want to call on is her younger sister, Mika."

"Oh, really? Quite some time ago, Mika went to live with family in Numazu and she still hasn't returned. I have heard that she was tired of living in Tokyo."

"Yes… Yes…" was all I said in response, since I hoped to bring our meeting to a rapid conclusion. I had already concluded that those now part of their lives were people I could feel no natural affinity for.

On the way home, I bitterly regretted both my infatuation and my hesitation in pursuing a woman's love. After I'd reached a teashop quite near Akasaka that we often used to go to, I decided to push open the door and walk in so as to rid myself of my agitated mood.

I began to use my days off to travel that October. I had always felt that leaving Tokyo allowed me to regain a sense of freedom, so I went out sightseeing each Sunday. I went to Nikko, Enzan, the Bōsō Peninsula, the Miura

36. Longing for the Past

Peninsula and elsewhere. I would stay for one night and then return home. It was right at this time that I arrived in Numazu.

Although nobody I spoke to there could tell me where the Tokioka family was to be found, scouting around a small place such as that did not pose any sort of challenge for the likes of me. Then, just past noon, I found a tidy little house near Otsuka Park and I attempted to contact its owner by telephone. The person who answered the telephone was a young woman with a clear voice.

"Oh my! It's you, Mr. Yoshikawa! I really never imagined this. Where are you now? Please come up here and we'll have fun. As it happens, Mr. Iwashita is here right now. Stop it! Hey, hey! That's my fiancé. I will introduce you two right away."

"Well then, why don't we all take a walk? By the entrance to Otsuka Park. That's right, please just wait around a little while. In ten minutes or so we'll be there. Well, see you soon!"

After she had put down the telephone, I could not help but feel that it was now too late to worry about my foolishness. The reason I had come to Numazu was to find out whether or not Mika was married. If she was not, I hoped to ask her to marry me.

Since Mika was Chika's younger sister, she had a few physical characteristics in common with her elder sister. While it seems ridiculous now, I hoped that the shape of the younger sister's face would help me cherish her elder sister's love.

Mika's personality was somewhat different to that of Chika. While her elder sister was a refined woman of pure Japanese style, Mika was an easy-going, lively, candid girl who usually wore western-style clothing and loved to have a laugh. However, with her body she too displayed some of her elder sister's natural grace.

After just a short while, she and a tall young man came walking up and as soon as she saw me she waved her hand and called out. It had been three years since we had last seen each other and she had already grown up. She was wearing a red jersey and her bosom was particularly eye-catching. Her western-style trousers were similarly form-fitting.

Through her introduction I learned that her fiancé was one of her mother's distant relations and that he was from Tokyo. He had enlisted and was studying to become an officer with the Azabu air squadron.

There were not many tourists in Otsuka Park. When looking between the trees from within the pine woods you could see right out to the ocean. With each step through the woods, the trees seemed to move as if in a cartoon. At times, she wanted to hold hands with the young man and he was obviously somewhat embarrassed. I sincerely wished the two of them well.

"…From here to there it takes eight minutes. No, seven minutes and twenty seconds," said the young man, as if he were trying to think of something to say.

And then he said, "From here to there the total distance is 545 meters."

Judging from the precision with which he measured distance and time, you could tell what sort of personality he had. Generally speaking, men in the army enjoy this sort of talk. Yet did this young man actually have an exceptional disposition or was he putting on a show for his fiancé because I was on the scene? Once all of this had occurred to me, I did not feel it was proper to say much more. I simply walked along with them in Otsuka Park.

As far as my daily working habits were concerned, it basically mattered little to me if I approximated by one or two minutes or 30 to 50 meters. On occasion I had been incorrect by one or two days or several hundred nautical miles. However, each of these discrepancies was dealt with accordingly and that was the end of it. And yet, as far as that day's circumstances were concerned, hadn't my romanticism caused me to make a huge mistake? I could only smile bitterly about my lot in life.

It was all over now. In the end, each of the two sisters had made her life with another man of this world. All I could do was wish the two of them well and hurry back to the train station. From there, I planned to travel to Hakone.

One day, near the end of that year, I had just returned home from work when the building manager approached me.

"Mr. Yoshikawa. Today a very beautiful woman came looking for you. She said that she was just passing by and wanted to collect some rationed goods."

"Uh, who was she… What was her name?"

"What's that? You don't know about this? What's this all about?"

My heart began racing and I thought to myself that, if it was her, I might be able to see her!

"Did that person leave any address?" I then asked.

"No, nothing."

"Really?"

She was just like me. I was certain that she hadn't wanted to complicate things any further by chancing a meeting between us.

"It will be for the best if we don't see each other," I advised myself after this had occurred to me.

I had not attempted to enquire about her address during my meeting with her mother, nor afterwards when I saw her sister. Furthermore, it wasn't as if I would not have been able to seek her out if I had truly wanted to do so. As a man with real aspirations, I did not want to get into the business of chasing married women and I was even less willing to do something that would cause her heart any unnecessary pain.

Around that time, I received a letter from my mother that pressed me to

36. Longing for the Past

get married. Included with the letter were three photographs, one of which I was to choose before returning immediately to my village to get acquainted with my potential spouse.

In order rid myself of this recent emotional instability, I decided to heed my mother's wishes and return to our village. I got married the following year and then returned to Tokyo with my wife. We established our household in the Suginami district.

37

Interrogating Prisoners of War

After leaving the train at Ōfuna Station, you followed the river until you reached the turn that led you up the mountain. Once there, you saw a cave. You could pass straight through that cave to arrive at an open area that was enclosed by hills of white clay. This was a detention center for prisoners of war (POWs) and the cave was the only way in or out. American POWs from every battle front were sent there and locked up, without having been officially processed. As a result, all of them were terrified about their fate. "Are we going to be registered as POWs as decreed by international conventions? Or are we going to be killed?" they wondered.

I was hoping to obtain some military intelligence information from these POWs who had just arrived from the frontlines. The interrogation of POWs for the purpose of gathering intelligence was, of course, a violation of international law and this fact was already common knowledge all over the world. Yet when the POWs were confronted by powerful people who held the balance of their lives in their hands, there really wasn't any room for resistance.

To resist or not to resist? This was not actually a life-threatening question, but a prisoner's answer to it did have the potential to influence the handing over of a cigarette or the provision of a meal. Thus, for each and every one of them, it was a question of feeling extremely happy or greatly pained. Consequently, the POWs had no choice but to swallow their hate, hide their rebelliousness, and pretend to submit.

Even so, there were some very self-confident and proud young officers among the POWs and they adamantly refused to discuss questions concerning their country. Yet as the Japanese officers present during the interrogations were also young and vigorous, an atmosphere of antagonism would build up between the two sides and this soon became out-and-out hatred. Tempers would then flare up repeatedly and give rise to situations where force was used against a POW. At times they simply cursed the POW and said "You bastard!" At other times they actually beat up their adversary, sometimes going to the extent of knocking out teeth and causing faces to bulge and swell. Yet the results produced by all of this were very poor because the more this went on, the more the other side was glaring angrily and not uttering a word.

As a result of these incidents, the U.S. High Command cited the provisions on the treatment of POWs as the basis for charging all members of Section 5 at the Navy General Staff with war crimes at the end of the war. Without exception, all of us were sentenced to 20 years in prison. Rear Admiral Takeuchi (our Section Head) and I were the only ones to get wind of this beforehand and we fled to the countryside, escaping by the skin of our teeth.

But let me return to the day I first arrived at the detention center. The POW I was assigned was a first-lieutenant pilot. While still wearing my overcoat, I sat down on a chair inside the interrogation room. It was in a simple wooden building that lacked a fireplace. The person called in to sit opposite me was a morose young officer who kept his head bowed. He was pathetic-looking since his trousers were mud covered, his chestnut colored hair was also flecked with mud, and dust (that had darkened until it looked like oil) covered the back of his head from his neck to just behind his eyes. One look his way was enough to make you feel sorry for him.

After walking into the interrogation room, he took a very quick glance at me and then remained standing with his head bowed. Oh that posture! After bravely volunteering to fight for your country during its hour of need, and then going through many arduous battles, you find that you have ended up a POW. It was that wretched posture, wasn't it?

"Sit down, please."

I had used a solemn tone when speaking these first words.

"Today I would like to have a chat with you," I began. "During our chat I am going to ask you various questions. If you don't want to answer at times, you don't have to answer. However, because I am carrying out my duties by interviewing you, I hope you can tell the truth."

"Yes sir," he said with a nod of his head.

Once the customary questions about name, rank, and command were answered, the questioning began.

"Would you like a cigarette?"

"Thank you, sir!"

He drew very deeply on the cigarette. Although registered POWs were said to receive three cigarettes per day, I did not know whether he had previously received any. The two of us began chatting as we smoked.

"How many people are in your family?"

"Both my parents, my two younger sisters, and me."

"Are your parents worried about you?"

"…"

"Anyway, you were very brave and you joined the war effort. One day you will be welcomed home as a wounded war veteran."

"Let's hope so."

For the first time he showed his teeth as he looked at me. But as it seemed that day was far off in the distant future, he then bowed his head dejectedly.

"But when you were shot down, where was the place? And on what battle front?" I asked as I pointed to a map that I had spread out in front of him.

"Here."

He used a trembling hand to point it out. It appeared that he was greatly upset by any discussion about the battle front.

"Do you feel cold?"

"Yes!"

I took off my coat and draped it over his shoulders. The first-lieutenant raised his head and looked at me in amazement. And a teardrop fell on the table.

"Did you fly from the aircraft carrier *Enterprise*?"

"Yes, the *Enterprise*... But, could you please wait a minute!"

The first-lieutenant raised his head and when he was looking straight at me, he continued speaking.

"Could I please ask you a question? Are you a serviceman?"

"Yes."

After hearing that, he again lowered his head. He then became somewhat emotional as he spoke.

"You, sir, have been very kind and I am extremely grateful. I was shot down off the east coast of Bougainville Island in the South Pacific. Unfortunately, I was taken prisoner and immediately after that I was put in irons in the extreme heat of a ship's hold. I was interrogated and beaten there. And I nearly passed out many times. But I would rather die than answer any questions that might bring harm to my country.

"After that, I was taken on a long voyage over the high seas and with much difficulty I was finally brought here. When I first saw you here today, I thought that you were a true gentleman. If Japan's leaders were like you, there wouldn't have been a war in the first place. Okay, you can ask your questions, I'll do my best to answer you."

The first-lieutenant took a long sniffle. I too felt somewhat dejected, but there was no help for it. Things had reached this pass despite the fact that the first-lieutenant and I both lamented mankind's miserable lot.

It occurred to me then that I was once one of those who had taken up the burden of war and I too had been detained. In addition, I had undergone interrogation by the FBI. Yet for some reason, the tables had turned and I had become someone who carried out interrogations.

Perhaps because I had met with the same sort of misfortune, in my heart of hearts I always wanted to show a bit of warmth and kindness to those little birds who found themselves surrounded by wilting vegetation and were suffering from the cold. In this place, I did not want to go back to thinking that there was here an enemy and myself.

"Please have a cigarette!"

"Thank you!"

"We will leave the questions here for today… You might not be able to smoke there, but here you can smoke as much as you like. However, you cannot take any back with you."

"Thank you!"

The first-lieutenant looked out the window at the scenery outside with an interested expression while drawing heavily on a cigarette.

The lunch bell rang a short time later and a soldier came in to take the first-lieutenant away. The first-lieutenant returned my coat while thanking me sincerely. He no longer looked like a POW, he simply had the bearing of a young American gentleman.

Some of my readers may believe that I was led astray by American sweet-talk and thus made the error of showing mercy while in the midst of war. Such criticism is ill-founded since it was through this method that I had reached my objective during the interrogation. It was at the very moment that he was expressing his gratitude that he said "Yes, the *Enterprise*," and I believe that his words were truthful. As long as I was able to prove that the aircraft carrier *Enterprise* was in a given location on a given date, I had reached my objective.

War on the frontlines is a complicated business and during repeated confrontations both sides will suffer losses. As a result, some naval vessels will leave the battle front for repairs while others will make for the frontlines at top speed to renew the battle strength there. In addition, there may be newly built vessels making their way to the battle front.

At the Navy General Staff, intelligence reports were being received continuously from all corners of the world. Among them there might be a report sent in by a reconnaissance plane saying that they had discovered an enemy aircraft carrier and another report from a cruiser saying that they were "engaging in combat while caught between two enemy battleships." Once provided with these intelligence reports, we had to soberly determine what sort of vessels had been sunk or stricken and that was no simple matter. How could it be otherwise at a distance of several thousand nautical miles from the edge of the South Seas? Nevertheless, the orders handed down to us at the Navy General Staff made it clear that we had to be intimately familiar with the details of any given situation and precise regarding its facts.

Five people in our Section were largely responsible for ensuring the accuracy of our intelligence reports. Naturally, we were not superhuman and thus we could not provide 100 percent accuracy but we did our utmost to make sure our work was accurate.

One day, a member of the royal family paid our Section a visit without having given us any prior notice. He served as an assistant to His Majesty the Emperor and worked in the War Operations Bureau at the Navy General Staff.

"Greetings, Section Head. What is the actual strength of the U.S. forces deployed in the Pacific?" he asked.

"Of course, in the past, we provided reports about this to the War Operations Bureau. Yet because we were not able to keep their trust, we recently stopped sending them our reports. But we are at this very moment preparing such a report."

His Highness wore a smile while listening to Rear Admiral Takeuchi's grumbling.

"Bring me your trump card quickly and let me have a look!" he then said.

"Certainly. Mr. Yoshikawa, go and get it please!"

From my drawer I fetched a table that showed various coordinates and I laid it out before His Highness before taking a step back to the sidelines. The table was titled "The estimate of enemy troop strength."

His Highness looked at it closely. "Hmm, there are that many!" he noted perplexedly. "There is a significant discrepancy between this and the estimate made by the Operations Bureau…"

His Highness was fully engrossed while examining the table. Finally, he put forward a critical question.

"…And so as a result of this, it will be necessary to draw up a new war plan… But first, Section Head, how do you rate the accuracy of this table?"

"While it's not spot on, it's not far off either," the Section Head stated confidently as he raised his head. He then added, "I guarantee that it is 80% accurate."

The Section Head immediately seized upon this rare opportunity to go one step further.

"Because our troops' reports of the sinking of enemy vessels on the battle front have been so numerous, we have been ridiculed during enemy radio broadcasts. 'The Imperial Japanese Navy doesn't seem to know how to do basic arithmetic,' they say. 'If you add up the vessels they claim to have sunk, the U.S. fleet would have long since been reduced to zero.' For the moment, we can forget about the enemy's scorn. However, I'm afraid that we believe we must come up with a new war plan quickly.

"We definitely are not 'going beyond the excesses of American propaganda' or 'Americanized,' although this is what those in the Operations Bureau make us out to be. We come up with our statistics on the basis of verified material and by using cool-headed judgments. And for this reason, there are some people who dislike us. Your Highness, it's time to ask you to think about all of this seriously."

37. Interrogating Prisoners of War

Although Rear Admiral Takeuchi was an unyielding sort of man, all of the words that he had bottled up inside had come pouring out.

"Hmm. I see," His Highness said after listening to Rear Admiral Takeuchi. "Uh, let me borrow this table now. I'll give it back to you shortly…" Having said this, he snatched up the table and walked over to the office that faced ours.

Even though we made use of material facts to calculate the crucial figures that detailed the strength of the enemy's forces at the frontlines, because the views inside the Navy General Staff were not unanimous, and because other problems existed, we could not work together properly as a team. As a result, we had no choice but to go and do the hateful work of interrogating POWs with the hopes that we could sort out the main threads of this great hodgepodge, little by little.

I have yet another story about the interrogation of POWs.

This time, the POW that I had to interrogate was a submariner whose submarine had been sunk in northern waters. He was so very young and short that he appeared to be a child. His skin was swarthy, his eyes were very round, and his nose extremely short. Despite this, he was certainly a white man. He had apparently grown up in a mountainous region and because of that he had always yearned to go to sea. Then, after hearing the call to enlist, he joined the navy. He had already been serving for three years. As he had been selected for promotion and was made the submarine's steward, it was clear that his service record was not bad and that he was quite clever.

After he had been brought into the interrogation room, questioning began in the customary manner and he seemed to respond in the very same way that he had responded to another officer's questions. Regardless of the question, he always had a ready reply. Nevertheless, every topic that we discussed was of no real significance and this put me in an awkward position. Furthermore, he kept eyeing the package of cigarettes that I had put on the table. Whenever I offered him a cigarette, he immediately stretched out his hand to take one and said "Thank you."

He seemed to love smoking. Yet as soon as he lit up, he didn't seem to understand anything of my questions and even went so far as to ask me to repeat them. Despite that, speaking with someone of his type was actually quite relaxing.

Well then, how was it that he had managed to escape with his life after his submarine had been sunk? It turned out that he was fortune's favorite. He had managed to turn bad luck into good.

Apparently, while navigating through fog on a northern battle front, a Japanese destroyer suddenly brushed up against an American submarine. At first, both sides mistakenly believed that the other vessel was one of their own. However, a moment later, the Japanese crew discovered that the submarine was an enemy vessel and the order to open fire was given.

"Thirty degrees left, enemy submarine. Fire!"

"Prepare to release depth charges!"

Yet because there was too little distance between them, the ship's main guns were of no use. A round of machine gun fire splashed against the water, "ta-ta," while the sound of the enemy craft hurriedly submerging could also be heard. At that instant, there was a submariner on deck who had failed to enter his vessel's cabin on time. He was the very man that I was interrogating.

The destroyer did not waste any time in pursuing the submerging vessel and it sank the submarine with depth charges. Heavy oil floating on the surface of the water soon proved that the enemy craft had been sunk. However, the submariner who had been standing on his vessel's deck was also floating on the icy sea water. He was then rescued by the destroyer's crew and taken back to Japan aboard the victorious warship in order to serve as a witness to its victory.

"May I have a cigarette, please?"

"Well now, let's talk about the period from the time you enlisted to the time you were taken prisoner…"

"Okay!"

Though he began to talk a lot of nonsense, he eventually went on to say "…and after that we went south to the base at Guadalcanal."

"And how many months did you stay? Please take a cigarette."

"Hmm, we stayed there a pretty long time. It was around a month. We were waiting for them to kit out our vessel with something."

"What sort of thing was it?"

"Radar."

"What is radar?"

"It's a device that can detect all enemy vessels in your area and tell you their distance and direction."

"Hmm. Explain that to me again, carefully. Just a minute, let me get a pencil and paper…"

After hearing his explanation about radar, I was very excited. I had now learned that radar was a device used to detect movement and it was very likely that this was a new sort of weapon. I could not say that I did not know what it was, however. I would have met with his scorn if I had not given the impression that I had long known about this sort of device.

After further discussion with him, I gained a deeper understanding of the matter. With this device that made use of the feedback from electrical waves, American troops were able to accurately determine a target's direction and distance and this greatly reduced the margin of error. He told me that all of the U.S. Navy's ships and submarines had been equipped with this sort of device. "You guys have probably known all about this for some time now," his tone of voice seemed to say.

I hurried to conclude my discussion with him and then I rushed back to the Navy General Staff and reported this information to my superiors. A news bulletin about this was sent off to all branches of our military soon afterwards. At the time, the Japanese navy had still not sufficiently mastered radar technology.

No wonder the Japanese submarines that had joined the Battle for the Northern Seas (which included the Battle for Midway Island) were suddenly met with enemy fire while they were navigating through the Aleutian Islands in heavy fog in June 1942. Following that, during night fighting in the Solomon Islands, Japanese naval vessels once again met with enemy fire coming from an indeterminate direction and heavy losses were sustained. The traditional Japanese tactic of using the cover of night to draw near to enemy ships and carry out torpedo attacks had been rendered completely useless.

Just prior to the start of the war, in October, I had sent Tokyo a coded cable that read more or less as follows: "Recently, a rack-shaped antenna installed at the top of the masts of the heavy cruisers has been observed. Its purpose is not known."

In addition, in July of the same year, the Japanese military attaché to the U.S. received an intelligence report from the Italian military attaché to the U.S. under the auspices of the intelligence-sharing pact between Japan, Germany and Italy. The report explained that America had developed a new type of armament called "radar."

It was expressly because of this that the Japanese military attaché's office dispatched Commander Sakamoto to the U.S. West Coast to carry out an investigation. In the end, he was only able to verify my cable report. Meanwhile, the Navy General Staff was so busy preparing for war by then that it had not yet started the work of developing its own radar.

The information concerning radar that I had fortuitously gleaned from the POW on this occasion was later confirmed by several other POWs. They unanimously declared that the capabilities of this device were truly outstanding, which finally compelled the Navy General Staff to pay more attention to the matter. Consequently, the navy's research and development unit was urged to speed up its development program.

Unfortunately, the problems with the radar device that they completed were so numerous that it did not function. Thus, there was no alternative except to send a submarine to Germany to ask for assistance. Its crew was obliged to bear the scorn of the German Navy.

"Since you are coming from Japan to demand radar from Germany," they said, "it seems that Japanese technology isn't up to much."

Even though Germany presented Japan with a radar set, the Japanese flotilla transporting it home was sunk before it had completed its return journey. Consequently, we were not able to produce a fully-functional radar system.

38

Cipher Code and the Death of Commander Isoroku Yamamoto During Combat

On 20 April 1943, the Navy General Staff received the sad news that the Commander-in-chief of the Combined Fleet Isoroku Yamamoto had been killed in action. Although very few high-ranking officers were notified of this, some other officers who sat at their lunch tables soon learned the news as well. The entire Navy General Staff was enveloped by an atmosphere of great sorrow that day.

The death of Commander Isoroku Yamamoto during combat was a tremendous humiliation for the Imperial Japanese Navy and it greatly damaged our navy's prestige. Subsequently, after the shock had begun to wear off, everyone began to discuss the same questions:

"What are our men on the frontlines doing?"

"Did the Commander disembowel himself because the war's outcome seemed so unpromising?"

In former times, the deputy commander would immediately lead the troops back home as soon as the commander had died in action. For example, in the days of Imagawa Yoshimoto and Takeda Shingen this was what happened after a warlord died in action.[1] In present-day warfare, however, soldiers are no longer recruits in a warlord's private army and a successor is immediately appointed to continue leading the battle as soon as the commanding officer dies in action. This policy aims to prevent the weakening of morale among the troops.

The death in action of Commander Isoroku Yamamoto was kept secret until the end of May, when the news was finally made public. It was then decided that a state funeral would be held on 5 June. All personnel, without exception, were ordered to attend the funeral.

I was one of Commander Isoroku Yamamoto's subordinates and he knew of me, although I had never seen him nor spoken to him personally. This was

38. Cipher Code and the Death of Commander

because he was both the architect of the surprise attack on Pearl Harbor and the top commander leading the Carrier Striking Task Force on that attack. He apparently attached great importance to "A's" intelligence reports, which were delivered to him by the Navy General Staff. "A" was the code name attached to my intelligence reports.

Some of the staff officers who were assisting him a few hours before the attack on Pearl Harbor was launched have told me about his reaction to the final cable that I sent from Honolulu, in which I had written that eight battleships were anchored in the harbor and that the two aircraft carriers that had entered the harbor on the previous day had already left port. "Two aircraft carriers have given them the slip!" he said while reading that cable, stamping his foot to express his displeasure.

Since then, the Imperial Japanese Navy had suffered defeat at Midway, Coral Island, and Guadalcanal. Large numbers of our troops had been lost and the shipping lanes in the South were under serious threat of attack from enemy aircraft.

In order to change our position and create new possibilities, Commander Isoroku Yamamoto had ordered his staff to draft a new battle plan and this was code-named "Operation *I–Go*." According to that plan, all our carrier-based airplanes were to be transferred to the air base at Rabaul to wage a fight to the death against U.S. air troops over the Solomon Islands and thereby foil an offensive by U.S. forces based on Guam. Once those battles had been won, a second line of defense would be established in the South Seas. Since the maxim "attack is the best form of defense" was long cherished in the Imperial Japanese Navy, it might be said that this battle plan was both a timely measure and somewhat belated.

Commander Isoroku Yamamoto was the type of commanding officer who was very often present at the frontlines to direct the troops. In order to raise the morale of the officers and troops who were fearlessly waging war as Operation *I–Go* began to produce the expected results, he decided to go to Balalae Airfield (the frontline air base at the southern tip of Bougainville Island), the Shortland Islands, Buin, and to other sites to personally inspect the bases there.

Very specific measures should have been adopted to safeguard this inspection tour by the Commander-in-chief of the Combined Fleet and they ought to have been prepared for every possible contingency. However, it's worth noting here that the only enemy aircraft activity around Bougainville Island at that time was that of reconnaissance aircraft and there were not very many of them. Furthermore, there had never been a large-scale air raid in that area.

Since a new cipher book had gone into use on 1 April, it was thought unlikely that the enemy would be able to decipher the latest cables. Consequently, it seemed appropriate to notify each base about the tour by sending them the commander's itinerary in advance:

> At 06:00 on 18 April, the commander will leave Rabaul accompanied by the chief of staff to the fleet and various assistants. They will fly to Buin aboard two medium-sized attack aircraft, under escort from six fighter planes.

On 18 April the sky was clear and visibility was excellent. Flocks of birds were singing away, while the rosy clouds that are so characteristic of dawn in the South Seas were already glowing above the commander's quarters in the mountains at Rabaul. Tavurvur Mountain, which overlooks the airport, appeared just the same as ever as it spewed white ash up into the azure sky.

Commander Isoroku Yamamoto was famous for being punctual and the aircraft carrying him and the staff officers took off from Rabaul Airport on time. Once the commander's aircraft had reached an altitude of 1,500 meters along the west coast of Bougainville Island, it began heading south towards Buin and Balalae Airfield, their first stop. Just then, it suddenly came under attack by 16 U.S. fighter planes.

Although the commander's aircraft dived sharply to the level of the dense jungle below in an effort to escape the enemy aircraft, those planes stayed in hot pursuit. In the blink of an eye, the commander's plane was shot down and crashed into the tropical wilderness north of Buin. Meanwhile, the chief of staff's aircraft was shot down over the sea. In this great tragedy the commander was killed in action, the chief of staff suffered serious injuries, and various other personnel were killed.

A special search team rushed to the crash site and discovered the body of the commander in the dense jungle the next day. The tremendously powerful and renowned admiral of the Imperial Japanese Navy had apparently kept a tight hold on the hilt of his traditional sword and he had remained in his seat.

Who could have foreseen that Admiral Isoroku Yamamoto's fate was already sealed? This was so because the commander of U.S. forces at Camp Henderson on Guam had received an order from U.S. Navy Command on 17 April:

> In the early morning on 18 April, Commander Isoroku Yamamoto will be leading a party of staff officers to inspect the frontlines. He is expected to reach Ballalae at 06:45. Order your air troops to carry out an air intercept and attack. Spare no effort in shooting down Isoroku Yamamoto's airplane and its six escort aircraft!

It was not until after the war that we finally learned the reason behind all of this: U.S. forces had cracked the telegraph code used by our troops on the frontlines. Exactly how was a cable code that had just been changed at the beginning of April decoded in less than a month's time? Some of the main reasons for this were as follows.

38. Cipher Code and the Death of Commander

After U.S. marines had landed at Guadalcanal on 8 August 1942, the Japanese forces that were fighting the first Battle for the Solomon Islands found themselves on the defensive. Soon after this, on 17 August, a total of 222 U.S. marines traveling aboard two submarines landed on Makin Island at dawn. Makin Island is in the Gilbert Islands Archipelago, which marked the eastern limit of Japan's mandate for the South Sea Islands.[2]

At the time, the only presence on the island was that of 43 special marines under the leadership of Petty Officer Yū Kanemitsu. They were engaged in the work of intercepting intelligence report transmissions. Despite the extensive security measures they had put into place there, the asymmetrical troop levels (43 servicemen versus 222) meant that the outcome of this battle was never in doubt.

Added to this was the fact that Makin Island was vulnerable to attack and very difficult to defend. The entire island was made of coral, flat, and wonderfully tall coconut palms were the only things that grew there. Water was present everywhere throughout the island and it made the digging of defensive trenches more or less impossible. Thus, there was nowhere to hide nor any place to run to. Although repeated bombing sorties were carried out by Japanese aircraft, the numerical superiority of the U.S. troops was not diminished.

The U.S. Navy had dispatched the landing force simply to cause the Japanese navy to focus its attention there, they had never intended to occupy the island. Their troops had originally planned to return to their submarines after having forced the Japanese troops to flee. Yet because of repeated bombing by Japanese aircraft, those submarines did not dare surface.

After some time, the submarines were able to take advantage of a break in the bombing to resurface. They were unable to find the troops that had landed, however. As a result, the U.S. marines were obliged to seek out the Japanese troops defending the island and prepare them for their surrender. Then, while searching hither and yon, they found some classified documents inside a Japanese garrison. After quietly seizing those documents, they made use of the cover of night to withdraw and return to their submarines.

From this incident it is apparent that even the tiniest complement of our troops could take extremely important top-secret documents to a very remote and minuscule island, which was utterly absurd. This sort of incident had become a deadly tradition for Japan's navy.

In January 1943, there was yet another incident during which a cipher code book was lost. It occurred after a Japanese I-1 class submarine was attacked just off the coast of Guadalcanal. This incident came to pass because the commanding officer had not completely destroyed his code books before his submarine was dashed, which allowed some U.S. Navy submariners to seize an invaluable book from the submarine. However, Japan's navy was still making use of that cipher to carry out its operations one month later since it was unaware that its secret code book had been obtained by U.S. forces. What a tragedy!

Between the summer of 1942 and the spring of 1943, large numbers of Japanese aircraft participating in naval battles around the Solomon Islands were shot down and all such airplanes carried secret code books. From these downed aircraft, U.S. troops were able to get hold of large numbers of cipher books that had not been destroyed. When these secret materials were collated, an ordinary person with minimal knowledge about deciphering code (never mind a cipher expert from the U.S. military) would have been able to break our cipher. Even after a change to the cipher code, it would not have been difficult for anyone armed with these materials to work out the key to deciphering the new code.

There was yet another such incident, which involved the sinking of the *Nachi* (a heavy cruiser) in the shallow waters of Manila Bay. When compared to the above-described episodes, the seizure of documents by U.S. forces during the so-called *Nachi* incident was far more disturbing to our navy's commanders.[3]

During this incident, all of the Imperial Japanese Navy's classified files (stored with their seals still unbroken and "only slightly dampened by seawater") were seized by U.S. troops. Not only were there secret code books among those files, there were documents outlining the navy's battle tactics, the battle plan for "Operation *Sho-Go*," documents concerning troop strength and deployment, and more.

If there is anything to be gained from recalling these defeats when we study the Pacific War, I believe it is the many painful lessons that came from them.

Naturally, several thousand personnel and specialists within the intelligence-gathering network on the Japanese side were charged with the work of deciphering codes and gathering intelligence information. Each of the four Bureaus at the Navy General Staff played a part in this. At times, we too were able to learn about the enemy's plans in advance and that set the stage for great successes in battle. This fact is beyond dispute.

In order to improve the reader's understanding of secret communications, I would like to leave this discussion for a moment and turn to secret coding in pre-war Japan and during the war. I may then tell the story of the breaking of our secret telegraph codes by the U.S. military.

39

Japanese Secret Code Before the War

After the war, we learned that the Americans had been able to decipher 108 top secret military intelligence cables sent between Japan's overseas embassies and consulates and the Japanese Foreign Ministry during the four months that preceded the surprise attack on Pearl Harbor. One must admit that this was a remarkable achievement.

As a consequence of this, there are to this day a few smug know-it-alls who do not seem to have tired of making the following argument: "Since all of Japan's intelligence reports were completely deciphered by the Americans, it's abundantly clear that America lured Japan into launching its surprise attack on Pearl Harbor."

In response, I would like to ask something of those people: On what grounds are you entitled to comment?

Since the end of the war, the question of America's knowledge of the planned attack on Pearl Harbor has remained unresolved. It is to this day a "mystery" in the USA, the very country it concerns most of all. Nonetheless, two camps have long been quarrelling about it with their competing theories. One camp says that the Americans were well aware of the Japanese plan to attack Pearl Harbor and purposely allowed Japan to fire the first shot. The other camp says that America simply did not understand the situation and was blindsided by the attack. In the following section, I would like to carry out a new study of this matter by examining some of the cables that were intercepted and deciphered by the Americans.

The Japan-U.S. peace talks had just about reached the point of collapse by the summer of 1941. Yet while Japan (which considered itself the leader of the alliance of the Axis Powers) was having talks with America (which considered itself the leader of the "liberal" camp), there never really was any chance that their discussions would lead to an accord. It did not matter how much Ambassador Nomura patiently tried to persuade, or that Ambassador

Kurusu put on a smile to show his amity, or that the greatest of efforts was being made. After the U.S. government had resolved to curb Japanese territorial expansion, nothing was capable of moving the talks forward in any meaningful way.

Seen from this perspective, one can argue that the U.S. clearly had decided to force Japan into firing the first shot so as to be able to stand at the head of the liberal camp, rescue Britain, and then go on to smash the Axis powers: Germany, Italy, and Japan.

President Roosevelt evidently believed that if Japan's external capital were frozen, and if oil exports to it were prohibited, Japan would find it was being slowly strangled to death and feel compelled to take its chances. Consequently, regardless of the risks, Japan would enter the South or Hawaii and that would provide America with the suitable pretext it needed to confront its enemy. America could then gather together its numerous, disparate people, drunk or disoriented by American wealth and culture though they might be, and urge them to take up the cause. While doing so, America would earn the support of each and every country in the free world and draw other countries over to its side as well.

They had also concluded that they would have to suffer Japanese attacks during the conflict's initial phase, but this was a pain they would have to bear for a time in order to procure the final victory. And while seeking to ensure its losses would be kept to a minimum, the U.S. government must certainly have wracked its best brains trying to determine the answer to a key question: Was Japan actually going to aim its attack at Hawaii or would it target the South instead?

"Did the U.S. know beforehand that Japan was going to attack Pearl Harbor?" someone is said to have asked the U.S. Secretary of State Cordell Hull after the war. The Secretary of State simply smiled and made no reply. To this day, no one knows what sort of secret Roosevelt and Secretary of State Hull kept hidden. This is a mystery that remains unsolved.

It might be best to allow this "mystery" to remain as such. However, as I am the sort of person who enjoys getting to the bottom of things, I have adopted the historian's approach in my attempt to solve this puzzle (albeit with the pocket money that remains after my living expenses have been covered).

First of all, the Americans had already reached one conclusion: Japan is definitely going to attack the South. Therefore, we must concentrate our efforts on gathering intelligence on the South. I believe that this was what both the U.S. government and President Roosevelt had resolved to do at the time. Now allow me to speculate on how the situation then was seen from President Roosevelt's perspective.

Hawaii was, without doubt, the U.S. Pacific Fleet's largest base and it

39. Japanese Secret Code Before the War

would be no trivial matter if that fleet were to meet with a devastating attack. Yet was Japan truly capable of making the long push necessary to attack Hawaii? If Japan wanted to take on the U.S. Pacific Fleet, it would certainly have to mobilize its entire fleet. Furthermore, it would have to traverse 2,000 nautical miles of high seas and get past the security corridors around both Midway and Wake Island. Although the odds of success for such a mission were estimated at 2:3, the U.S. Pacific Fleet (which possessed ten air bases on land) had every reason to feel reassured about its chances.

Therefore, from Japan's perspective (which was that of a country suffering a penury of materials), there was no way it ought to run a risk of this sort when it offered no practical rewards. Consequently, it could be deduced that the South was going to be the focus of Japan's attack. The Philippines and Guam would naturally be the first to fall, but from the Americans' standpoint those attacks wouldn't really hit a sore spot. Hong Kong, Singapore, and Indonesia (which was under Dutch jurisdiction) would fall underfoot after that. Yet if things were to come to such a pass, the United States, Great Britain, and Holland could easily form a united front.

Since Japan needed to focus its attack on the South, a way of cracking its secret cables had to be found before it made its move. This would enable the Americans to determine how best to deal with the situation. In other words, if you were able to keep abreast of current developments by way of the cables dispatched back and forth between the Foreign Ministry in Tokyo and its overseas embassies and consulates, you could implement your plan to force Japan to risk a desperate gambit and do this at the lowest of costs. I am quite sure this was the analysis that the office of the U.S. Commander in Chief made at that time.

It is undeniable that America's intelligence network had an almost complete grasp of the situation in Japan. However, I know from my work in the Intelligence Bureau at the Navy General Staff that Japan's intelligence services had a firm grasp on the situation in the United States as well. During the war we knew everything about the U.S. Navy vessels that were going to be launched two years hence, including their names, their class, and launching points. So-called "intelligence gathering" is able to achieve precisely this sort of result.

Large numbers of U.S. military personnel and secret agents lived in the "villa belt" around the Yokosuka Naval Arsenal. They kept an eye on things there just as I kept watch on the U.S. Navy's fleet in Honolulu. They were constantly vigilant, and kept their eyes open wide while peering through every possible nook and cranny to follow the activities of Japan's warships. Additional undercover agents, such as Sorge, operated within Japan's political and financial circles.[1]

Since Japan urgently required oil supplies, it needed to adapt the collaborative approach taken by the army and the Manchuria Railway to a new region.² Thus, the navy began coordinating its activities with the South Seas Development Corporation and the South Seas Society along the same lines that activities were being managed on the mainland. Both of these organizations were placed under the protection of the navy while they carried out the operations necessary to extract vital oil resources from the South.

By the time Japan's oil reserves were no longer ample enough to support the activities of its naval fleet for longer than three months, the intelligence services in the U.S. were already well aware of the situation. The best method of keeping abreast of Japan's policies, both general and specific, was simply to crack the secret cables sent back and forth between the Japanese Foreign Ministry and its embassies and consulates overseas. In the pre-war period, the U.S. achieved a fair number of successes in this area. Japan successfully carried out activities of this sort as well, most notably with intercepted navy intelligence reports sent by post. The quality of that work was so high that great achievements were made.

There were three methods of cracking secretly coded telegrams:

Method 1: Intercept enemy cable communications and subject them to thorough analysis in order to determine their meaning. Generally speaking, a cable could be cracked within 20 days regardless of the code used. However, at times it took as long as 60 or 70 days to decipher a cable.

Method 2: Take photographs of a secret code book without tipping off the enemy.

Method 3: Seize documents through force, from downed aircraft personnel, or from the cabins of bombed or sunk vessels.

The last two of these methods ensured that only two or three days were needed to break a code. Since the useful life of a secret code book was not very long, couriers were frequently sent out to replace code books and new cipher instructions were often sent out from the central office via cable.

The U.S. Army and Navy, U.S. diplomatic personnel, and the FBI made use of all three of these methods and were thus able to decipher some of the many secret cables sent between Japan's Foreign Ministry and its embassies and consulates abroad.

According to statistics compiled on this subject, 107 cables were deciphered during the pre-war period from 1 August 1941 to 8 December 1941. A further 25 were deciphered after the war began.

According to material from the Joint Committee for the Investigation of the Pearl Harbor Attack established by the U.S. Congress, many Japanese cables were deciphered during the six months prior to the war and just after the start of the war. They can be divided into regions as follows:

39. Japanese Secret Code Before the War

Cables Sent From (Region)	Cables Deciphered (Pre-war)		Cables Deciphered (During War)
Tokyo	15		3
Hawaii	3		8
Panama	20		6
Manila	54		5
S.E. Asia, & U.S.A West Coast	15		3
Subtotal	107		25
Total Cables Sent		132	

This table appeared in a report published by the above-mentioned congressional investigative committee, which was charged with finding out who was responsible for the Pearl Harbor Incident. Among the report's contents were the texts of secret telegrams, relevant dates, the names of personnel assigned translation duties, the classification levels of the secret communications, and more. It is very reliable source of that information.

From this table, it can be seen that only three ciphered cables sent from Hawaii to Tokyo were fully deciphered during the pre-war period. However, the number of cables Tokyo sent and received from Manila and Southeast Asia that were deciphered during the same period amounted to more than 70. It is not difficult to conclude that there is something peculiar about this.

Since the number of secret code books held by each of Japan's embassies and consulates had to be more or less the same, Manila definitely was not furnished with just one low-level secret code book. At my place of work, the Japanese Consulate-General in Honolulu, the number of secret code books was no less than ten. I reckon that our embassy in Manila would have had a similar number of code books, if not more. Despite this, the number of cables sent from Manila and Southeast Asia that were deciphered by the Americans was extremely high. This is somewhat suspect, isn't it?

Here I invariably return to the thought that there might have been an undercover agent at work inside our embassy in Manila, or at the Foreign Ministry in Tokyo. What's more, that undercover agent must have been a person of significant authority. Furthermore, he would have been acting under direct orders from the U.S. government. Naturally, the possibility that the Americans had simply poured all of their effort into cracking the intelligence reports sent from Manila cannot be ruled out either. Whatever the case, anyone can see that the Americans put a lot of effort into intercepting the intelligence reports from Manila and that they used nearly every available means to do so. On the other hand, they did not spend very much time deciphering intelligence reports from Honolulu.

If one considers these 132 cables a representative sample, the rate at which the U.S. Army and Navy respectively deciphered intelligence reports was 3:2. The U.S. Army was at a bit of an advantage, perhaps because it assigned greater numbers of its personnel to the task and because of the more than 20,000-character codes it made use of.

Yet when it came to the deciphering abilities of their staff, the U.S. Navy had a slight advantage. Furthermore, they required shorter periods of time to crack a code.

All of the various methods used by the U.S. Army and Navy to decipher codes are summarized by the following seven "channels." Each one of these channels was a classification assigned to encrypted Japanese cables by U.S. intelligence services.

1. J17K6
2. J18K8
3. J19
4. J19K9

    These four cable types were ordinary coded cables sent by the Imperial Japanese Navy and intercepted by American forces. Generally speaking, deciphering cables of these varieties required relatively long periods of time.

5. PA-K2

    This refers to top secret Imperial Japanese Navy cables. In all probability, they were deciphered after a code book had been seized. Not much time was required to crack intelligence reports of this sort.

6. Secret Purple[3]

    This refers to coded Japanese diplomatic telegrams. They were probably cracked after an undercover agent surreptitiously photographed a code book. They could be deciphered within a short period of time.

7. Secret Red

    This refers to intelligence reports that concerned the Soviet Union.

The majority of the intelligence reports sent between the Foreign Ministry in Tokyo and Japan's embassies and consulates in the Philippines and Southeast Asia used a Secret Purple cipher. A total of 65 of these were intercepted and deciphered.

Given that each of these telegrams was deciphered in just one to three days, while the fourth telegram channel (J19K9) required 30 days or more to decipher, one can infer that those responsible for reporting about Secret Purple cables likely used special methods to make timely, secret reports to the U.S. Although the personnel responsible for deciphering coded cables would have been well aware that no single secret code book was in use for long since frequent changes were made to the ciphers, no more than three days were needed before the codes used on these cables could be broken. This is sufficient to give one to pause for thought, is it not?

In order to further explore this matter, allow me to present several cables that were intercepted by U.S. forces at that time:

(1)
From: The Minister for Foreign Affairs, Tokyo
To: The Envoy to Mexico
23 June 1941
(Secret Purple)

Regarding the plan to gather intelligence reports on transportation along the Panama Canal and maps of its surrounding areas. Under the auspices of an official business visit, you may send Military Attaché Kihara to the Panama Canal Zone. Furthermore, you may send Secretary Yoshinaga along with him.

If they return by airplane with the maps, please give them to Naval Attaché Sato who will bring them home to Tokyo. We are certain that the Americans have increased their surveillance. As there are signs that suggest our codes have already been partly deciphered, we hope that you will adopt all necessary precautions to complete this task.
(The U.S. Navy deciphered this cable on 24 June 1941)

The above text shows that Tokyo sent this cable on 23 June. It was immediately deciphered on 24 June. In addition, since the above telegram notes specifically that "our codes have already been partly deciphered," the person responsible for leaking the code may have been in Tokyo.

(2)
From: The Envoy to Manila
To: The Minister for Foreign Affairs, Tokyo
12 August 1941
(Secret Purple)
RE: The reply to cable #25

1. According to a non-commissioned U.S. naval officer, the British warship I reported in my cable #414 was the *Warspite*. At first, I too believed that this was the case. But the name of that British warship had been obscured and a secret agent who witnessed the vessel entering the docks said that it was actually a 7,000-ton vessel. Was it really? A ship had been moored at the Cavite naval base earlier, but given the shallowness of the waters around those docks it is not clear that it was the *Warspite*.

Then again, judging by the shape of the vessel, it looked very much like one of the Royal Navy's Leander-class light cruisers (When entering those same

docks, the *Cincinnati* had let off water in order to lighten its load.) According to other reports, the ship weighed 8 tons. These reports have been confirmed.
2. There were some sailors wearing hats with silk ribbons, of George V style, among those who disembarked from the vessel. According to another undercover agent, the ship was carrying 48 people who had been wounded during battle on the Mediterranean Sea.
3. Subsequent to the dispatch of cable #451, the movements of this vessel are unclear. No other Royal Navy ships have entered port recently.

(The U.S. Navy deciphered this cable on 16 August 1941)

This telegram's long text was deciphered in three days as well. The reason I have selected this cable is to draw my readers' attention to the fact that Japan may have hired a foreign secret agent in Manila. Furthermore, he may have made frequent visits to our embassy there. However, that foreign agent might have been a double agent hoping to catch a big fish by giving up a smaller one. I wonder whether or not those at our embassy noticed this.

(3)
From: The Minister for Foreign Affairs, Tokyo
To: The Embassy in Manila
4 October 1941

Cable #318 (Secret Purple)
Please thoroughly scout out all new defensive fortifications under construction along Luzon's east, west, and south coasts, and then report on their state of completion and the troops deployed to them. In addition, you may investigate things that are of interest to you and make a report about them.

(The U.S. Army deciphered this cable on 8 October 1941)

(4)
From: The Envoy to Manila
To: The Minister for Foreign Affairs, Tokyo
1 November 1941

Cable #723 (Secret Purple)
(In reply to Cable #318)
Although I have run into some difficulties while gathering information because security is very tight, I am still trying to come up with a way of conducting a secret survey. For the time being I will report the following information, which was provided by newspapers and reports from foreign embassies.

1. Philippine Army troops have been recruited to carry out construction work on the eastern side of the country, the progress of which is ever more rapid. By the end of this year it is estimated that their numbers will reach 120,000.

    In numerous areas, military camps are being built and the rate of their construction is quickening. The purpose of all this seems to be to increase the strength of the ground forces.

    The sites are located at: Cabanatuan, San Mariano, __ __ __, __ __ __, __ __. (Several site names are unclear.)

    Furthermore, from November onwards, the numbers of ground troops

39. Japanese Secret Code Before the War

stationed near Lingayen are set to increase rapidly and military exercises are scheduled to be held there by the middle of the month. It's possible that those exercises will be temporary in nature.

2. Near Mariveles, they have hired 3,000 workers in order to rapidly carry out various construction projects. Yet the number of cavalry and army troops stationed in the area is not more than 300.

   The 2,000–3,000 ground troops that I detailed in the report I sent on the 27th, which had already left the north side of Manila by bus, were perhaps heading to the zone that I have just described. I am currently investigating this. At the zone in question, three airfields are now under construction and a shipyard seems to be undergoing expansion.

   The security measures in place in the Bataan Zone are particularly strict and even the local residents are barred from entering it.

3. The pace of the road construction between Dingalan and Laur is quickening and they reckon that it will be finished shortly. Prior to the middle of October, only 5 kilometers of this construction project (Hwy #80) had been completed.

   The road between Infanta and Manila is currently being broadened to a width of 5 meters.

   Engineering operations are being carried out both day and night and the speed at which they are progressing is truly astounding.

4. According to reports, there are 30–40 fighter aircraft, 20–30 bombers, and (?) high altitude aircraft at the base in Iba.

A more detailed report about this situation will be sent on by post.
(The U.S. Navy deciphered this cable on 4 November 1941)

Within three to four days, the U.S. government had deciphered the last two above-detailed telegrams (numbers 3 and 4).

Exactly what sort of determination did the Americans make on the basis of these two cables?

One can imagine that the U.S. government must have believed that the Philippines was certainly going to be one of Japan's targets for attack since Tokyo was so keen to learn about the Philippine Army's defensive installations and also sought detailed information about the numbers of troops deployed to them. Furthermore, members Japan's diplomatic corps in the Philippines were carrying out a wide variety of reconnaissance missions, in accordance with Tokyo's instructions, and sending back reports about them.

(5)
From: The Minister for Foreign Affairs, Tokyo
To: The Embassy in Manila (for Secretary Yuki)
5 November 1941

(Secret Purple)

The Navy General Staff wishes an investigation of a list of items. Please adopt the most appropriate measures to investigate thoroughly before reporting.

The items to be investigated are as follows:

i. The situation at the army's air bases
ii. The types of aircraft at each airport and their numbers
iii. The equipment used to kit out warships and landing troops
iv. Miscellaneous equipment and installations, their state of development or deployment

(The U.S. Navy deciphered this cable on 13 November 1941)

(6)
From: The Envoy to Manila
To: The Minister for Foreign Affairs, Tokyo
6 November 1941

Cable #735 (Secret Purple)
  Cable of the Highest Importance concerning corrections to my cable #743
  The following report is a compilation of information reported by two undercover agents:

1. There are 50 U.S. Army officers and 1,200 Philippine Army officers and men stationed at Bugallon in Pangasinan Province. Furthermore, there are 8 light-weight tanks, and 8 anti-aircraft guns (which sit upon fixed mounts). And there are many American artillery troops in the coconut palm covered hills between Santa Cruz and Lingayen.

2. At Iba in Zambales province, there are 10 twin-prop light bombers, 190 P-40 Warhawk fighter aircraft (one undercover agent had previously reported that there were 60 of these aircraft, but recently their numbers have increased), as well as 400 American air troops and officers.
    A division of Philippine troops, 15,000 strong, is stationed at San Marcelino. Within this division there are 3 regiments of foot soldiers, 3 field artillery companies, and 3 armored mobile artillery companies. In addition, it is possible that there are many tank reinforcements. They have recently started the construction of a new air base at this site.
    Apart from this, a further 320 Philippine troops are stationed at Botolan.

3. At present, on the either side of the road that leads from Tarlac to Santa Ignacia (Hwy #84), there are three sites where they are building barracks capable of housing 500, 1,000, and 1,500 troops respectively.
    Additionally, at the site of a new airfield 5 kilometers south of Tarlac, they have already completed the work of making the ground level.
    The military road from Camp O'Donnell in Capas to Botolan, Zambales is more or less finished now. We discovered that troops have been camouflaging it recently.

4. 200 lightweight tanks were recently unloaded at Fort Stotsenberg in Pampanga.

(The U.S. Army deciphered this cable on 15 November 1941)

It took eight days to decipher cable (5) and nine days to crack cable (6). The rate at which these cables were deciphered was relatively short to average.

On the basis of these two deciphered cables, it can be surmised that the High Command of the U.S. Armed Forces must certainly have devoted a great deal of time in the middle of November to careful research about the targets Japan would attack.

39. Japanese Secret Code Before the War

(7)
From: The Envoy to Manila
To: The Minister for Foreign Affairs, Tokyo
13 November 1941

Cable #757 (Secret Purple)

1. The heavy cruiser that I reported in my cable #753 is the American ship *Portland*.
2. In the morning on the 13th, the British destroyer *Guardian* entered port.
3. Of the 9 submarines reported in my cable #742, I can now confirm that there are as many as 8 vessels (or perhaps as few as 4 vessels) of the 129-class. These submarines all entered port recently, but the precise date and time of their entry is unclear.

(The U.S. Navy deciphered this cable on 13 November 1941)

It is difficult not to attach any importance to the fact that this cable (7) was deciphered the very day it was sent. I am afraid that no coded telegram from any country is decoded on the very day it is sent. Even if several thousand decoding personnel were mobilized, it would be very difficult to attain such a high degree of efficiency. Furthermore, from a practical standpoint, this sort of telegram would certainly go through a relatively high-level cipher before being sent. It definitely would not have received light coding before it was sent off.

In short, when we consider that 69 of these intelligence reports and instructions were deciphered within roughly a week of being sent, the idea that the U.S. government had poured all of its resources into gathering intelligence on the South becomes highly credible. They achieved such great success in this area because they added staff to deal with this work, deployed excellent decoding personnel, dispatched undercover agents, had photographs taken of secret code books, and more.

Now please allow me to further explore the communications situation with respect to Hawaii.

From 1 August to 8 December 1941, they deciphered a mere eight telegrams. Of those deciphered cables, five were instructions sent from Tokyo while only three were reports sent from Honolulu. Furthermore, the time required to decipher those cables generally ranged from 15 to 19 days. Of those cables, five were not deciphered until after December 5.

In light of this, one may conclude that the U.S. was not adequately prepared to defend itself against a surprise attack on Hawaii by Japan. The average amount of time the Americans needed to decipher the telegrams sent between Tokyo and Honolulu (almost all of which took 16 to 19 days to crack) was three times longer than was required to crack Tokyo's communications with the South. This clearly demonstrates that while the U.S. did take note of the cable transmissions to and from Hawaii, it did not attach a great deal of importance to them.

In fact, reports concerning naval vessels sent from Honolulu were ten a penny because each and every other country was sending such cables. Thus, I'm afraid that no one who had noticed those three cable reports about naval vessels would have been likely to believe that Japan was on the verge of attacking Pearl Harbor. While I was watching over Pearl Harbor like a hawk at that time, I never noticed anything out of the ordinary about the movements of the U.S. fleet.

Then again, according to documents that the Americans have published, the U.S. government gave the following order to its air troops on Midway and Wake Island near the end of November of that year: "If you happen to spot a Japanese submarine, you have the authorization to sink it."

Despite this, I'm afraid that the Americans never imagined that Japan would actually carry out a risky surprise attack at Pearl Harbor.

The FBI agents from the Honolulu bureau seized an ordinary cipher book and what the Americans called a "PA-K2" cipher book from our cryptographer after they stormed into the Japanese Consulate-General on the day that war broke out. By making use of this PA-K2 code book between the day the war began and 12 December, they were able to decipher nine telegrams in total. However, as the war had already started, this was of no real use.

According to FBI Bureau Chief Shivers in *The FBI Story*, he was filled with regret, bitterness, and rage because he had not uncovered Morimura's true identity in time. And yet I met with considerable difficulties as a result of those telegrams. I had to undergo very serious interrogations from the FBI while I was detained. "Were you the one who sent off all those telegrams?" they asked me over and over. "I don't know," I responded, time and again. In the end, they had no choice but to let me go.

In fact, almost all of the military intelligence reports sent from Hawaii had been drafted by me. I arrived in Honolulu in March to take up my post. From August (when the situation took a turn for the worse and continued to worsen by the day) to the start of the war on 8 December (129 days in total) I personally dispatched no fewer than 50 cables. Of those 50 cables, only three were deciphered.

From this it is clear that the Americans spent considerably more time deciphering cables from Japan's diplomatic missions in Manila and Batavia than they spent on those sent from Hawaii. Furthermore, through various means, they were definitely able to compile a significant number of military intelligence reports. On the basis of the facts these contained, the U.S. authorities probably concluded that Japan was going to start the fires of war by attacking and invading the South.

Once the U.S. had made such a determination, they began to gather the Pacific Fleet in Hawaii in an attempt to keep any potential losses to an absolute minimum. At the same time, they strengthened their defenses at Midway

39. Japanese Secret Code Before the War

Island, Wake Island, and the other advance bases, keeping watch on Japanese activity as it unfolded while waiting for the moment the first battle would commence.

If the Americans had actually determined that Japan was about to attack Pearl Harbor, they certainly would not have left the bulk of their fleet defenseless and exposed to the enemy there, no matter how careless they might have been. At this point it is abundantly clear that there is no basis to the argument used by those gossips who say that President Roosevelt deliberately left a few decrepit capital ships in Pearl Harbor as bait to reel in the Japanese and thereby incite the populace.

During the first six months that followed the start of the war, America had no choice but to look on, eyes agog, as control over the Pacific was effectively assumed by Japan. This clearly demonstrates that the U.S. was then in a disadvantageous position. And from this it can be determined that when the U.S. government was in the process of considering the question of a Japanese attack on Pearl Harbor, it made an error in judgment of the most deadly proportions.

In other words, because they did not detect that nearly every secret cable that they transmitted was being deciphered by the Americans, Japan's diplomatic missions in the South helped to create the conditions that led the Americans to make an error in judgment. All of which facilitated the success of Japan's surprise attack at Pearl Harbor.

In summary: Although the strategic thinkers within the U.S. Navy had long since determined that Japan was likely to make a surprise attack against Pearl Harbor, the argument that Hawaii was going to be attacked became less and less compelling. This happened because Japan was so obviously intent upon attacking the South and because the intelligence information coming from deciphered cables was making this increasingly clear. Consequently, they quite naturally began to relax their state of readiness. I'm afraid that this is what people tend to do when they have too many things on the go!

Having said all of this, I don't think it is too difficult to understand the meaning of Secretary of State Hull's smile.

In order to be able to clearly understand an issue, you ought to analyze it from various points of view. I am simply presenting my own views here and I speak without having access to any restricted intelligence reports about this matter.

In what follows, please allow me to return to my own story so that I can discuss my memories of some miserable times I lived through.

40

Walking Away

A total of 110 battles were fought in the air and at sea during the 16-month period that began with the first naval battle for the Solomon Islands (8 August 1942) and ended with the sixth air battle for control of the seas around Bougainville Island (3 December 1943). A life-or-death struggle was underway in the Solomon Islands region at that time and it brought both victory and defeat to our forces. This struggle eventually became a brutal war of attrition that sent huge numbers of our navy's most outstanding pilots, and precious extremely well-maintained aircraft, to the bottom of the seas around the Solomon Islands. The situation then degenerated to such an extent that it was no longer possible to replenish our forces. In fact, Japan was compelled to abandon its outermost territories by the end of 1943 because the situation was steadily worsening. At the start of 1944, U.S. forces began the aerial bombardment of Japan's "inner defensive perimeter" and our position was further degraded.

A long series of dispatches containing bad news had arrived one after the other during the period between the Doolittle Raid on 17 February 1942 (a bombing attack on one of Japan's Home Islands) and Commander Koga's death in action at Davao on 31 March 1944. By then, however, the public had already begun to sense that there was something prophetic about these inauspicious events.

During the previous year (1943), Japanese forces on Attu Island were completely wiped out on 19 May. On 8 August, Italy had announced its unconditional surrender. On 25 November, all of our troops on Tarawa and Makin Islands were slaughtered. Even more notable, however, were the deaths of Yamamoto and Koga (both of whom were commanders of the Combined Fleet) within a single year's time. These various incidents plainly revealed that combat on the frontlines had reached the level of absolute cruelty. A feeling of hopelessness then began to spread right across the Imperial Japanese Navy.

At the start of June, a majority of the enemy's naval vessels began to appear in the zone around Saipan Island. Judging from the reports provided by our reconnaissance aircraft, which we recorded on nautical charts, the U.S.

40. Walking Away

Navy now possessed a large and aggressive fleet. Units comprised of its battleships and aircraft carriers were everywhere to be seen.

At the time, I was responsible for making estimates of the enemy's strength on the basis of sightings that provided us with dates, times, and positions. I used a nautical chart, a compass, and a ruler to plot my measurements while I attempted to determine the actual strength of the enemy's forces. Unfortunately, because I could no longer get hold of sufficient intelligence reports, I often lacked one or two key pieces of information that would shore up my estimates. Thus, I began to feel both worried and uneasy.

As our war effort was reaching this stage, the accuracy of the reconnaissance work done by the scouts on each vessel was similarly in decline. They would very often mistake a destroyer for a battleship and then send in a cable with that information. Sometimes they would lose track of an enemy vessel, perhaps the intense flashes of light during a night attack had caused their vision to become blurry, and yet they would immediately send in a cable with the news that an enemy vessel had been "hit with a large explosion and sunk."

Ever since the outbreak of air and sea battles around Bougainville Island during the previous year, such occurrences had become increasingly obvious. Consequently, the battle results reported from combat zones by our own troops could not be fully trusted. Nevertheless, the Communications Office at the Imperial General Headquarters would take the reports sent in by the troops in battle zones as the basis for its own boastful reports. They basically had no qualms about making such reports part of their intelligence reporting. Consequently, our Bureau was often at loggerheads with the Communications Office about the reporting of exaggerated battle results.

However, this was how the Communications Office responded to us:

> Those of us here in the rearguard have no reason to complain about that which concerns the officers and men on the frontlines, who risk their lives to get results in battle. Furthermore, you don't have any evidence whatsoever to demonstrate that these battle results aren't accurate.

As soon as this "emotional" argument was employed by way of rebuttal, there was nothing left for us to do except remain silent. However, they then took this matter even further by commenting on me and on my work duties: "A guy like you, someone who handles U.S. intelligence reports, can fall prey to the aims of American propaganda and become 'Americanized' without realizing it."

In the end, I was removed from my intelligence reporting duties and ordered to take up the job of investigating U.S. economic power. By that time, however, I didn't feel that there was any point in investigating the production levels of American iron, aluminum and the like with outdated materials. Consequently, because I could not bear to be in the position of merely observing the war from a comfortable post, I submitted my resignation. Although my resignation was not accepted, I left the Navy General Staff that day.

As absolute obedience was so greatly emphasized in our military, regular servicemen believed that an officer ought to die for his king even when he did not behave like a monarch. Yet because I was a retired serviceman, and because I had adopted the habits of an undercover agent and had been thoroughly tainted by them, I was ready to walk away as soon as the monarch stopped behaving like one. After leaving the Navy General Staff, I lived in seclusion at home for a time.

The situation grew progressively worse from 1944 onwards. On 7 July all of the troops defending Saipan Island chose death to surrender and thus one corner of our "inner defensive perimeter" was smashed. The entire nation was utterly astonished by this. Then, on 17 July, Prime Minister Tojo's entire cabinet was forced to resign.

The new government formed immediately afterwards was led by General Kuniaki Koiso. Admiral Mitsumasa Yonai took a ministerial position within its coalition cabinet. The new cabinet wished to replace the previous plans for "Victory" with emergency measures aimed at saving Japan's armed forces from the situation they were in. They hoped to "redeem the military from its steady decline, create new and more favorable conditions, and seize the opportunity to hold peace talks." However, in the aftermath of air and sea battles fought across the Philippine Sea and off Formosa's coasts during which the Imperial Japanese Navy had suffered disastrous defeats, the situation was worsening far too quickly to allow this.

Nevertheless, the reports from the Imperial General Headquarters still continued to announce "glorious results from the frontlines." In the following section, I would like to present the battle results issued by the Imperial General HQ at that time along with the losses that were actually suffered by the enemy's forces:

> General HQ announces that on successive nights beginning 12 October, our troops fiercely attacked the enemy's mobile forces off eastern Formosa and eastern Luzon, causing the loss of more than half the enemy's strength and forcing their retreat. In total, the victories in battle earned by our forces were as follows:
> 1.
> Vessels sunk: 11 Aircraft Carriers, 2 Battleships, 1 Cruiser or Destroyer.
> Vessels damaged: 8 Aircraft Carriers, 2 Battleships, 1 Cruiser or Destroyer, 13 vessels of indeterminate type. Of these damaged vessels, 12 caught fire after being struck.
> 2.
> The losses in battle suffered by our forces were:
> 312 aircraft that did not return to base.
> This battle has been named "The Air battle for control of Formosa's seas."

And yet, according to an investigation conducted after the war, two badly damaged cruisers were the only losses actually suffered by the enemy during this battle. They incurred no other losses.

There didn't seem to be any way of disputing the Imperial-edict-like report of the sinking or damaging of 50 enemy vessels at that time, even though there were in fact only two vessels involved. Looking at this matter today, it truly seems like a huge farce. Oh my! How on earth did this come to pass?

I can recall Prime Minister Kuniaki Koiso ranting "Victory lies just before us!" around that time, which made the uneasy public wildly happy. Meanwhile, its own reports about the frontlines had made the navy drunk with glee at the thought of victory.

Yet on 17 October, the day after the glorious results of the "Air battle for control of Formosa's seas" were announced, our reconnaissance planes discovered four separate enemy mobile force units off Formosa's east coast and in the seas to the east of the Philippines.

Some officers at the Combined Fleet and at General HQ then began to have their doubts about the battle results from the "Air battle for control of Formosa's seas." Thus, Captain Fukada and Captain Suzuki (the former a senior staff officer from the Combined Fleet, the latter a staff officer from General HQ) were dispatched posthaste to investigate the materials Lieutenant-Commander Tanaka had used to report the results of that battle. They concluded that only four enemy aircraft carriers had been damaged, if one made the most generous interpretation of the available evidence.[1]

To this day I firmly believe that Japan met with a crushing defeat in the Pacific War precisely because of erroneous reporting of this sort.

Following immediately upon this, on 25 October, Japan caused an uproar by sending *kamikaze* attack aircraft into action. These aircraft attempted to stop the advance of the enemy's mobile units by imploding against them during sea and air combat around the Philippines.[2]

The fighting during the subsequent battle, the Battle of Leyte Gulf, was extraordinarily fierce and both sides mobilized the bulk of their armaments and troops. Our side's losses were absolutely disastrous in the end. In truth, Japan's navy was utterly destroyed.

At the end of that campaign, the enemy merely needed to wait for a moment before knocking down the door and forcing Japan to reveal her nakedness. Saipan became a base for American B-29 "Superfortress" bombers, which were mustered in a calm and orderly fashion. And then many columns of such aircraft, numbering more than 100, carried out the first large-scale bombing of Tokyo on 24 November.

When that city's inhabitants first saw those silver wings dazzling in the glare of the searchlights, they quite simply became panic-stricken. Since they were panic-stricken, and because the enemy was putting on such a show of force, they were cowed into submission. Even so, they could not have imagined that those silver wings were just about to turn our Imperial Capital into a demonic sea of flames.

Soon after the new year (1945) was underway, metropolitan Japan found itself under attack by enemy aircraft on an almost daily basis. A quarter of the city of Tokyo went up in an enormous, raging fire. Nearly 300,000 buildings were razed and 250,000 citizens were killed or injured. Countless numbers of people were left homeless with nowhere to go to except air-raid shelters because so many buildings were burned down.

As panic about the lack of foodstuffs gradually grew ever more serious, the population was forced to scatter. Some heads of families, obliged to look on while their sons and daughters went away on their own, felt as if their hearts were being ripped out of their chests. People everywhere were living in a state of constant anxiety. Nevertheless, despite having to doggedly endure their lot, the people were also expected to respond to appeals to join the so-called "Decisive Battle for the Mainland."[3]

However, only a few housewives accepted the idea of going through air defense drills or taking up bamboo gun training. Meanwhile, most intellectuals were working to heighten the anti-war mood. And then there were the profiteers, who were taking advantage of the shortage of material goods to do a roaring trade on the black market.

I was working for an aircraft manufacturing company by this time. I had reasoned that I might as well take on a low-level job to help to produce more aircraft. Although I was fully aware by then that raising aircraft production would be of no real consequence, I wanted to do whatever I could for the nation. I was still willing to do anything, even risk my life, for the cause. By so doing, I hoped to dispel the unhappiness that I felt deep within me. Every day, from early morning until late at night, I worked alongside several thousand women and children and shared their joys and sorrows. We were all repaying our country.

Businessmen were not of the same outlook, though. They entered into agreements with the military and the government to buy up rationed goods, which they subsequently sold on the black market at a huge profit. Before long, the watchwords that the government leaders shouted out at the top of their lungs did not have any effect since they no longer had the confidence of the people. The reasons for this were twofold: the chaotic state of the nation's economy and their perverse tendency to say one thing and do another. Consequently, Japan found itself slowly wading into the quagmire of defeat.

One day around this time, I was aboard a tramcar when I heard two female students having a discussion:

> "I could eat an entire bowl of rice porridge with vegetables. And I really wish I could eat some buttery bread. I'd eat as much of that as I could."
>
> "Hmm, that's … so good to eat. It's my very favorite too."

40. Walking Away

I never noticed whatever it was the two of them were speaking about before or after this discussion. Yet it was obvious that food was something that they longed for as soon as they began to talk about it, because their voices were so very loud. This showed quite clearly that even young girls had missed out on the important things that they ought to have had in their lives.

Once further aerial bombing was underway at the beginning of May, Tokyo was transformed into a giant ruin that stretched out as far as the eye could see. A putrid stench floated in the air everywhere you went. Weak light came from small houses that sat alongside the remnants of scorched trees and this gave you a feeling of desolation that is difficult to explain.

After the two atomic bombs were dropped, the Soviets entered the war.[4] And this meant the only path that would have allowed Japan to sue for peace had been blocked off.[5] As a result, Japan was forced to surrender unconditionally. On 15 August the Emperor announced an "armistice" during a broadcast to the entire nation. The Pacific War's final curtain had come down.

41

On the Run

The war finally ended after more than 3,700,000 Japanese citizens had been killed on various battle fronts. Things were in a state of total disarray after the war's end. Food, clothing, and accommodation were all in very short supply because American bombs had razed the majority of Japan's buildings. As a result, people found themselves running around in circles without really knowing what to do.

In the midst of all the chaos, the only thing that was still working normally was the railway system. City dwellers were fortunate to be able to make use of it. Some of those who used it were demobilized troops, others used it to return from the areas they had scattered off to, there were also those who used it to move away from Tokyo, and those who used it to transport foodstuffs.

At that time, more than anything else, people wanted to find a place to live, a way of making a living, and sufficient food to live on. As for the future, that was not even a consideration. (At any rate, people had no illusions as far as that was concerned.) For a while, nearly everyone seemed to be closely observing social changes as they unfolded before taking any decisions. I myself was one of their number. When I realized that I needed to make it easier to see for myself how things were developing, I began preparing to send my wife back to our village so that I would be left without a household to manage.

Tokyo was rife with rumors at that time. Once it became widely known that Chinese military police were to be garrisoned in the Suginami district where we lived, local authorities began to go up and down the streets exhorting women to cut their hair short. Soon after that, the news arrived that a violent incident involving the "Three Countries" (i.e., the three powers of the Potsdam Declaration: USA, Great Britain, China) and China's communists had occurred.[1] Consequently, city dwellers were becoming increasingly anxious.

Yet as far as I was concerned, those were the least of my worries. My biggest fear was that they were going to punish war criminals, in accordance with the Potsdam Declaration, once troops from the United Nations were stationed in Japan. I realized that this would be most unfavorable for me.

41. On the Run

Troops from the countries that had emerged victorious from the war would be riding high on the emotion of their victory and I did not know what they would be capable of. More importantly, it was unclear whether or not they would decide to preserve the existing Japanese state. If they did, to what degree would it be maintained? Nor was the extent to which they would actually punish war criminals clear to me. In short, I felt that I was going to be given some sort of punishment.

My wife agreed to return to our village to live with our child. She left Tokyo three days after the war ended to return to our family village in Shikoku, while cradling our not yet 6-month-old daughter (who held a milk bottle in her mouth) aboard a train that was overflowing with demobilized troops.

My wife and I were married in 1943, right in the middle of the most intense period of the war. Not long after we were married, the bombing of Tokyo by U.S. forces began. Our daughter was born amidst a storm of incendiary bombing.

My wife wished to remain with her husband in Tokyo in spite of the situation there; she was determined that we should share life or death together. As a result, she had at times sought cover in air-raid shelters with our baby. At other times she had carried her on the street when buying food. In the process, my wife had a taste of extreme hardship. She had been willing to do her utmost to fulfill her duty as a citizen in the "Decisive Battle for the Mainland," even if that meant climbing through the mountains or lying low in the countryside. To that end, she had even saved a pint of salt for a long period of future use.

Now she was leaving me. While I was seeing her off at Tokyo Station, for some reason that I cannot explain, I felt that this was to be our final goodbye and I was heartbroken...

Yet after that, I felt as if I had finally become much lighter. Even though they were going without me, I knew that they were on their way to a place where they would find it possible to live and that was a great consolation. When night arrived after my wife had gone away, I was all on my own in our home. The first question that I was faced with was how to make a living. Even though I had already experienced a life of poverty, my situation at that point was such that I did not have any income whatsoever. So how was I going to live? This truly was the most bothersome problem that I was facing.

I was lying down in a room, surrounded by mosquito netting, thinking day and night about this for an entire week. Nevertheless, I failed to come up with a good plan. Get a job? That would expose my true identity. Start up a business? I did not have any capital. Furthermore, I lacked any sort of skill that would allow me to earn any money. Really and truly, I was at the end of my rope.

I thought it all over. And then I thought it over again. There really was just one path for me to take and that was to get into the black market.

"Now that the war is over, I am sure that the foodstuffs requisitioned by the military need to be disposed of," I reasoned. "I might somehow be able to buy those foodstuffs and then sell them. That is illegal, but there really isn't anything immoral about it."

Sure enough, just as I had imagined, food products of all kinds were being kept in the Agricultural Co-operative Society's management zone in Chiba Prefecture.

During the war, my wife and I knew nothing whatsoever about the black market. Now, I simply had to get into it. Consequently, one week after the end of hostilities, I withdrew ¥20,000 from my savings account and I borrowed ¥40,000 from my paternal uncle. Using this as investment capital, I bought white rice and peanuts and I transported those goods back home with a truck I had hired on the black market.

Back inside my home I stacked more than a hundred sacks of rice and peanuts, I even piled them up on the floor in the living room. Yet once I had brought the goods in, I still did not know how I was going to sell them. All I could do was leave them sealed in their sacks for quite a few days.

It was right at this time that more and more demobilized servicemen began appearing on the streets. All of them were looking around everywhere for a way to make some money. Some of them were navy veterans wearing the light clothing designed to prevent heatstroke and that white hat with the black line all the way around it. Then there were the soldiers, each of whom wore a blanket over his back. All of them were willing to go out and sell foodstuffs for me. They took the goods to a place near the Shinjuku train station and sold them in a trice.

From then on, the back and forth of buying and selling was constant. I made money and they profited too. I was soon running around all over the place thinking of other ways I could get foodstuffs into Tokyo because I could not get enough of a good thing. After the supply of those foods began to dwindle I moved on to selling radishes and green vegetables, which also proved to be profitable. I quickly became one of the very few black-market businessmen in the vicinity. There were piles of foodstuffs, car tires, tools, and many other goods in my home.

I also went running off to the Atsugi Air Base, which was very far from Tokyo, and I got hold of the petrol that the American troops didn't want (which had originally belonged to the Japanese military). I shipped it back to Tokyo without having paid a penny for it. At that time, a barrel of petrol sold for ¥10,000 on the black market in Tokyo. After I had been doing business on the black market for just four months, ¥1,000,000 filled my pockets.

When that year was nearing its end, the allied countries solemnly announced a list of wanted war criminals. At the top of the list were politicians, followed closely by members of the military. What's more, a large number of them had already been arrested.

Then, from the Navy General Staff side of things, I got wind of the fact that all personnel who had worked on American intelligence in Section 5 were going to be put on trial. The charges were for the interrogation and maltreatment of POWs in a temporary holding site. This had come about after the released POWs had provided testimony, which was then investigated.

As I had gone to the place in question many times to interrogate POWs myself, I decided to flee. I reasoned that I had already gone through enough hardship at the Triangle T Ranch in America and I was determined not to go through that sort of suffering again on Japanese soil. Despite the fact that I had never mistreated any of the POWs during the interrogations I conducted, the Pearl Harbor question would eventually be investigated and the truth revealed. When that time came, I was certain that I would suffer their retribution.

Consequently, I thought over my situation. How could I find myself in Japan and yet be stupid enough to allow them to catch me? "All right then, if they're any good, let's see if they can catch me!" I said to myself after deciding I would live in hiding.

I was undaunted at this prospect. In any case, I didn't lack funds and it made no difference to me whether I went up into the hills or out into the open country. I decided I would hide myself hither and yon and keep on lying low. I quickly returned all our borrowed furniture and other household items to those I had borrowed them from and then I gave the keys to my home back to the landlord. At that point, I found that I had been utterly transformed. I was now the commanding officer of an army without any troops.

I didn't dare return to my village, of course, because I had no idea when I would be caught up in the dragnet wielded by the military police there. For the time being, there was nothing for left me to do except wander aimlessly like a drifter. I had to keep a careful eye out for the MPs (the U.S. military police), and perhaps the Japanese Military Police as well. Changes of name and disguises were my specialty, but things here were not the same as they were abroad. Since everyone here was Japanese, I could relax and boldly wander about like a tramp.

In the areas near Tokyo Station, quite a few rowdy, spoiled-rotten American troops were on the scene. So, I brought a somewhat old camera of mine there and sold it for a high price to an American flight sergeant who had just arrived from the South that very day.

After that, no matter where I went, the extremely sad things that I saw and heard all around me were enough to leave me speechless. Yet after I remembered that Japan had been defeated in the war, and that I was now a fugitive, all that was left for me to do was to hold my temper and get aboard a train that was leaving the capital.

I disembarked at Shizuoka. I had not done so because I had friends or family there, but for quite the opposite reason. I was simply doing my utmost to find a place to wander where I knew absolutely no one. At that very moment, I could not help but let out a sigh while I thought about my cussed lot in life. Just when exactly was I going to become a free man? And why had all the bad luck in the world landed on me?

In that place, you only had to look around you to see the omnipresent scars of war. The people's faces looked old, darkened, and frail. Only their eyes had a hint of light in them. The sight of them looking around everywhere for food was enough to make anyone sad. Was there any way that a place such as this could harbor a drifter?

I staggered out of the railway station and began to wander the streets aimlessly until I found myself on a small, quiet lane. Initially, I had hoped to find a guesthouse where I could rest my feet. However, I soon realized that someone like me, a bachelor without any worldly possessions, would be regarded with great suspicion. I thus waited until dark and then, with some difficulty, I finally found a small inn to stop at.

Yet it was not a place I could stay at for any length of time. It was dangerous for me to stay anywhere for very long. There could be no doubt that the occupying forces had already begun to make use of the Japanese Military Police's investigative networks. As Japan's police were the best-equipped in the world, all the occupying powers needed to do was to give the order and they would have ferreted me out even if I had been hiding inside a hollowed-out log.

The possibility that I would be discovered was with me at all times. When fugitives are thinking about where to hide, they generally choose to work as a miner, a worker, or a temporary worker. Thus, they make use of their professional abilities after fleeing somewhere. I was not able to do any of those jobs, though. What's more, having colleagues and supervisors was a part of such jobs and that certainly was not safe for someone like me.

Well, what was I to do? As I squatted in that dreary little inn, I began to think this over. It was then that I suddenly came up with the idea of becoming a monk and living in seclusion. I resolved to use my situation as on opportunity to reflect on all of my past behavior and deeds, meditate, and do some soul searching to find closure to the difficult times that I'd had in life.

My youth had coincided with a militaristic era. Consequently, I was naturally inclined to feeling either kindness or hatred. I was either blindly hating the enemy or vainly bewailing the inconstancy of others. Yet despite the fact that I knew a great many things, I did not possess the ability to judge right from wrong. Nor did I meditate or engage in self-reflection in my free time.

41. On the Run

Now that the war had ended, I began to think calmly. What exactly was the point of that "holy war" in which all the members of our nation had given of themselves unstintingly, some even sacrificing their own blood? Were the positions advocated by the victors truly correct? Were the defeated to be blamed for taking the road that they chose to travel along? My 35-year-old self could not yet provide any clear answers to these questions.

Japanese society might consider me a lackey to those who had started the war, but it never was my intention to make myself useful to them. However, little by little, the cruel and merciless nature of war had compelled me to take that path.

A lot of people in Shizuoka venerated Ryūtaku-ji, the ancient monastery founded by a Buddhist monk named Hakuin Ekaku.[2] So, I took up my religious calling at a certain Buddhist temple and then I became a wandering monk. I swept temples and monasteries clean every day, meditated, begged for alms, and cut firewood. Apart from that, I visited monks in various localities to learn from them.

The following is a poem I wrote at that time:

> The old pine trees at Ryusawa Mountain are graceful and tall
> Rinzai meditation, unhurried and enduring
> Can the Regent hear the sound of one hand clapping?
> An old monk gives a shout and calm fills the skies

By this time, I was already beginning to turn away from a Kumagai Naozane–like mindset and becoming open to following Kamo no Chōmei's example of living a life of solitude in order to fulfill my desire to study and learn.[3]

Despite this, I was at the same time suddenly impatient to see my wife in our old village. I began to feel an urgent need to return home and see her again.

42

The Family Village

    The world outside was beset by food shortages, high prices, high unemployment, difficult living conditions, the problems that emerged from the need to build anew, and the great clamor that went along with it all. Monastic life was completely detached from the burdens of those affairs. Life as a monk was calm and peaceful, rather like going swimming on a warm and sunny spring day.

    If there wasn't enough, there wasn't enough. If there was any left over, it was given to charity. There was no corruption, nor any asking for more. Giving yourself over completely to this life was like freeing yourself to follow the natural order that reigns between heaven and earth. Although I was not immediately able to rid myself of all earthly desires, I had been attracted to Buddhism from the time I was a child. Thus, I gave myself over to this life relatively easily and in a calm frame of mind.

    While living alongside my monastic brothers, I discovered something quite uncanny about them. At times they were fierce and indomitable, in the style of Hōjō Tokimune. Yet at other times they were as devout and pious as one can be when one prays to the Buddha.[1] So I seemed to find myself in the midst of a violent storm at times, while at other times life was as peaceful and gentle as a breeze on a spring day. This was actually quite difficult to grasp.

    I enjoyed the monastic life. On a whim, the monks might decide that we should focus all our vital energy and sit up through the night to enter a state of deep meditation. At other times we would do ordinary activities that were of more general interest, like going on an outing and having fun for an entire day.

    One warm and bright spring day, we were sweeping the temple when one of my monastic brothers put his broom aside. "What is your lay-Buddhist name anyway?" he asked me.

    Since I did not have a dharma name upon arriving there, everyone called me "the lay-Buddhist."[2] In fact, that's all I had ever been called since taking up this life. I subsequently gave the matter some serious thought. The "boat" character seemed to be the most suitable to use for my lay-Buddhist

42. The Family Village

name, because I had been in the navy. However, it then occurred to me that Yagū Munetoshi (the master swordsman of the Sengoku period), Tesshū (the famous samurai from the late Tokugawa period), and the expert marksman Dorobune were among those who had used the "boat" (舟) character in their names.[3]

Since each of those men was beyond compare, I felt somewhat hesitant about my idea. But in the end, I decided to adopt that character and the jasper character from the pseudonym that my father used when writing haiku poetry. Ishiba (溪碧) was his pen name. And so, I became known as the lay-Buddhist Hekishū (碧舟).

"What would you say if I were to be known as lay-Buddhist Hekishū?"

"Hekishū," my monastic brother replied casually. "That's a good name!"

I believe that names are merely symbols. Taro is a good name, Jiro is a good one too. Anyone can be called by any name. I chose the name Hekishū because jasper is a moss that has been slowly transformed into stone over a very long period of time. If you were to make a boat out of jasper, it would sink to the sea bottom and never surface again. Naturally, my monastic brother had no way of understanding the true significance of this name.

That monk, who was already 40 years old or so, had been a practicing Buddhist in various locales for nearly 30 years. Since he had never married, and because he was unsuitable for the post of abbot, he contented himself with his ethereal, transient life. Despite the fact that he was very learned, and a deeply moral man, he was quite odd.

He was apparently the son of a Kyoto teahouse owner. His mother was a deeply devout Buddhist who urged him to his calling. "All of the members of our family will be saved if you become an abbot," she said to him repeatedly. So, he shaved his head and became a monk when he was 13. He subsequently became a wandering monk and roamed the entire country, stopping at temples in each and every district.

He did not make a habit of nitpicking with me, even though he was better-versed in the faith than I was. At times, he would even bring out some of the pungent wine that he kept hidden on the other side of the mountain and the two of us would sit facing one another under the light of the moon and continue drinking until the night fell silent. As I had become a monk on my own initiative without having been formally initiated, and since I had not trained as a monk from a young age, I would not be reprimanded as long as I did not violate any of the important rules of the temple.

Whenever my monastic brother got drunk, he would always repeat the same tale:

> In the autumn when I was 13, I ran away because I couldn't stand life in the monastery any longer. Run… Run… Run… I ran until I reached Yamashina. By then, I was so hungry that I couldn't go any further. So, I sat next to the trunk of a pine tree and

went into a deep meditation. A pinecone from one of the higher branches of the tree fell down just then. "Dut," it hit my head with light thud. And then a bird that was sitting on the pine tree suddenly called out, "Gwaah" …

And all of a sudden I came to an understanding that has stayed with me. When I think about it now, it was only a small insight. But actually, there is great enlightenment too! Do you understand? Ha, ha, ha.

When he had stopped laughing, he would continue:

You know Tosa, at Cape Ashiguri, don't you? Right, right, it's just over there. I built a grass temple there and I lived in it for around three years. I also preached Zen Buddhism to the locals every day. One day, a local bigwig came by with some liquor. "Come and have a drink, beggar monk," he said to me, more or less. So, I became enraged and we came to blows. I twisted that guy's arm and pushed him down, right against the ground. From then on, the two of us got along much better.

That day, I drank four pints of spirits all on my own. After that… My lay-Buddhist friend, can you guess what happened? I ran to the seaside to pull myself together and sat on the rocks, which were exposed since the tide had gone out. The water around me was up to my waist after a while, but I didn't even notice.

That was because I had reached a state of deep meditation! After the sun came up, the people on the beach mistakenly believed that I had been caught in the tidal waters, so they hurried here and hurried there to try and rescue me. But I didn't actually realize that any of these things were happening… And because of this, everyone said "That beggar monk is an extraordinary guy."

So, the women folk sent some food to me and they also mended my clothes. It caused quite a stir for a little while! Ha, ha, ha… Of course, Zen Buddhism became more popular there too.

His words went a very long way in helping me to purge myself of my vulgar habits, but the worries that kept raging in my mind were anything but forgotten.

In late autumn that year, I decided to pay a visit to a renowned monk at Tenru-ji.[4] So I set off with a book that I was going to offer as a gift. The streets of Kyoto, where the temple was located, had been spared from the rages of war and had not actually suffered any damage at all. The dazzling lights of the neon billboard signs there were mesmerizing, and material goods plentiful. Judging from their expressions, it appeared that the local people were quite content.

However, I was shocked by the very large numbers of foreign troops there. The reason the Americans had chosen not to bomb the city of Kyoto was so that they might live a life of pleasure there after they had begun their occupation of Japan. When I looked at their self-satisfied faces, I was simply filled with hatred. They had used every possible means to ensure that Japan would lose its will to fight, even going so far as to drop two atomic bombs on innocent civilians. However, they had preserved this seat of Japanese culture in order to escape charges of cultural destruction. How cunning that was! Nevertheless, I could not help but admit that their ruse was first-rate.

42. The Family Village

When I learned just how numerous the prostitutes selling themselves to the occupying army's troops were, and how the city depended almost entirely upon the sale of black-market goods to American troops to support itself, my anger became difficult to control. Yet there was little that I could do other than make my way to the temple at Sagano.

There the misty mountains and red autumn leaves have been the same throughout the ages. While absentmindedly crossing the Togetsu Bridge, I noticed that the fully red-colored mountains were being reflected by the crystal-clear river water. I glanced into the distance after walking across the bridge and I noticed a tall old cedar tree in the temple grounds, standing proudly amidst all the autumn colors.

Then, as I followed the path that led to the main gates, I saw the Imperial Mausoleum that stood on the right. While I looked over the Imperial burial grounds, I could not help but think about the Nanboku-chō period and the long years of war that the competing courts waged against each other.[5] All of that history had been wiped away indifferently by the passage of time.

The lion's den that I wanted to visit was on the left. Hanging by the gate was a scroll covered with the amazingly flamboyant calligraphy of the lay-Buddhist Tesshū. Once inside, I presented the book that had been recommended by my superiors, a tray of noodles, and a box of steamed bread rolls stuffed with red bean paste (all of which were regional specialties), along with my wish to be allowed to live alongside my fellow monks in their lion's den so that I might share in their difficult life.

By the end of that year, I had decided to return to my family village to get news of what was going on there. It was only half a day's journey from Kyoto to Matsuyama. To get there, I took one of the Kansai Steamship Company's ships across the inland sea and it reached our destination after nightfall.

I took a taxi from the docks and traveled along roads that were familiar to me, though they had been scarred by the flames of war. I finally got back to my family home in the middle of the night. I had planned to arrive at that hour in order to avoid being seen or heard by others.

There were two things that I was quite concerned about:

1. Whether or not the military police had already been to my home with the order for my arrest.
2. How my wife and child were doing.

After sending the taxi away, I went for a short walk before approaching the front door of my family home. I looked at my watch as I stretched out my arm to knock on the door. It was nearly midnight.

"Hi, Emi!"

At first, I spoke in a low voice and called out several times but there was no reply. I then looked all around me, but there was not a sound to be heard anywhere. So, I went around the house and knocked on two or three other doors. And then, it sounded as if someone was getting up inside.

"Who's there?"

I knew it was my wife's voice. As I had expected, she was staying in the single room at the back of the house.

"It's me, open up!"

"What? Is that really you?"

"Keep your voice down!"

It was as if I were a petty thief for a moment. Then, in the darkness, I could smell my wife's body odor. She had draped an old, worn-out silk kimono over her pajamas.

"It's my girl's daddy!"

She was surprised and happy, though her voice was somewhat hoarse. She held me tightly and sobbed audibly while her shoulders trembled. In the coldness of the night, I could feel that her shoulders had become very thin. I stood mute in the dark; words failed me.

I hadn't seen my daughter in a long time and she had grown so much I wouldn't have recognized her. Her formerly pale white cheeks looked ruddy now and she was sleeping soundly. A little while later, my mother (who had always had keen ears) came in from one of the main rooms. Our family was reunited at last.

My mother then told me that a police officer had been to visit two or three times while I was away. He had asked if there was any news of me. My family said that I was still living in Tokyo and provided him with my former address. Before leaving, the police officer told them that they were to make it known to the police right away if I returned. However, the police officer was very sympathetic in his approach.

Even though there was no way to establish exactly who had given him his orders, nor any way to find out what the charges against me were, there was no doubting the fact that I had become a criminal at large and that they were searching for me. I had long expected that this would prove to be the case. However, I was still unsure about the severity of the charges against me.

Of course, there was no way I could freely pay a visit to the GHQ (the general headquarters established by the allied forces) to make inquiries about turning myself in. Nor would it be practical to send someone else there to make inquiries for me. Among my fellow servicemen at that time, there were ruffians who habitually put the blame on others. There were also cowards who, for their own personal safety, refused to get involved in any affairs that involved others. Furthermore, there were some shifty toadies who would try to cozy up to the occupying troops by telling tales about other people. As a consequence of all of this, I decided that I still could not lower my guard. I had to stay on the run.

42. The Family Village

My wife went out to get me some liquor in the middle of the night and returned carrying a small bottle. She had apparently managed to persuade the tavern owner to provide her with a bottle, even though he felt somewhat dubious about doing so. Soon I could smell the sweet fragrance of freshly made rice and my heart was overcome with emotion because my wife was carefully preparing some food for me. Although it was simple, it was far tastier than the most exotic of delicacies. There wasn't anyone else in the entire world who could welcome me as sincerely or as passionately.

I left my family the next evening. Naturally, I still had no particular destination to get to. My mind was blank as I sat on a boat that sailed to the prefecture on the opposite shore. After I reached the Kunisaki Peninsula, I began visiting ancient monasteries and praying at stone Buddha sites. Just as before, I continued to live as a wanderer.

During this period, I made several furtive visits to Tokyo where I made some inquiries here and there to get the latest news. Since the rebuilding of Tokyo was underway by then, I would either put up a street stall to sell ice cubes or simply stand in the bustling streets of Tokyo's Ginza district selling flavored ice sticks. Bit by bit, people were slowly rebuilding our homeland. Wooden houses were put up where the air-raid shelters had been during the war and lights could be seen shining inside them. Meanwhile, the shops that lined the streets had opened for business.

By that time, several of the most wanted war criminals who had been condemned to die had suffered the punishment that had been handed down to them. Those who had been sentenced to time in prison had long since been locked up.

And then, finally, the tempest raised by the GHQ (the paramount power in the land) blew over. By piecing together bits of information in the newspapers, I was able to determine that they had more or less stopped carrying out investigations aimed at pursuing war criminals. Upon learning this, I could not help but let out a heartfelt sigh for those who had been called to account for crimes committed during the war.

Our people had been forced to swallow their bitter tears. Despite this, and all the other difficulties they had met with, they put on a brave face. Such hardships had ended, finally. Exactly four years had passed since the end of the war, and numerous high-ranking officials had committed suicide, one after the other. Others still had been locked up all that time. Japan was at last seeing its wounds beginning to heal; the process of reconstruction was well underway.

It was then that I started to act somewhat more boldly. At times, I returned to stay at my wife's side for several days at a time. Otherwise, as I still did not have a fixed abode, I continued to wander and make stealthy visits to

Tokyo. Yet this was no longer as nerve-wracking for me as it had been in the past and I was able to lead a relatively relaxed life.

That was how things remained until 4 September 1951, when Japan signed the San Francisco Peace Treaty and war criminals were pardoned for their "past misdeeds." At long last, I was once again able to come and go as I pleased.

43

Green Vegetable Juice

In this chapter, I would like to tell the story of a "discussion of times past" that I was a party to.

Soon after the war ended, all personnel from Section 5 of the Intelligence Bureau at the Navy General Staff were charged with war crimes relating to the interrogation of POWs. Those charges were merely a pretext. In fact, the American authorities had been greatly angered by the thorough investigation of America carried out by the personnel in Section 5 for the purpose of providing the intelligence reports needed to wage war. It was for this reason that they had retaliated. Yet while they were taking the personnel from Section 5 into custody, something unexpected happened: Rear Admiral Kaoru Takeuchi (the Section Head) and myself, both of us key members of staff, went on the run.

Rear Admiral Takeuchi went into hiding the day before he was supposed to be arrested. His Chief Staff Officer, Captain Minoru Matsuzuro, was sentenced to 20 years in prison soon afterwards. Commander Yokura, his second in command, was sentenced to 15 years in prison.

Rear Admiral Kaoru Takeuchi reappeared in public in 1951 and I subsequently paid him a visit. As we were both "war criminals who had escaped through sheer luck" when we met up once again, we could not help but discuss the years that we had spent on the run as well as what the future might hold for Japan.

"They came and asked about your whereabouts repeatedly, Mr. Yoshikawa, but I simply said that your house had burned to the ground and that there had been no news about you. Could we have allowed them to catch us? What do you think, Mr. Yoshikawa?"

Together the two of us laughed bitterly about our fates because we were, in a way, complicit. That is to say both of us were quite unwilling to submit to any humiliation brought on by the U.S. Navy, even though our side had been defeated.

I recall one of Rear Admiral Kaoru Takeuchi's frequent admonitions: "We are all spies and it is our duty to use every possible means to uncover details about the enemy that have heretofore remained unknown to us. And if defeated, we simply have to die quietly. There is no way that we will suffer the indignity of humiliation merely to survive."

He was imbued with a will of iron. When our navy was on the verge of giving up all hopes of winning the war, he noticed that the battleship *Yamato* was still in good condition and thus repeatedly petitioned Vice Admiral Ito to put him aboard and send him into dangerous combat zones so that he might preserve the reputation of the Imperial Japanese Navy.

During our conversation, he told me the full story behind his decision to go on the run.

"The highest authorities in our navy put the blame on me for every offense committed against the United States, from the start of the war until its end. Consequently, I was called into the GHQ on numerous occasions so that they could make inquiries of me. In the end, they decided to arrest me. But that was something that I simply refused to accept, so I became a fugitive the evening before they were supposed to take me into custody. Ha, ha, ha…

"How could I have allowed them to catch me? Had I been able to die as a martyr in combat, my wishes would have been fulfilled. Wouldn't you say so? In any event, it must have been very difficult for you to be on the run so far from home and for such a long period of time…"

"That was all thanks to the guidance that you gave us day after day, Section Head." I replied with a laugh. "It was nothing other than the spy's art of remaining invisible!"

At that moment, Rear Admiral Kaoru Takeuchi seemed to be lost in thought. Then, in a reproving tone, he said: "Anyway… Have you published some silly nonsense in a magazine or some other publication recently? Writing in some magazine, for an undercover agent such as yourself, is not something that one ought to do. You're not meant to reveal secrets. What's more, didn't you write that when a spy is on his deathbed he ought to follow the example of Sarutobi Sasuke and burn every last piece of evidence?"[1]

After that, he straightened his back. "My door is always closed to journalists," he said. "Anyone who comes around making inquiries, about any sort of nonsense, is sent packing."

After hearing him out, I put forward my own position:

"Your views on this matter are quite interesting, Section Head. However, isn't it necessary to have discussions about the past that reveal the truth and lead to self-reflection? Isn't that the only way we will get to a better future?"

"My views are not at all the same as yours," said Rear Admiral Takeuchi.

I further explained my thoughts.

"But, Section Head, reconstruction is the most significant problem Japan is facing. At this crucial moment, isn't it time that we all told the whole truth so that everyone, our entire nation, can avoid repeating the mistakes of

43. Green Vegetable Juice

the past, carry out some self-reflection, and begin to think seriously about the path we ought to take?

"As for the self-discipline of an undercover agent, I share the view of your Excellency and I have always done my utmost to keep it in mind.[2] In a similar vein, the undercover agent's guiding maxim is 'Do not waver!' Despite our having been defeated in the war, we should now move quickly to secure a brighter future, shouldn't we?"

I moved my knees forward so as to draw closer to him and then I continued.

"Just wait and see, sir! The Americans will inevitably find themselves at their wits' end regarding the problems and disputes in China and Southeast Asia. And when that time comes, they will finally understand the true significance of Japan. That redneck MacArthur punished any old veteran, just to vent his spleen, and thereby made a mockery of the investigation of war crimes and settling of accounts. However, in the not too distant future when the United States comes up against problems in East Asia, they will certainly need help with defense matters. And then the people of Japan will stand tall once again.

"As you say, Japan's citizens were very naive in the past and remain 20 years behind their counterparts in the other advanced countries. Well then, should we not eliminate the 'do not allow it to be made known, do not allow word to be sent' mindset, which pervades our government, the military, diplomacy, and the public, to come together as a people and reflect on what sort of future we want?

"To reach that objective, might it not be necessary to say that nothing is taboo and that everything should be revealed? By engaging in self-reflection, mightn't we inoculate ourselves against such mishaps in the future? This is what I have been thinking about."

"Yes, I see. There is a certain logic to what you are saying, but my view on this—"

His Excellency got to this point before stopping for a moment.

He then continued speaking.

"I firmly believe that those of us in Section 5 never really lost the fight against the Americans. Furthermore, we were spot on when we predicted that the Americans would attack Japan's Home Islands. Yoshikawa you agree, don't you?

"Ever since I was a boy, I have poured my energy into learning everything about America. I considered myself the foremost expert on America within the Imperial Japanese Navy. However, our navy's leaders never sent me to the United States to see things there for myself. All I have been able to see is American troops, after the war during the occupation. What's more, despite the fact that we knew the enemy's situation just as well as we knew the back of our hands, they did not formulate their strategy on the basis of our knowledge. So how exactly do you change this, hmm?"

"But, Section Head, where did you end up hiding in the end?"

"The answer to that is a riddle within an enigma. Ha, ha, ha…"

Our conversation went back and forth and we ended up getting off track. However, I could tell from his manner of speech and by his tone that Rear Admiral Kaoru Takeuchi had gone into hiding by taking shelter in temples and monasteries, just as I had done.

Although we were both Buddhists, I was with the Rinzai school while he belonged to the Sōtō school. Yet I'm afraid that my brothers in the faith would never have believed that the Section Head belonged to the Sōtō school, nor would they have believed that he had gone into hiding by staying at Buddhist temples.

"Your health is still not very good," the Section Head said to me when it was time to say goodbye. "From now on you need to drink a lot of green vegetable juice. And you must tell your wife to go out and buy you a copy of Dr. XX's book. Your health is the most important thing of all. If you want to stay healthy, drinking green vegetable juice is of the utmost importance."

His Excellency the Section Head clearly believed very strongly that drinking green vegetable juice produced positive health results. By then, he and his wife had not eaten rice or meat for many years. In fact, they did not eat anything other than the small quantities of barley and vegetables that they grew for themselves. Furthermore, their door always remained firmly closed to any and all would-be visitors.

Despite the fact that five years have already passed since this meeting, I have not yet had any green vegetable juice to drink nor have I followed the other instructions given to me by the Section Head. At some time in the future, however, I will have to give it a try.

44

War History

After the Peace Treaty was signed at San Francisco on 4 September 1951, Japanese and American historians began to engage in frequent exchanges while carrying out their research into the Pacific War. While conducting their research, they realized it was necessary to compare materials from all of the warring countries if they were to clearly understand how events had unfolded during that huge military conflict. Any historical research that relies exclusively on materials provided by just one of the belligerent countries will result in a war history that is biased and unjust.

The following examples are instructive in this regard.

During the war, the Japanese were at times rejoicing over what they supposed were successes in battle (the alleged sinking or damaging of enemy vessels in battle) when the Americans had not actually suffered any losses at all.

At one point in the war, the Japanese believed that a cruiser they had sunk simply represented another battle prize. Meanwhile, the Americans were greatly worried that the cruiser in question was the very one transporting the atomic bombs that were to be used to strike Japan.

Japan's initial battle results for the surprise attack on Pearl Harbor are likewise instructive in this regard. Even though the Japanese carried out a fairly thorough evaluation of those results, the true figures could only be arrived at after comparing both Japanese and American materials.

The battle front figures and accounts of the attack on Pearl Harbor provided below are a synthesis of both Japanese and American materials. They provide an accurate description of the event, which was in no way arrived at as a result of my own views.

1. The Japanese Attack Force

(i) Air Units
    40 Torpedo Bomber Aircraft
    104 High-altitude Bomber Aircraft
    130 Dive-bomber Aircraft
    80 Fighter Aircraft
Total 354 Aircraft
(ii) 5 Special Midget Submarines

2. Objectives

(i)
Total: 70 warships berthed in Pearl Harbor
24 service vessels
94 vessels

(ii)
381 Aircraft stationed at various airfields

3. Battle Results

Type of Vessel	Vessel Name	Anchoring Place / Targeting Location	Torpedo Strikes	Bomb Strikes	Personnel Killed
Battleship	Pennsylvania	Southern End of Docks	0	?	?
Battleship	Oklahoma	Outside the harbor	3	--	415
Battleship	Maryland	Inside port, right side	0	2	4
Battleship	Tennessee	Inside the harbor	0	?	5
Battleship	Arizona	Outside port, large explosion	?	?	1,103
Battleship	Nevada	Moored at north end of port	1	--	50
Battleship	West Virginia	Outside the harbor	6–7	2	105
Light Cruiser/ Small Ship		Many such vessels sunk various locations	?	?	?
Land Installation		Many destroyed various locations	?	?	?
Airfield-based Aircraft		188 aircraft destroyed at several air bases	?	?	?
		155 aircraft damaged at several air bases	?	?	?

4. Japanese losses

Aircraft Lost   29 Aircraft
Special Midget Submarines   5 Vessels Sunk or Scuttled

44. War History

A photograph taken from a Japanese plane during the Pearl Harbor attack. Ford Island and the Navy Yards are clearly visible (Naval History and Heritage Command).

5. The situation in the battle zone

The Carrier Striking Task Force, a flotilla comprised of 33 ships, left Etorofu Island's Hitokappu Bay on 26 November 1941. This strike force was comprised of 6 aircraft carriers, 2 battleships, 3 cruisers, 11 destroyers, 3 submarines, 8 fuel tankers, and 423 carrier-based aircraft. Under the command of Admiral Chūichi Nagumo, the strike force made its way east while staying close to the parallel at 40 degrees latitude north.

At 5:30 in the afternoon on 2 December, the strike force received the message "Climb Mount Nikita 1208." This was the order that set the date of the actual attack for 8 December Japan time.

On 6 December, the Carrier Striking Task Force arrived due north of Hawaii and turned abruptly to the south. The next morning at 6 o'clock, when they had reached waters 275 nautical miles to the north of Hawaii, the aircraft taking part in what was to be the first wave of attack took off from the aircraft carriers.

Commander Mitsuo Fuchida, the leader of the first aerial attack squad, circled his plane in the air for a time while his wingmen in the first attack squad took to the skies from the motherships. When a total of 183 aircraft had taken off and arranged themselves in columns, they began flying south.

As the aircraft drew very near to Oahu, Commander Mitsuo Fuchida gave the order to attack: "Strike, strike, strike." Then the fighter planes converged upon aircraft that were sitting in rows on the ground at the air bases and began strafing them with machine gun fire. Meanwhile, torpedo bomber aircraft dropped their shallow-water torpedoes from a height of 10–30 meters into the calm waters below. Following immediately upon this was a wave of dive-bombers, which was in turn followed by a squadron of high-elevation bombers.

From the time that the first bomb was dropped at 7:50 am (Hawaii Time) until more than one hour later, the entire Pearl Harbor complex was in a state of paralysis. Huge billowing clouds of smoke began floating southwest as the anti-aircraft fire going up into the skies above became increasingly sparse.

After Commander Mitsuo Fuchida was certain of the success of the surprise attack, he sent out the radio message "Tora, tora, tora."

This meant: "Our surprise attack has succeeded. Our torpedo aircraft have struck the enemy's vessels and we have achieved a great success."

As the noise of the bombs, artillery fire, and warning sirens fused into a single sound, the following call came repeatedly from Honolulu's radio stations: "Air raid Pearl Harbor. This is no drill! All Army and Navy personnel must return to their posts immediately!"

6. A Comprehensive Analysis:

i.

Although the Carrier Striking Task Force sent to attack Pearl Harbor included a total of 423 aircraft, only two waves of attack aircraft, 354 planes in total, took to the air. After that, further air attacks were called off. How was it that repeated air attacks were not carried out? It was precisely because of this that the shipyards and docks were left almost completely intact, which allowed the harbor to serve as the U.S. military's central hub during the Pacific War. This in turn led directly to Japan's capitulation.

All U.S. Navy vessels struck during the surprise attack, with the exception of the battleship *Arizona*, were repaired, brought back into service and fighting in the Pacific War within two years.

ii.

Despite the fact that the Japanese navy's torpedo bomber aircraft were aiming at stationary targets, they only managed to hit 35% of those targets.

iii.

The battleships moored within the inner-harbor suffered relatively minimal damage and losses.

iv. A majority of the aircraft stationed at air bases were destroyed and thus Japan obtained temporary control of the air. Exactly why it was necessary to make a hasty retreat remains unknown.

v. Why didn't Japan's military commanders order repeated air attacks? And why weren't Japanese warships called in to attack so as to make use of their firepower?

The following text summarizes the views on the war shared by both Japanese and American historians:

> "All in all, the attack on Pearl Harbor was a less than thorough operation because Japan's military commanders were satisfied with just a little success and because they were guided by a paternalistic approach. Consequently, they gained nothing while they provided America with a reason to rise up and ultimately lay waste to Japan.
>
> "War ought to be waged in a way that brings about the utter destruction of the enemy. Any paternalism that exists among those waging war will lead inevitably to defeatism.
>
> "Since the idea of a 'partial success' governed the thinking of the Japanese navy's commanders, it led directly to Japan's defeat. One cannot help but say that this was highly regrettable."

As noted earlier, it's not difficult to determine what errors of judgment occurred during a war when a thorough investigation of materials from all the countries involved is conducted. When this is done, it is possible to ascertain whether the errors made were the responsibility of the commanding officers or a result of the strengths and weaknesses of the troops in the field. An investigation of this sort will always provide food for thought.

In the midst of the present analysis, the most thought-provoking and polemical question concerns the motives that led to the start of the war. That is to say, did President Roosevelt know that Japan was going to attack Pearl Harbor? Or did the Japanese military claim this was so just to stir things up, even though Roosevelt had not known about the attack beforehand?

If one claims that President Roosevelt and his top military advisors knew that Japan was going to attack Pearl Harbor beforehand, how was it that they never warned either the Commander of the U.S. Pacific Fleet in Hawaii or the U.S. Army's Commanding Officer there?

In America, two schools of thought have emerged about this question. The "anti-Roosevelt" school believes that while neither Admiral Kimmel nor General Short was responsible, President Roosevelt himself was responsible for the tragedy at Pearl Harbor. For its part, the "pro-Roosevelt" school believes that the war was started by Japan and thus was definitely not Roosevelt's responsibility.

Both schools of thought have published research papers and debate about this question is ongoing in the United States. Yet because many of the people directly involved in the matter have already died, and because conclusive proof has yet to be found, it is very difficult to predict when this debate will finally be settled. However, U.S. historians are still doing their utmost to make a breakthrough by working tirelessly to discover new research material on this question.

Among those at work on this subject is Dr. Gordon Prange, the former chief historian at the GHQ's historical research office and a historian of maritime warfare. Before obtaining a post as professor, he earned a doctorate with his thesis on Christopher Columbus' logbooks. He came to Japan to serve as a member of staff at the GHQ and to investigate the Pacific War by gathering Japanese material about it.

In order to understand both government policy and military strategy, Dr. Prange intended to research Pearl Harbor at the time that the war broke out. Yet because the Imperial Japanese Navy burned all of its records shortly after the war came to an end (just before the country surrendered), it was impossible for him to recover records of any real significance. Therefore, he actually went looking for Pacific War veterans who had survived. He carried out his inquiries all around the country, asking servicemen to explain what things had been like during the war. For example, he went through the following dialogue with eight servicemen who had worked aboard the aircraft carrier *Akagi*.

"Back then, what time did they wake you up and who woke you up?"

"It was around 4 in the morning; one of the sailors on duty would come to wake me up. He would shake my hammock to wake me up. I'd say it was about five minutes before four then."

"After you got up, what did you do?"

"After you got into your plane, how did you feel? What was the weather like then?"

His questions quite often concerned the most trivial of matters, yet he never grew weary of asking them over and over again. This clearly shows how tirelessly he worked to discover new evidence that might greatly enlighten him about some aspect of his research.

The Commander of the air troops that attacked Pearl Harbor, Mitsuo Fuchida, and Staff Officer Commander Minoru Genda of the First Air Fleet were two of his most frequent interviewees. He also tracked down the former Section Head from the War Operations Bureau at the Navy General Staff, Captain Sadatoshi Tomioka, and other personnel from that Bureau for questioning. Furthermore, he made use of the GHQ's powers to investigate deciphered cables sent to and from the Foreign Ministry.

While carrying out his investigation, there were two questions that instantly filled him with doubt when they came to him:

44. War History

Why did Japan decide to fix the date for the start of the war on 7 December?

How did the Japanese military predict the date at which the greatest number of navy vessels would be anchored in Pearl Harbor?

Despite mulling these questions over for some time, he apparently remained puzzled by them. The peculiar thing about this was that nobody else had carried out any sort of investigation about those questions until then.

A careful reading of the telegrams sent from Japan's Consulate-General in Honolulu left him even more perplexed. How had the Japanese Consulate-General in Honolulu managed to acquire expert military intelligence reports about Pearl Harbor?

There were very large numbers of citizens of Japanese ancestry living in Hawaii and it was estimated that up to one or two thousand of them might be hostile actors assisting the Japanese military. While this thought was not particularly surprising to the American, his examination of the intercepted cables revealed that each one contained information that the Japanese military was most anxious to learn about. That information focused upon points of strategic importance: the operations of the fleet, the positioning of battleships, obstruction balloons, anti-submarine netting, berthing and anchoring locations. Moreover, one cable suggested that "a surprise attack on these sites is almost certain of success."

There was no getting away from it, all of this information gave Dr. Prange pause. He then realized that there must have been an undercover agent active in Hawaii at that time. Although he was still not sure whether that agent was Japanese or American, he was quite sure that an undercover agent had been involved.

He carried his investigation further by following up every possible lead. Finally, after making contact with a Japanese naval officer named XX, he came to learn that I had been in Hawaii at that time. He then made some inquiries and got my address. I subsequently received a letter from Dr. Prange. Essentially, the letter was an invitation to go to Tokyo to help him with his research on the history of the war. He wrote that he himself was extending this sincere invitation, that it definitely was not a subpoena from the authorities, and as such there was no need for me to worry. In addition, he promised to take care of all my expenses.

Furthermore, he stated quite pointedly that the fact that I was present in Hawaii at the start of the war was of critical importance. I was to be an important eyewitness for his research on the history of the war. He asked me to remain as discreet as possible while ending his letter with what seemed to be a threat: I was not to divulge any information to anyone else. If I were to divulge information to others, I alone would be responsible for any unfavorable consequences while he would not be to blame etc. Consequently, I accepted his invitation.

I reasoned that since they were about to sign a peace treaty, this might not be some sort of ploy to arrest me. My bold nature led me to agree to his request in the end. I was thinking all the while that this was a good opportunity to find out what the GHQ made of me.

I remember going to call on him at the GHQ in Tokyo on the eve of the signing of the San Francisco Treaty in 1951. After going through the main entrance at the GHQ, you had to pass through countless checkpoints. American troops wearing clean uniforms and Japanese troops in scruffy uniforms were on sentry duty everywhere. After I had passed through the final door, someone telephoned Dr. Prange and a secretary emerged. She then led me to the Imperial Hotel.

He said to me later that it was not appropriate for us to talk at the GHQ because his invitation was a personal one. Therefore, he had invited me to the Imperial Hotel. I felt that this was ample proof that the Americans were a very calculating bunch.

I stayed there for a week. Every day, I drank Coca-Cola and whiskey while answering his questions. He was greatly interested in what I had to say and he told me that after he returned home he was going to write a book that he was sure would sell very well. He also said that he was going to send me a sum of money to remunerate me for my assistance.

It would be remiss to suggest here that I was helping him to write a book. It would be more accurate to say that I was using that occasion to discuss some of my knowledge of the war because it offered me the opportunity to enlighten Americans. I was hoping that they might thereby come to understand the tenacity that so characterizes the Japanese people. While Japan certainly needed to pause and reflect on its past behavior and deeds, I also hoped that the Americans would come to know the unyielding quality of the Japanese character so that a deeper mutual understanding might exist between Japan and America in the future.

There was something else that I wanted Americans to understand. Mutual understanding really cannot be developed in a relationship of dominance and submission, where one side is expected to bow and scrape. In fact, the Americans were not people of the spoiled and naive sort who would to this day feel compelled to criticize the wrongs committed by a secret agent. Nevertheless, I fully understood why the Americans expressed very deep, and sometimes violent, regrets about the Incident at Pearl Harbor. However, it only came under Japanese attack as a result of the miscalculations made by U.S. authorities.

In the present day, the Japanese navy has nothing to boast about in comparison with its American counterpart. Nor can the leaders of a defeated military speak about bravery. Nonetheless, in terms of military strategy, Japan certainly managed to carry out a splendid surprise attack.

44. War History

Yet as soon as one brings up the war, Japanese people immediately feel as if it was all their fault. (This has been the case for some time now.) This is particularly true when the discussion turns to the attack on Pearl Harbor, at which point they feel as if they cannot even raise their heads.

Despite the difficulties our situation presented us with when we found ourselves under the control of the all-powerful GHQ, I didn't believe that we Japanese were anything like acquiescent slaves who ought to feel compelled to bow and scrape. As a result, I said only that which needed to be said and I keep hidden that which ought to have remained hidden. There was no room for compromise. He may have felt that I was an arrogant so-and-so, but as far as the GHQ was concerned I had always been unyielding.

I had no qualms about taking the roundabout route into the GHQ. After lying low for a stretch of time, I finally make an appearance there. In so doing, I demonstrated just what sort of resistance I was capable of.

45

CBS

After the San Francisco Treaty had come into effect in 1951, I returned to my family village to live quite openly alongside my wife and I began selling petrol to make a living. Fortunately, business was good. As a result, I was fully prepared to spend the rest of my days living anonymously in the countryside and selling petrol. I had no plans to take on any public duties ever again.

Yet after the San Francisco Treaty entered into effect, the government's very first decision was to scrap the "Banish from Public Office" law.[1] Consequently, I began to work as a member of the local government council after being elected by the people in 1953. I was later re-elected to serve a second term. By that time, I already had two children (a girl and a boy) and I was living a fairly peaceful and comfortable life.

In 1960, people from various magazines, radio stations, and other news organizations began to come to see me, notebooks in hand, even though I didn't have the vaguest idea where they had got word of me. Soon afterwards, the newspapers began printing elaborate stories about my past deeds and I rather unexpectedly became the famous resident of our district. Before long, I had become a prominent figure in the news.

In the summer of that year, the U.S. Ambassador to Japan sent me a letter from Tokyo requesting that I write an essay for the students of the U.S. Naval Academy at Annapolis, Maryland, which would be published later in *Proceedings*, the U.S. Navy's prestigious journal. As I was more than happy to write something for those young students, I went to Tokyo to visit the U.S. Embassy.

Fourteen years had already passed since the end of the war and Tokyo was by then busying itself with all the work that had hitherto been neglected. As I stood at the busy Toranomon Gate junction, I looked down the road toward the government ministry district and noticed that nearly every single government ministry building had been completely restored. However, the red bricks of the Navy Ministry building were nowhere to be seen. When I cast another look toward the roof of the South Manchuria Railway Company building, the flag flying in the wind there was no longer Japan's national banner but rather the American Stars and Stripes.

45. CBS

The Navy Ministry building was a place that I had entered and exited every day, both before and during the war, and it had left a deep impression on me. Yet the site had been completely transformed and it was now legally under American jurisdiction. A large portrait of Abraham Lincoln was hanging in the hall near the building's front entrance.

The naval attaché's office was on the fourth floor, so I asked someone at the central reception desk to telephone Lieutenant-Colonel Norman Stanford and explain the reason for my call. He then gave me permission to visit his office.

As soon as our eyes met, Lieutenant-Colonel Stanford extended both of his large hands in order to welcome me inside. "Sir, you are welcome," he said several times. As I recall, that great burly fellow must have been around three or four years younger than me. After he had introduced me to his colleagues in a very forthright manner, they shook hands with me and welcomed me most earnestly. Then we began to introduce ourselves in a very cordial way, which made me feel slightly embarrassed. Yesterday's enemies had become today's friends. It doesn't seem to matter what country a military man comes from, since all are equally plainspoken.

A photograph taken at a battle front during the Korean War, which showed a marine rushing into battle, was tacked on a wall in the office. "That's where I was wounded," Lieutenant-Colonel Stanford told me as he pointed to the photograph. He was a decorated member of the marines.

Of all the troops from the various branches of the U.S. armed forces, the marines possess the greatest fighting spirit. Therefore, the marines are always called in to make the first strike wherever there is a difficult battleground. They visited tremendous adversity on Japan's troops during the battles for Guadalcanal, Saipan, and Iwo Jima.

The two of us immediately got down to the work of investigating the history of the war. Our conversation was carried out in a haphazard mix of both English and Japanese. Lieutenant-Colonel Stanford had worked very hard to learn Japanese and spoke it relatively fluently and I could speak English fairly well. However, I always used Japanese when telling him my story so that he could fully understand my meaning. Yet on the most important points he often interrupted me and asked if I might "use English and say that once again."

He had a very straightforward disposition and his manner was very much that of a military man. All those who worked in the offices of Japan's Self-Defense Forces knew him and showed him great respect. They said that he was a good person.

It took the two of us three days to complete our work. After that, we had a draft typed up and sent off to the Annapolis Naval Academy. I then hurried back to my village.

The account that we had co-written about our memories of the war was published in the December 1960 edition of *Proceedings*. After our account was published, there was a lot of reaction to it in the United States. The New York Times, The International Herald Tribune, and other newspapers and magazines were all vying to be the first to reprint the story. Various French and Canadian newspapers and other publications also contacted me to sound me out about reprinting the story. Furthermore, the Canadian Broadcasting Corporation (CBC) came by and spent four days taping.

After that, in the spring of the following year (1961), the American broadcaster CBS and the makers of its television series *The Twentieth Century* agreed to collaborate on the shooting of a television documentary about me. Their plans called for filming on location at the sites where the past events had taken place.[2]

The drafting of the script for the television program was done in Washington, D.C., and negotiations about the project were held there with U.S. authorities. At the very start, the Pentagon and the U.S. Defense Department were apparently unwilling to agree to it. There was no need for any further discussion of "that Yoshikawa" they said. They added that if anyone wanted to use the great blemish on American history that was the attack on Pearl Harbor and intended to carry out filming at the site for the purposes of a historical documentary about the incident, there was no way that they were prepared to authorize it.

However, CBS personnel kept running over to the Pentagon day after day to request that authorization be given. In the end, permission was given for filming at the site on the condition that no images of shipwrecks appear in the film. As a result of all of the twists and turns that this process involved, the process of putting together a script was a greatly troubled one.

In addition, the producers felt (and had planned) that there should be a scene in the program during which I would mark the noteworthy twentieth anniversary of the Pearl Harbor Incident by admitting my guilt and showing signs of my remorse and soul-searching. However, I categorically refused to do so. Although I have to this day been engaged in soul searching, I have never felt the slightest bit inclined to show feelings of regret.

We were in a dispute over this question for a period of time until they finally decided that they would only film "Yoshikawa's personal story" and that no part of the program would reenact my espionage activities in Honolulu. In addition, the program's most important storyline was shifted to the post-war era, right up to the present day. The Pentagon was prepared to permit this as well.

Just before taking the decision to begin filming, we had a small meeting at Lieutenant-Colonel Stanford's villa in Hayama to talk things over. I was subsequently running back and forth between Shikoku and Tokyo, month after month.

45. CBS

Although the remuneration I was to receive for appearing in the program was quite meager, I realized that this opportunity was a means by which I might see Pearl Harbor once again. That thought alone left me feeling greatly consoled. Consequently, I had no wish to haggle over my salary. This was ever more the case as I recalled the days when I had been pacing back and forth, wishing that I could get a better look at Pearl Harbor. Now I would be able to take a good look at it. That thought alone left me indescribably happy.

Apart from looking forward to filming during a visit to Honolulu, my innermost heart held four special wishes:

1. Since the feelings of enmity and gratitude that the war had initially given rise to had already begun to die out, nearly twenty years after the end of hostilities, I wanted to recall the Japanese and Americans who had been killed in action while saying prayers for them beside their gravestones.
2. I felt the need to bear witness to all American citizens that Hawaiian residents of Japanese ancestry were loyal to America.

After my article entitled "I was the Pearl Harbor Spy" was published, a majority of the Americans who read it seemed to respond in the same way:

> Since he's waited up until now before finally speaking about all this, his story must be a load of nonsense. How could a young officer have completed such a huge task on his own, without any of the 150,000 Japanese-American residents in Hawaii assisting him? He couldn't have gone ten months without being informed on once, not even with superhuman powers. Can his account be considered anything less than dubious? It's safe to say that it was thanks to the help of his 150,000 compatriots that he was up to the task.

Moreover, I had heard that ordinary American citizens were not alone in holding this view. Some American historians shared this assessment and that was no trivial matter. As a result, it occurred to me that I had to find a way to clearly explain the truth to the American people in order to dispel their doubts.

If the loyalty of Japanese-Americans became a cause of concern for the rest of America's citizens, it would inevitably affect the lives of Japanese-Americans and their activities within the wider society. This matter of erroneously placed blame was a really painful problem for me.

In fact, the work was done by me alone. There were no others assisting me. Yet, and I must stress this point, any affirmation of this fact is quickly denounced as "the blowing of one's own horn." As a result, I am somewhat reticent to speak about it. Nonetheless, the truth is the truth and I sincerely wish to make an appeal to the American people. Please do not cause Japanese-Americans to suffer any injustice.

I believed that once I had reached Honolulu I could certainly find an opportunity to say all of this by way of newspapers, radio and television.

3. I needed to know how my friends, both male and female, were faring. Had all of them been living happy lives? I particularly wanted to know about those people who'd had dealings with the consulate-general, since I had heard that some of them had been charged with crimes during the war.

And what had become of those who had worked on the plantations? And what about those young people who had renounced their Japanese nationality and enlisted in the U.S. military? What had become of them? I simply wanted to get some news of them.

4. I wanted to return to my old haunts and once again enjoy the great natural scenery there. I cherished my memories of all the mountains, seashores, and islands I had seen during the ten months that I spent in Hawaii.

46

Filming

Finally, the time came to start shooting the film. But before we could begin filming, we had to do some test shooting in Tokyo. As rainy-season clouds filled the Tokyo sky early on that day, the cameraman told us that we needed to wait until it cleared before we could shoot our test film in Shimizudani Park.

I then realized that I had never been in a film before and I began to doubt my ability to put on the appropriate facial expressions. Despite this, I was going to have to act. What sort of impression was I going to make with my mouth full of English words that I was barely familiar with? My heart was thumping quite a bit when it suddenly occurred to me that I was already aboard this "ship" and that all I needed to do was to listen to the people in charge. I thus made myself psychologically ready for the experience.

The cameraman was grinning broadly when he explained to me that the camera would be trained on me in such a way that my acting would show what it needed to show. Thus, there would be no way to confuse the face of the businessman with that of the spy. It was for this reason that he would only be filming close-ups or scenes of me walking down the road on this shoot.

The next consideration was the lighting. In aid of this, he requested that I remain a very precise distance from the camera when walking. To ensure that I would do so, he attached a wire to my trousers that compelled me to walk in a straight line. The face that I wore then was simply that of a trained monkey.

Afterwards, we filmed a recollection scene. For this he sat me down on a boulder and had me smoke a pipe filled with tobacco. "Take your positions! Scene Three. Take One," he then shouted while snapping the clapperboard shut. As soon as the camera began turning, I began to discuss a memory.

"You really aren't apprehensive when you're in front of the camera!" the cameraman happily said to me after the test filming was completed. In fact, the very first time that I looked into the camera I was stunned and somewhat lost. Fortunately, I had long since been prepared to make a fool of myself in public.

In the middle of June, it was decided that we would go to my family village to film. On the evening before the first day of filming there, a truck equipped with an electric generator arrived from Tokyo. I had assumed that, at best, they would be filming with an 8mm camera and that after shooting away, "clickity-click, clickity-click," that would be the end of it. Who would have imagined that they were actually going to send in large quantities of top of the line filming equipment? This ended up attracting crowds of people and received a lot of attention.

As I ran a business, they filmed me filling up my customers' cars with petrol, accepting payment, and giving thanks. The purpose of this shoot was to record the actual conditions of my everyday life without resorting to any falsehoods or trickery.

While filming me, pen in hand, inside my study the Ancient Light Hermitage, they told me to put on the robes of a monk and sit in a meditation position. Furthermore, they asked some monks from the local temple to assist with the scene by taking a hose to the rooftop and spraying what was supposed to look like rain dripping off the edge of the roof. They roped in large numbers of people to accomplish all of this and our time there really was busy.

The following day, they had to film a scene in which my wife and I were shown walking together. I felt truly embarrassed since we were surrounded by a crowd of people and I couldn't stop myself from breaking into a sweat that soon covered my entire body. Fortunately, the work of filming in our village was completed in just three days.

Here, I would like to add a comment in passing. My photograph was taken while I was wearing a monk's clothing and seated in a meditation position during the filming, and it appeared in a New York newspaper the next day. For those who saw the photo, it may have looked as if the former Pearl Harbor spy had decided to become a monk and was now spending the rest of his days as such.

In August, my passport and visa were properly sorted out. Shortly afterwards, I received a cable notifying me that I was to depart on 15 August and that I needed to get to Tokyo as soon as possible. The day that I got to Tokyo happened to be Armistice Day and media organizations were everywhere very much in view because Mikoyan, the Soviet Deputy Premier, had come to Japan on an official visit. When Hagerty was in Japan on a visit just prior to this, left-wing groups were out causing disturbances for a time.[1] On this occasion, however, there was a chance that right-wingers would come out to cause a stir. Consequently, the authorities had taken the precaution of deploying 9,000 police officers.

The cameraman was already waiting at Haneda Airport when he telephoned me to say that we would probably have to postpone our departure.

46. Filming

However, he telephoned again later that evening to say that we would proceed as scheduled and leave aboard a plane that was to take off at 11:40 pm. I then hastily made my way to Haneda Airport.

On the morning of 15 August, we reached Wake Island. We then flew over the southern half of Midway Island, where so many of my brothers-in-arms perished. In the afternoon (local time), the huge body of our passenger jet aircraft tilted smoothly to the left and then to the right before facing towards Honolulu. When the aircraft dropped below the clouds, it was already possible to see the waves of the Pacific Ocean. I then realized that I was just about to see all of the Hawaiian Islands and I began to feel slightly unsettled. The previous night, I had not been able to get to sleep as the thought that I was just about to reach Pearl Harbor kept swirling around in my mind.

Mr. Bingham, who frequently traveled on this route and was sitting in the window seat, suggested that we change seats so that I might get a better view.[2] Then his large and agile hands darted into his carefully packed bag and he produced an 8mm camera that he was obviously familiar with. After checking the film and cleaning off the dust that was covering the lens, he concluded by putting it through a trial run.

I fastened the seatbelt and then pressed my forehead against the window and looked downward. The airplane broke through the sea of clouds and dropped its speed while its silver wing glistened in the blue sky, wobbling slightly. Little by little, I became ever more excited until I reached the point where I could feel the pulse in my forehead as it pushed against the glass.

The airplane continued to fly toward Honolulu and I thought to myself that the Japanese strike force might have taken this very flight path 20 years earlier. Wearing headbands emblazoned with a red sun, their hands gripping onto their joysticks so tightly as to nearly crush them to bits, they fixed their eyes upon Pearl Harbor as they slowly drew closer and closer to it, pressing on until the attack was launched. The surprise attack on Pearl Harbor, an incident that lasted but an hour, would ultimately change the course of history and decide Japan's fate.

I then thought about the 20 years that had passed since the attack on Pearl Harbor. All I could do was let out a deep sigh. "Alas!" And that put a stop to my deep pondering and wistful thinking. I wouldn't say that I had at that very moment come to some sort of understanding about the loyalty those warriors showed our ancestral land, right to the very end, as they carried out their bounden duty. I would rather say that I had a thought that was special and difficult to express.

The airplane banked to the left, then to the right, and soon afterwards it began to descend. Pearl Harbor, which looked like a white starfish, leapt into view. The Aloha Tower, Cape Diamond, and Nu'uanu Pali followed, the sight of each and every one of them served to bring back my memories of the past.

I was so excited that my eyes became teary and my lips began to quiver. Here was the island that I had taken great pains to scout out. I had poured my youthful energy into completing my work there. It was stretched out in the shade, looking just as it had before, and I was utterly overcome by an indescribable emotion.

Just then, I heard the sound of a movie camera that was filming. When I turned my head to have a look, I saw that Mr. Bingham, an indefatigable worker, had been aiming his camera at me while I was in this emotional state. That is to say, he was already getting down to the work of filming.

"Hey! Please keep on looking!" he said when he saw that I had discovered him filming me. Immediately after that, he changed the position from which he was filming and continued to shoot.

Since I was now an object, it didn't matter what sort of ineffable emotions I was feeling. I had become a spectacle that people could enjoy.

On the stairs down from the airplane, smog could be seen hovering over Pearl Harbor and the imposing sight of the U.S. Pacific Fleet's main base was on full display. From here the defenders of the free world clique sent off their directives to Okinawa, Dutch Harbor, Guam, the U.S. Seventh Fleet, and to Polaris missile equipped submarines.

Twenty years earlier, I too had lofty ideals that I cherished. Pearl Harbor … what had it all been for? Had it not been about launching a surprise attack on that hateful U.S. Navy with an oath to fight to the very end?

Our group was staying at a hotel in Waikiki. The director, assistant director, and interpreter had all flown in from New York. Our filming continued for two consecutive weeks at outdoor locations and the work went on non-stop. At times there was heavy rain, but the skies always cleared up before too long. The filming thus went ahead smoothly and stayed on schedule regardless of the weather.

Successive days were spent filming at the elevated sites overlooking Pearl Harbor that I had so often gone to, such as The Shunchoro Teahouse, the Kolekole Pass, Mount Tantalus (with its view of the coast), the sugarcane fields, and elsewhere.

Filming inside Pearl Harbor went on for three days. The officer assigned to supervise our group, who also served as our guide, was constantly alongside us. This was the first time I had been able to strut right into the harbor in broad daylight. I hadn't realized that the inner harbor was cramped into such a small space.

We took a motorboat for a short trip to the memorial that is the battleship *Arizona* and from there we went over to Ford Island. Within the harbor we saw vessels with obscenely large guided missiles aboard, while the air pipes of submerged submarines circulating inside the harbor protruded from the water.

46. Filming

Since the *Arizona* was so badly damaged, it was not possible to carry out a salvage operation on it. Most of the unbroken hull of the sunken vessel lies foundering under water while the U.S. flag flies over the ship's midsection. Only a bit of the vessel's hull comes out of the water and the upper-level structures have been removed. The warship now serves as a permanent memorial and is to remain in place.

On the day that the war broke out, this very stretch of peaceful water was transformed into a sea of fire and over a thousand U.S. Navy seamen were burned to death there. Also resting on the seabed below were Japanese special midget submarines smashed to pieces by explosions. When I realized that the white bones of the young officers aboard those special midget submarines were still scattered there, I could not help but press my hands together and say a prayer for them.

After we completed outdoor filming at a sugarcane plantation in the afternoon on 23 August, the filming moved to the Shunchoro Teahouse and continued well into the night. The landlady at the Shunchoro Teahouse was still there and in good health. She said that their establishment had received the cold shoulder from American servicemen from the war's start right to its end. Consequently, they had been forced to close up shop. Her son and his wife had only reopened the business a few years earlier. She was now retired and living life on her own.

"I'm very sorry for causing all of you so much trouble," I said to her in order to apologize.

She smiled a charming smile and said: "Not at all, not at all. You were doing it for the homeland. You and Mr. Kita certainly did come here quite often! At the time, I felt that there was something a bit suspicious about you. However, I definitely did not imagine that you, Mr. Morimura, were actually that… Oh, I'm speaking impolitely now."

As the filming went ahead on the basis of an "express" schedule, my eyes became bloodshot, my face darkened, and my cheeks were afflicted by a painful burning sensation. Then finally, at long last, the work of acting while following the schedule fixed by Mr. Bingham and the Pentagon came to an end. I was then able to calm down and catch my breath.

While we were filming on the beach, a few tourists who were out swimming came up to see what the fuss was all about. Among them was a brawny fellow who came over to me and shook my hand. "I've read some news reports about you," he said to me, smiling. He was a captain in the air force and had apparently just come back from Japan. He was just wearing swimming trunks and had a very hairy chest. His expression was full of life and he made a deep impression on me.

There was also a young lad who stood alongside us.

"What grade are you in?" I asked him.

"Seventh grade," he replied.

He told us that his summer holidays would continue until September 6 and that he was going to keep on swimming as much as he liked.

"I too am an expert swimmer," I said, proudly vaunting my own skills.

He blinked as he looked up at me. "Hey mister, are you a movie actor?" he asked.

"I am not a professional actor," was my less than candid reply.

Upon hearing this, his expression showed that he had not fully understood.

I once had my own youthful passions, but I had given them up and put my life at risk so that I might make the greatest of efforts. And yet it had all been for naught.

Had any good come of the price that was paid?

Just like footprints in the sand washed away by the tide, everything had vanished without a trace…

There the natural sights and scenery were no less beautiful than they had been in the past. Turbulent waves from the other side of the Pacific Ocean came rushing in, pushing the waves ahead of them onto the beach with a splash, and lining the shore with a string of white spray for an instant.

47

Strolling Around Honolulu

After the filming had ended, my first thought was to rest for a while. Yet various local newspapers, broadcasters, and people that I used to know in Hawaii kept ringing me up non-stop and asking me to satisfy their requests. I had no idea how they had managed to get news of me.

However, the contract that I had signed with CBS stipulated that I was not permitted to agree to any requests from other organizations. Consequently, I was left feeling slightly embarrassed. At just that time, the landlady from the Shunchoro Teahouse rang to invite me over to see them. Her invitation got me out of my predicament at the opportune moment and I rushed out of my hotel to go and pay them a visit.

"This is the room that you used to stay in 20 years ago," the landlady told me in a low voice as she patted me on the shoulder. "During the war, the business was closed. How we suffered! So very many hardships!" she added.

Then a long-time geisha told me that so-and-so had become a mother of two children, so-and-so had already died, so-and-so was now a beautician, and so-and-so had been out of touch for a while. All of this news was of great interest to me.

A short time later, a few women came running up happily with the young landlady in the lead. There was Kiyoko, Yoshiko, and others. They had all acted alongside me during the filming there earlier. Today, it seemed as if we had been friends for years as they gathered around me to discuss Japanese things that they were obviously completely familiar with.

And then they spoke about the American troops who had gone over there looking to cause trouble during the war.

"Back then, we told those American troops: 'We have not done any bad things. How can you not know that we are good citizens and that we always do our best for America?' Then they slowly began to understand and they didn't come back to cause any more trouble."

"Just after the war began, we really did suffer a lot. But whenever the Japanese scored victories in battle, we always cheered them on in our hearts."

"During the war I sold whiskey to American troops on the black market and I ended up making a fair bit of money."

"So-and-so cozied up to some American troops and then, quite unexpectedly, she slandered so-and-so, which caused so-and-so a lot of trouble. Even though that charley still comes around here looking to have fun, everybody hates her."

Then the old landlady spoke about the time she worked on a sugarcane plantation, just after her arrival in Hawaii. She had pulled up weeds in the sugarcane fields all day long and had suffered quite a lot. And yet, the young landlady asked an insolent question about this: "Didn't all of us have to do exactly the same work during the war?"

"And I worked in a tuck shop selling things to the troops!" said another.

The conversation kept growing louder and everybody had to say their piece. One and all wanted to fascinate and charm with their loquaciousness.

In any case, those second and third-generation Japanese-American women were more partial to Japan than their menfolk were. The women all felt profoundly attached to Japanese kimonos, grass sandals, our language and customs. Most of all, they enjoyed Japanese magazines, films, and song. This had been the case in the past and it was still true now. The sight of those girls, who didn't understand much Japanese and yet were able to get such enjoyment from Japanese things, was truly fascinating.

When the sound of some drunken white people shouting came up from the main hall downstairs, I mistakenly believed that I had detained the women. "They are shouting for you downstairs," I said. "Why don't you go and have a look!"

However, they simply ignored the shouts of those white people. "It's no problem," they replied. "Anyway, white folks hate lazy people! Just ignore them and they'll leave after a while."

They used proper Japanese when they were putting on their acts, but during their more casual moments they mixed various languages together and their speech became a hodge-podge of English, Japanese, and the local dialect.

In light of this, I said: "It doesn't seem as if there's any need for Japanese schools in Hawaii, because Japanese-Americans all study English. And they all become real Americans."

Upon hearing that, they all objected to my words at once. "No, no. Japanese is absolutely necessary."

The next evening at nightfall, Roberts from the Pineapple Company telephoned to extend me an invitation. "Let's have a drink together!" he said. "Okay?"

After I agreed, he immediately sent a car over for me. I did not know him, but he and his son had apparently come over to see what all the fuss was about while we were filming outdoors a couple of days earlier. It was only after I had taken a look at the business card he had given me that I learned he was the head of his company's marketing department.

We began by having a drink at a nearby bar. After that, he invited me to have dinner at his family home and added that everything had already been prepared. As it was difficult to refuse such warm hospitality, I had little choice but to go.

Mr. Roberts was a cheerful sort of man, very good in conversation, and he had obviously received a good education. He was roughly two or three years older than me. His wife was apparently a well-known musician who gave performances around the country, but I didn't understand much about the musical world she belonged to.

When we were leaving the bar, he said that we had to visit a colleague's apartment for a "surprise attack." Once there, he induced his friend to bring out some whiskey. He was just that sort of easy-going, hospitable person.

Lights from the rows of tall buildings and villas that lined the beach at Waikiki were glimmering in the night. His home was situated on a high terrace that overlooked the seashore. That evening, his 17 or 18-year-old daughter took on the role of hostess and was either pouring drinks or playing the harp. She was completely attentive and considerate. As for their home, it was immaculate and utterly tranquil.

It appeared that Roberts could drink like a fish, since he would drink fine Scotch whiskey while putting on a record.

"…To tell you the truth, I received some property from my father when I was young and I turned that into cash. Then, using Paris as my base, I wandered around Europe for many years. After that, when I didn't have a single penny to my name, I returned to New York. For this, all of my friends criticized me. 'What did you actually get out of squandering so much money?' they asked. And I replied, 'I got the ability to see clearly what people are all about.'

"When I first said 'Takio,' I was depending on that ability; I felt that you were a real kind of guy as soon as I met you. And that's why I invited you over. Hey, come on! Let's keep drinking…"

"Takio"? Ahh, he was just using my given name "Takeo." But he had made a mistake with the spelling of my name in using T-a-k-i-o instead of T-a-k-e-o.

I was nevertheless a bit taken aback because, according to Japanese tradition, calling someone by their given name is a practice reserved exclusively for parents. Even then, the given name is used only when parents want to show that they are pleased with their children.

"Thank you. I fully agree with your view. I also feel that when people are brought together, honesty is always a mutual feeling. It's the same all over the world."

"Right. You Japanese enjoy '*Kamishibai*,' but people in real life aren't allowed to act that way together." (He was referring to a type of Japanese comic theater that is similar to *Kyōgen*.)

His voice, emboldened by the alcohol, had become increasingly loud.

"Dad, don't you think it would be better if you didn't have another drink?" his daughter, who was at his side serving him, asked somewhat anxiously.

Regardless of the country, it seems that all other family members are helpless when it comes to the drinking of their elders.

The next day, I had tours of a factory and a sugarcane plantation with Mr. Roberts serving as my guide. At the former, there was a cloyingly sweet smell in the air that was extremely irritating. The factory, which covered a vast area, stood alongside Dole's pineapple factory and was one of the biggest in the city. It had been established many years earlier and employed several thousand workers. Before the war, I had secretly reported to Tokyo that the site should be considered a target for bombing because, in my estimation, the factory was certain to be used for military purposes as soon as war broke out.

While reading the information booklet given to me while I was having a look around the factory that morning, I was able to confirm that the factory had in fact been used to can pineapple for the troops during the war. Furthermore, it had been running at full capacity to satisfy the needs of the military. Inwardly, I laughed a bitter laugh. However, I did not discuss the matter with Mr. Roberts.

In the afternoon we set out again, this time to visit the Wahiawa sugarcane plantation in the flatlands of central Oahu. We sped along the highway that runs past Pearl Harbor and arrived at Wahiawa very quickly.

When having a look at our surroundings from the heart of the plantation, all we could see was a research center set within a seemingly limitless expanse of sugarcane. Wheeler Field, the air base, was in the area. In the past, large numbers of P-51 fighter aircraft had been parked at that airfield and I had recommended that those fighter planes be attacked to prevent them from taking to the air during the initial stage of an attack on Hawaii. Similarly, you must first sprinkle petrol around the hive and ignite it so as to burn off worker bees on the wing when you want to get honeycomb from a beehive.

Since I had gone to check up on the activity at that airfield on a daily basis, I was very familiar with the area. As the car was passing the gates in front of the airfield, Roberts looked at me.

"You've been here before, haven't you?" he asked me with a laugh.

"Of course," I replied with a laugh.

In fact, they carried out very thorough attacks on Wheeler, Hickam, and Ewa airfields just before beginning the attack on Pearl Harbor. Thus, none of the aircraft stationed at those air bases took to the skies. Only 27 Japanese aircraft were lost during the attack and those losses were due to anti-aircraft fire from guns manned by U.S. ground troops. Meanwhile, the American aircraft

47. Strolling Around Honolulu

stationed out in the open and in air hangars at the airfields met with machine gun strafing and bombing from the Japanese planes. This sent them up in roaring flames. The losses suffered as a result were disastrous.

I thought about all of this while we passed the gates in front of the airfield and I couldn't help but lower my head to show my very deep remorse.

There was a group of people waiting to welcome us in one corner of the canteen. They were technicians who worked at the plantation's research center. After we had spent some time getting to know each other, we all shook hands without the slightest hint of reserve and wished one another well.

With a technician named Mercer as our guide, we then drove off for a visit around a pineapple plantation. Once there, Mercer used a machete to cut up a pineapple. After tasting it to see how flavorful it was, he threw it away. He did this five times in succession before he finally found one that he was convinced was of optimal quality. Only then did he let us try it.

I honestly had no idea that raw pineapple could be so luscious and sweet tasting.

"You have to select just the right time for harvest," he told us. "It's no good if it's done a day early, or a day late. But for productivity reasons, doing just that is extremely difficult."

Afterwards, he put a question to me:

"There's something I've been wondering about that I haven't been able to find an answer to. And I was wondering whether you might have the answer… Anyway, when the Japanese air troops came in to attack Pearl Harbor, why didn't they bomb the oil storage tanks in the area?"

His comments clearly revealed that he was a scientist and that he possessed the true scientist's honest character. He was the sort of person who made a good impression on others.

"There's no need to be so polite," I replied. "I can answer any question you may wish to ask, regardless of its nature. Mr. Mercer, those oil storage tanks were empty. … All of the oil used by U.S. troops was kept underground."

"Now wait just a minute. How could those air troops have known that they were empty simply by looking at them?"

"That was information that I had reported by telegram."

"But, how exactly did you…?"

"By knocking on their sides, it was easy to figure that out. I used my fingers to tap lightly on the containers' sides, in much the same way that you just did with the pineapples to determine their precise degree of ripeness. And then I knew right away."

Mercer couldn't restrain a loud laugh. "I understand, I understand," he said. "So that was why!"

As we stood in the field of pineapples, all four of us laughed quite freely.

48

Returning to the Mountain

When I returned home from Hawaii, the village was already filled with the sound of drumming for the *Bon Odori* dance. In our village, near Matsuyama in Shikoku, an old tradition sees nearly everyone in the area coming out to dance on the night of the full moon in September. On that day, there are always some dance masters and dance troupes from faraway places dropping by to take part in the festivities. The event has consequently become one of the region's finest and most famous *Bon Odori* dances. It quite often turns out to be a lively affair, with participants numbering in the tens of thousands.[1]

Although the full moon was still some days away, a few enthusiasts had already started to practice for the event.

Whenever I went away or returned home, I always did so in the most casual manner. As this was my customary practice, none of my family members thought it odd that this return home wasn't any different.

"Hello, it's me. I'm back!"

As soon as my wife heard this, she came running up to me. "Oh my! You're back! Look at you! Your face is so tanned now! And I was thinking of going to Haneda Airport to meet you!" she said.

"Would there be anyone there for you to meet now? Listen, going from Hawaii to Tokyo takes eight hours. But it's another 22 hours from Tokyo to our place. Ay! I'm already worn out."

I was walking towards my study, the Ancient Light Hermitage, as I spoke. Once there, I sat down heavily, opened my travel bag, took out the only local product that I had brought back with me, and gave it to my wife.

"What do you think of this traditional dress that Hawaiian women wear? Try it on and see!" I said.

"Oh, it's beautiful!" my wife replied. "It's a bit too colorful for me, though. But I could wear it as pajamas, couldn't I?"

Despite having taken many trips away from my family, I had very seldom brought home any local products purchased during my travels. Actually, it had never occurred to me that I ought to buy my wife something that she might want until this trip. And yet, now that she had made this determina-

48. Returning to the Mountain

tion, it so happened that I had gone all the way to Hawaii and bought my wife some pajamas.

"How was it? This trip to Hawaii?"

"Hmm, it was like going to sweep the tombstones clean."

"If I had known that you were going to be back so soon, I might have gone away with you."

"Perhaps."

The reason my wife was now having some regrets was because the Americans had said that I could bring along a companion. What's more, they had promised to pay for our accommodation. However, as I had originally hoped to spend much more time in Hawaii, my wife was somewhat reticent about going. As a result, she forfeited the opportunity to come along with me.

In fact, I did apply for a 6-month visa extension at the immigration office once the filming had ended. Yet after some U.S. Navy officials had interfered with that process from the sidelines, I was told that they didn't want me to stay in Hawaii any longer. Consequently, I had no choice but to return home.

"This world is too small! Judging from what I have seen of it," I said casually after remembering this.

"It's so good that you're back!" my wife said once again, although her incomprehension upon hearing my words clearly showed.

Evidently, she was only now able to stop worrying. In fact, right from the very start, she hadn't been keen on the idea of my going away to distant Hawaii to loll about.

"The kids have gone out to dance," my wife told me as she went into the kitchen and began to make busy. "They didn't know that you were coming home!"

"Did anything happen while I was away?" I hastened to ask her.

She took her time to sound out an initial reply. "Oh that, uh … just a sec—"

A short time later, she was smiling as she held out a glass of wine for me. She then sat down beside me and said: "Some people came around to collect money for the Bon Festival. 'The head of your household is certainly making a lot of money in Hawaii,' they said. 'So, we would like to ask all of you to contribute a bit more than you have in past years.'"

"Really?"

That sounded slightly ridiculous to me.

"The people who came by said that as soon as anyone, even a dog, showed their face on American television, they could earn tens of thousands of dollars!" my wife added slyly.

I couldn't contain a burst of laughter. And then I looked my wife in the eye. "I'm telling you Emi, a man isn't worth what a dog's worth! At best, I'm only worth as much as a mouse!"

I felt particularly happy upon saying those words. I was especially pleased because the comparison that I had made between myself and a mouse seemed so apt.

Perhaps the people who had come around collecting donations were only having some fun, but when Americans get involved in making business deals they are nowhere near that generous. All that was left in my travel bag were the two aloha shirts that I had bought to give to my kids.

It then occurred to me that if I had received the star treatment worthy of a dog, I might have brought home some high-quality local products to make them happy. In all honesty, there was nothing else from Hawaii that I could give to them now. There were plenty of Japanese things around, though, and they were of better quality. Besides, the shirts that I had bought in Hawaii might have been exports from Japan! The world was getting smaller, but economic competition was becoming much stiffer.

"Right, right. There's a dog there, what's his name? And he made a pile of money."

"All right, all right," my wife said when she noticed that I was chattering on about dogs. "Now you can tell me about the filming you did on location. Okay?"

"When will they be showing it on television?" she asked immediately after that. "Are they going to broadcast it in Japan or not? Did you see any of the people that you used to know in Hawaii?"

Although she was evidently keen to know about all of those things, I had already grown a bit tired of her chatter.

"Ahh… It's already autumn!"

"Yeah, just listen. The crickets are singing now!"

My wife stood up and opened the window.

The moon was high up in the night sky by then, its silvery light gently reflecting across the long dyke.

While everyone loves to take in a view that strikes an emotional chord, each individual has a unique frame of mind and this may cause the same scenery to give rise to various emotional responses. The moonlit landscape before me had brought back memories that I couldn't bear to recall, yet those images kept lingering in my mind: the giant moon above the beach at Waikiki; the cold wind blowing while the moon was setting over the Arizona desert; and the bright moon and sparse stars of Tokyo's night sky.

Why was human life, which follows the movement of the stars, so very unpredictable?

At one point during my most recent trip, a chance meeting had taken place. I had run into the two sisters, my former lady friends, in Tokyo. After 20 years, some major changes had occurred in their lives. The elder sister, Chika, had an only child who was apparently going to study in the United States the following spring. Mika, the younger sister, had lost her husband. He

48. Returning to the Mountain

died in China, apparently. Now Mika and her daughter were running a small restaurant. The old building by the Sannō woods, where she once lived, had been demolished and a modern tower block put in its place.

Near Nagatacho, we saw a group of demonstrators waving red flags. Ah, how everything had changed. The people that I had spent time with in the past had either died, fled, or completely vanished like smoke in the air. Meanwhile, the younger generation was now grown up, strong, and healthy. And they were building a new world.

But what about me? The life-or-death struggles during the first half of my life that I had carried on through, and the suffering that I had endured, all of it had been for naught.

It pained me to feel that I hadn't created or built up anything at all.

"What sort of achievements have I actually given this world anyway?"

I fell into deep thought.

"It's so late, but the kids are still…"

"Do you want to drink a bit more?"

It seemed that my wife had understood my pensive frame of mind and was actually urging me to drink, which was almost unheard of.

"Hmm," I said with a nod. I felt then that my wife, who had stayed with me through every hardship ever since she was a young woman, was simply to be pitied. I turned to her for consolation and completely depended on her. I could never find anyone to take her place.

"Emi, will you drink a little bit too?"

My wife wasn't at all used to drinking and just one glass was sufficient to leave her face looking completely red. However, I was feeling somewhat unrestrained as well.

And then it felt as if none of my myriad thoughts held any meaning, so I turned to a poem I'd written that was hanging on the wall of my study. I began reading it aloud.

> Like a bird weary of flying, which has returned to the mountain
> Man goes home to his village, when tired of the world outside
> I have rushed time away, gone to the back of beyond and returned
> Again and again seeking life's heart, broad and magnanimous
> I've become whole, hidden away in a grass hut
> In a peaceful frame of mind, writing texts

"At long last, I have returned to the mountain!" I said with great emotion.[2]

Having said this, I wanted to take my wife's hand. She pulled her hand away, however.

"Just think! The Master of the Dharma is watching you!"[3]

"Drink! Forget your vain hopes!"

The sound of my wife's gentle laughter went through the grass walls of my study and drifted off into the autumn night.

Chapter Notes

Chapter 1

1. The expression "second-generation" is used here to describe American nationals of Japanese parentage born in Hawaii or elsewhere in the United States.

Chapter 2

1. As Japan is located on one side of the International Date Line and Hawaii on the other, the Pearl Harbor Attack occurred on 8 December on Japan's calendar and on 7 December in Hawaii.

Chapter 3

1. Emperor Meiji reigned from 23 October 1868 to 30 July 1912. Emperor Yoshihito (Taishō) reigned from 30 July 1912 to 25 December 1926. Emperor Hirohito (Shōwa) reigned from 25 December 1926 to 7 January 1989.

2. The Rice Riots, which occurred between July and September 1918, were in fact a series of popular revolts that took place right across Japan after the price of rice shot up dramatically. At the end of July 1918 in the town of Uozu in Toyama Prefecture, some local women who were at work loading rice on the docks attempted to prevent a shipment of rice from leaving port. Although this incident was promptly dealt with by the authorities, news of it spread quickly and rioting broke out in several towns across Toyama at the beginning of August. Before long, riots had broken out in distant prefectures and an uprising in Kyoto soon followed. Subsequent to this, there were strikes in various large cities and industrial zones.

3. There is a Japanese Buddhist tradition of giving a new Buddhist name to a deceased child. This name is said to prevent the spirit of the child from returning when he hears his name called.

Chapter 4

1. Natsume Sōseki (1867–1916) was a well-known Japanese novelist who made use of his experiences as a teacher in Shikoku in his work.

2. In 1888 the Naval Academy, also known as The Imperial Naval Academy at Etajima, was established to train future naval officers in the military sciences. It was located on the island of Etajima in Hiroshima Prefecture. Graduates received the rank of ensign after completing a period of duty at sea. All Japanese naval officers, whether lieutenants or admirals, were required to have gone through training at Etajima.

3. Admiral Osami Nagano (1880–1947) was an admiral in the Imperial Japanese Navy. He was, at various times, Head of the Imperial Naval Academy, Commanding Officer of Japan's Combined Fleet, and (from April 1941 to February 1944) Chief of Staff at the Navy General Staff. At the end of WWII, he was made to stand trial as a war criminal. He died while his trial was underway.

4. The Five-Power Treaty or the "5:5:3 Treaty" refers to one of the agreements made at the Washington Conference, which was an international conference on disarmament held between 12 November 1921 and 6 February 1922. Delegations from nine countries were in attendance: USA, Japan, Portugal,

Holland, Belgium, Italy, Britain, France and China.

At the end of WWI, both the British and the Americans were concerned about what was to become of Germany's warships. Subsequently, the Treaty of Versailles (1919) set strict limits on the number of warships that Germany would be allowed to maintain.

Soon afterwards, a new naval arms race broke out with Japan, Britain, and the U.S. all announcing that they were constructing new warships. This arms race soon met with opposition from the public and from politicians in various countries. As a result, calls were made to initiate a process of disarmament. These calls ultimately led to the series of meetings known as the Washington Conference.

Three treaties were signed at the conference. Among them was the "Five-Power Treaty" (a.k.a. the 5:5:3 Treaty). This agreement was signed by USA, Britain, Japan, France and Italy. It stated that the relative power of the American, British and Japanese navies in terms of tonnage was to be maintained at the ratio of 5:5:3. The treaty prevented Japan from developing a navy more powerful than those of its main rivals.

Although Japan may have been reluctant to sign an accord proposing such terms, the treaty also stated that further construction of naval bases in the Western Pacific region was to be prohibited to all world powers. This provision seemed to ensure that Japan would remain the dominant naval power in the Western Pacific and likely prompted Japan's leaders to sign the treaty.

5. In 1918, Japan's parliament approved the "Eight-Eight Naval Fleet" plan. The plan called for the construction of eight battleships and eight battlecruisers. It also called for the modernization of the rest of the Imperial Japanese Navy's fleet. Although this shipbuilding plan was approved and put into effect, it was never fully implemented. Following the Washington Conference, Japan put off the construction of the battleships and battlecruisers that had not been built because it had decided to accept the Five-Power Treaty's restrictions.

6. The "Imperial Rescript to Soldiers and Sailors" (*Gunjin Chokuyu*) was issued to the troops by Emperor Meiji on 4 January 1882. The edict aimed to instill servicemen with a sense of duty and create an emotional bond between army and navy troops and their Emperor.

7. *Shaba* was a word used by both students and staff at the Naval Academy. The expression meant "outsider" or "brute" and it served to describe members of the wider society outside the academy.

8. *Manchukuo* was the large territory in northeastern China (otherwise known as Manchuria) that was occupied by Japan following the "Mukden Incident." Although the last Emperor of China, Puyi, had been forced to abdicate in 1912, he was chosen by the Japanese government to serve as the puppet "Emperor" of Japanese-controlled *Manchukuo* in 1932. Puyi remained the "Emperor" of *Manchukuo* until he was taken prisoner by Soviet troops in 1945 at the war's end. Hsinking is today known as Changchun.

9. The first Shanghai Incident or "January 28th incident" refers to the bombing of Shanghai by Japanese aircraft following an outbreak of anti-Japanese violence in the city.

Chapter 5

1. Iyo Province, in northwestern Shikoku, is the former name of present-day Ehime Prefecture.

2. Themistocles led an armada of Greek naval vessels to Salamis where the Greeks won a decisive victory over the much larger navy of the Persian King Xerxes.

3. The Manchurian Incident or Mukden Incident occurred in northeast China near the present-day city of Shenyang, which was known as Mukden at the time. On 18 September 1931, Japanese troops detonated explosives that caused minor damage to the Japanese-run South Manchuria Railway. After blaming Chinese terrorists for the staged attack, the Imperial Japanese Army used it as a pretext to invade Manchuria. After just a few months of fighting following the Manchurian Incident, the Japanese puppet state of *Manchukuo* was established and Japanese rule in northeast China began.

The "Marco Polo Bridge Incident" (July 1937) was initially an armed skirmish that pitted Kwantung Army troops (a Chinese private army, hired by the Japanese) against Chinese Nationalist Army troops near the

Marco Polo Bridge in Beijing. Although the incident was low-key to begin with, further skirmishes eventually caused the outbreak of the Second Sino-Japanese War.

Translator's note: The author describes both the Manchurian Incident and the Marco Polo Bridge Incident as past events at this point in the text. However, the Marco Polo Bridge Incident and the subsequent invasion of China by Japanese forces (i.e. the Second Sino-Japanese War) had not yet occurred at this point in the author's life. Takeo Yoshikawa's father would have had good reason to feel concerned about the worsening conditions in Japan and abroad following the Manchurian Incident, though. That conflict paved the way for subsequent incidents that ultimately pushed Japan and China into a prolonged war that would have serious consequences for both countries.

4. Kasumigaseki is a district in Tokyo's Chiyoda Ward. Many government offices and ministry buildings are found in the area.

Chapter 6

1. Ōtani Kōzui (1876–1948) was a bespectacled Buddhist monk from Tokyo and Abbot of Kyoto's Western temple of the Original Vow or Nishi Hongan-ji. While he was leading archeological digs in Central Asia, his prospecting activities caught the attention of some foreign intelligence agents.

Chapter 8

1. Sun Tzu or Sunzi (544 BC–496 BC) was a Chinese military strategist. He is said to have been the author of *The Art of War*.

2. The Hōjō school's military strategy was developed by the Hōjō clan in Awa Province during the Kan'ei period (1624–1644).

3. On 27 September 1940, an agreement formally known as the Tripartite Pact (or the Berlin Pact) was signed in Berlin by Germany, Japan, and Italy—the three largest fascist states. This pact marked the first stage of formal cooperation for the tripartite alliance, whose members were otherwise known as the "Axis" powers. Through their collaboration, these three powers aimed to establish a new world order in both Europe and East Asia.

Chapter 9

1. The Lytton Report was a League of Nations report written up by an international committee convened to investigate the Manchurian Incident, which occurred on 18 September 1931. Victor Bulwer-Lytton of Great Britain led the committee that included representatives from the United States, Germany, Italy, France and Britain.

During the Manchurian Incident of September 1931, Japanese troops deliberately detonated an explosion alongside Japan's South Manchuria Railway near Mukden (Shenyang). Although no significant damage was caused by the explosion, Japan asserted that Chinese terrorists had caused the explosion. Japan then claimed that the presence of terrorists acting against its commercial interests in China gave it sufficient grounds to send troops into Manchuria in order to establish *Manchukuo* (Japanese-controlled Manchuria).

The Lytton Report's findings included a call for the withdrawal of Japanese troops from Manchuria and it recommended that an international committee review the situation in China's northeast. After rejecting the findings of the Lytton Report, Japan announced its withdrawal from the League of Nations.

Chapter 12

1. Kamehameha I or Kamehameha the Great (1736?–1819) was the founder of Hawaii. He ruled the Hawaiian Islands from 1782 to 1819.

Chapter 14

1. Shinbashi, a busy district located near Tokyo Harbor, was formerly home to many brothels.

Chapter 16

1. The "ABCD line" or "ABCD embargo" was a Japanese concept that viewed The United States, Great Britain, China, Holland, and other associated nations, as members of an alliance that wished to constrain Japan economically.

Chapter 17

1. Although some U.S. media were voluntarily censoring sensitive military information as early as 1939, the U.S. government's ban on detailed weather reporting did not come into effect until after the December 1941 declaration of war.
2. The Inner South Seas is a Japanese geographical term referring to the maritime area that extends from the Malay Peninsula, across the South China Sea and over the Philippines, past Palau and the Caroline Islands, to the Marshall Islands in the central Pacific Ocean.

Chapter 18

1. The "Lahaina Roads" is the name of a deep-water sea channel situated between the islands of Maui, Lanai and Molokai. The channel's location and the depth of the water there make the Lahaina Roads a suitable anchorage site for large ships.
2. The famous "colony" for people afflicted by leprosy on Molokai's Kalaupapa Peninsula was run by Father Damien (1840–1889). He was a Belgian Roman Catholic priest assigned to minister to the Hawaiians quarantined on the Kalaupapa Peninsula because they suffered from leprosy (Hansen's disease). Father Damien began working with the quarantined sufferers of leprosy in 1873 and quickly improved their quality of life by setting up farms, building chapels and hospitals, and ministering to their community. Father Damien contracted leprosy in 1884 and he died of the disease in 1889. In his lifetime he received much recognition for his good works. He was officially declared a saint in 2009, after being canonized by Pope Benedict XVI.

Chapter 22

1. *The Treasury of the Loyal Retainers* (or *Chūshingura*) tells the story of the 47 rōnin (samurai without a master) from Akō who take revenge for the murder of their master, the lord of Akō, Asano Naganori (1667–1701).

Chapter 27

1. The elm woods described here were likely composed of gunpowder trees. Although it is not the American elm tree that once lined many streets across the USA, the gunpowder tree (*Trema orientalis*) does belongs to the elm family (*Ulmaceae*).
2. The special midget submarine, or Type-A *Kō-hyōteki*-class submarine, was developed by the Japanese navy in 1941. It was 24 meters long, carried two torpedoes, and was operated by a two-person crew. The submarine was designed to be transported by a full-sized submarine, or a large ship, to and from the battle front because it was not capable of covering long distances on its own power.

Chapter 28

1. *The FBI Story: A Report to the People* was written by Don Whitehead.
2. "Remember Pearl Harbor" and "Avenge Pearl Harbor" were watchwords used by the U.S. government after the Pearl Harbor Incident. These slogans were ubiquitous during WWII, appearing on billboards, commercial advertisements and packaging, and elsewhere.

Chapter 29

1. In Japan many farms take a single Hiragana character, such as *ni* or *ka*, for their name. Triangle T Ranch made use of a triangle and the letter "T" for its name, which was equally simple.
2. Japan's National Day is celebrated on 11 February.
3. *Kannon* is the Japanese name for the Buddhist Goddess of Mercy.

Chapter 30

1. Shinto or Shintoism, is Japan's indigenous religion. It is polytheistic and followers take the sun's "Great Spirit of the Heavenly Light" to be the focal point of their worship. In the 19th century, the Japanese Royal Family was included among its gods.
2. Bushido was a moral system that emerged at the time of the Kamakura shogunate (Japan's first military-led government). Its precepts were observed by samurai throughout Japan's feudal period. Faith-

fulness to the monarch, integrity, a sense of honor, bravery, and steadfastness were among its key principles. Bushido offered the samurai a code by which they could faithfully serve their lords.

Chapter 31

1. Yarihei Amano was an Osaka warrior and businessman during the middle Edo period. He fell afoul of the authorities after making arrangements to procure weapons on behalf of his lord, an Akō samurai. After the plot was exposed, he adamantly refused to admit to having any knowledge of it.

Chapter 34

1. Located in Portuguese East Africa (present-day Mozambique), Lourenço Marques is now called Maputo. Today, it is a large port-city with over 1 million inhabitants.

Chapter 36

1. The Warship March (*Gunkan kōshinkyoku*) was composed for the Imperial Japanese Navy by Tōkichi Setoguchi.

Chapter 38

1. Imagawa Yoshimoto (1519–1560) and Takeda Shingen (1521–1573) were both feudal lords (*daimyō*) during the Sengoku period (1467–1600). During that turbulent period, the armies of various regional clans were fighting for control of Japan.
2. Following the First World War, the victorious nations were given mandates to rule over territories ceded to them by the nations they had defeated. The new rulers were known as "mandatory powers" and their new territorial possessions were called "mandated territories." At the end of the First World War, Japan was granted mandatory power over various islands north of the equator in the Pacific Ocean because it had been one of the allied countries that opposed Germany. When the Pacific War ended, Japan's mandatory powers were rescinded and its mandated territories transferred to an international trusteeship.

3. The *Nachi* was sunk by U.S. forces in Manila Bay on 5 November 1944. Code books and other documents aboard the wreck were recovered by American divers in April 1945.

Chapter 39

1. Richard Sorge (1895–1944) was a German national who worked for the Soviet Union. He served as an undercover agent in Tokyo where he had many high-level contacts in the government. While undercover, he sought out top secret information about Japan and Germany and reported it to the Soviets. After his arrest in 1941, he was sentenced to death by hanging.
2. The Manchuria Railway was another name for the South Manchuria Railway Company, which was part of the infrastructure built by Japan within northeastern China. Established in 1907, the railway linked coal mines and iron processing facilities to ports in China's northeast. Those responsible for the railway sent intelligence reports on Chinese military affairs, politics, and economic matters to the Japanese army.
3. Secret Purple codes were used by Japan's Ministry of Foreign Affairs and its embassies and consulates overseas. The Japanese referred to these as "97-character print machine codes." These codes were changed regularly through slight adjustments to the 97-character encryption machines.

Chapter 40

1. The number of aircraft carriers was high because it included small vessels that had been refitted to carry a single aircraft.
2. The word *kamikaze* means "divine wind." It was first used during the Kamakura period (1192–1333) to describe the typhoons that twice helped to prevent ships carrying thousands of Mongol warriors from reaching Japan. Japan had never been subjected to an invasion by foreigners prior to WWII, and it was well-known that the "divine wind" had played a key role in this. When the Pacific War began going badly for Japan, some of its military leaders asked pilots to volunteer to use their aircraft as weapons in suicide missions against enemy naval targets. In so doing, they invoked the

"divine wind" because they hoped that the newly-dubbed *kamikaze* pilots would manage to thwart the enemy's goal of invasion. Although their desperate gambit ultimately failed to turn the tide, many of the *kamikaze* pilots who sent themselves crashing to their deaths inflicted tremendous casualties and devastation upon their enemies.

3. "The Decisive Battle for the Mainland" was announced on the eve of Japan's ultimate defeat. Some militarists then in power wanted Japan's people to fight to the very end. Efforts to turn Japan's Home Islands into a battlefield ultimately failed because civilians refused to be drawn into taking part in such a battle.

4. Two atomic bombs were dropped on Japan by the United States in 1945. The first bomb fell on 6 August at Hiroshima, the second on 9 August at Nagasaki.

5. Stalin had signed a neutrality pact with Japan in 1941. On 9 August 1945, following the bombing of Nagasaki, the Soviet Union withdrew from that pact and joined the Allies in the war.

Chapter 41

1. The Potsdam Declaration was also called the Potsdam Proclamation. The USA, Britain, China, and several allies issued this declaration on 26 July 1945 during a conference held in Potsdam, Germany. On 9 August 1945, after joining the war effort led by the allied powers, the Soviet Union signed the declaration as well.

The declaration made the following points:

1. The Allied countries shall continue to wage war on Japan until it announces its unconditional surrender.
2. Japan's armed forces must completely disarm.
3. Those Japanese leaders responsible for Japan's military aggressions must be permanently stripped of all power and influence.
4. Japan's sovereignty shall be limited to its Home Islands (Honshu, Hokkaido, Kyushu and Shikoku) and to some smaller islands to be decided on by the allies.
5. Japan must hand over its war criminals for punishment.
6. Japan must ensure that all impediments to democracy are removed and see to it that its citizens are provided with responsible government, universal suffrage, free speech, etc.
7. Japan may be allowed to keep those industries that might help with its reconstruction without in any way posing a threat to peace.

2. Hakuin Ekaku (1685–1768) was a prominent monk from the Rinzai school during the Edo period.

3. Kumagai Naozane (1141–1208) was a long-serving military officer during the Kamakura period. He fled to Kyoto and took up Buddhism after his troops suffered defeat.

Kamo no Chōmei (1155–1216) was a poet and Buddhist monk during the Kamakura period. He preferred to live a solitary life in order to study and write. *An account of my ten-foot square hut* is his most well-known work.

Chapter 42

1. Hōjō Tokimune (1251–1284) was the eighth ruler of the Kamakura period. He was a very devout man and is said to have been largely responsible for the spread of Zen Buddhism in Japan. He earned great renown after his forces successfully fended off would-be Mongol invaders.

2. A dharma name is a Buddhist name given to newly initiated monks and nuns.

3. Yagū Munetoshi 石舟齋, who was originally called Sekishūsai Songon (1527–1606), was a master of Japanese *kendo* (or martial arts swordsmanship).

Tesshū 鐵舟, more properly known as Yamaoka Tesshū (1836–1888), played an important role during the Meiji Restoration.

Kendo innovator Dorobune 泥舟, better known as Deishu Takahashi (1835–1903), served as a government minister in the late Tokugawa period.

4. Located in Kyoto, Tenru-ji is the main temple for Japan's followers of Rinzai Buddhism.

5. The Nanboku-chō period or Northern and Southern Courts period (1336–1392)

followed the end of the Kamakura period (1333). During this period, the Northern and Southern Imperial Courts were locked in a brutal struggle for power. The Northern Imperial Court eventually defeated its Southern counterpart.

Chapter 43

1. Some say that the popular fictional character Sarutobi Sasuke was based upon a real man. In films, Sarutobi Sasuke was known as *The Samurai Spy*.
2. The honorific "Excellency" *Kakka* (閣下) is a respectful form of address used for heads of state, top-level government officials, ambassadors, and military officers of the highest rank.

Chapter 45

1. In January 1948, the Japanese government adopted the "Banish from Public Office" law after it had been ordered to do so by the GHQ of the allied forces. The law required that all those who belonged to militarist or nationalist factions be forced out of their jobs in the national assembly, government, finance, and the media. The law was repealed soon after the San Francisco Treaty was signed in 1951.
2. The CBS television series *The Twentieth Century*, which was hosted by Walter Cronkite, ran from 1957 to 1966. "The Man Who Spied on Pearl Harbor" was the name of the episode that featured Takeo Yoshikawa. It was first aired on 3 December 1961.

Chapter 46

1. James Hagerty was President Eisenhower's Press Secretary.
2. Wade Bingham was an American cinematographer/cameraman whose work was frequently featured in episodes of the CBS television series *The Twentieth Century*.

Chapter 48

1. The Bon Festival is the Japanese "Ghost Festival" or All-Souls Day festival during which the souls of the departed are remembered. *Bon Odori* is a traditional dance festival associated with the Bon Festival celebrations. *Bon Odori* dances take place in many regions across Japan.
2. A "return to the mountain" is a Buddhist idiom. It refers to a monk's return to his temple after a lengthy period away from it.
3. There are no historical records about the Master of the Dharma, or Bodhidharma (circa 440–528). There are many apocryphal accounts of the man, however. Most of these accounts agree that the Bodhidharma was an Indian monk who brought Zen Buddhism to China. The Rinzai school in Japan is one of several Buddhist schools in East Asia that emerged from the teachings of the Bodhidharma.

Index

Akagi 264
Akasaka district, Tokyo 43
Alewa Heights, Honolulu 79
Allen, Riley 12
Amano, Yarihei 180, 293
USS *Arizona* 1, 82, 83, 146–7, 167, 260, 262, 276–7
Arizona, state of 166–7, 170
atomic bombs 250, 259, 294
Attu Island 236

Balalae Airfield 220
"Banish from Public Office" law 268, 295
Barbers Point 100
black market 55, 244, 251, 280
Bon Festival 285, 295
Borneo 36–7
Bougainville Island 212, 219, 236
Bushido 173, 292–3

Cam Ranh Bay 86
Camp Davis 131
Carrier Striking Task Force 219, 261–2
CBS 268, 270, 279
Chiang Kai-Shek 55, 194
Chiba Prefecture 244
cipher codes 51, 143, 220, 228
USS *Colorado* 82, 146
consul-general in Honolulu (Japan) *see* Kita, Nagao
consulate-general in Honolulu (Japan) 39, 62–5, 76–8, 81–2, 85, 112, 134–135, 137–9, 142, 145–7, 156
Cook, Captain James 67
Cronkite, Walter 295

"Decisive Battle for the Mainland" 240, 243, 294
declaration of war, Japanese 194
Decoux, Jean 86

Doolittle Raid 236
Dutch Harbor 47, 96, 101, 109, 276

"Eight-Eight" naval fleet plan 24, 290
Etajima 24, 289
Etorofu Island 116, 261
Ewa Airfield 99, 112, 131, 150, 282

FBI 40, 52, 63, 72, 77, 79, 95, 100, 119, 121–2, 134–5, 176, 198; *see also* Shivers, Robert
The FBI Story 156–7
firebombing of Tokyo 240, 243
5:5:3 Treaty 24, 289
Formosa 238–9
Fort Shafter 101
Fremantle, Australia 50
Fuchida, Mitsuo 2, 262, 264
Fukushima, Lt-Commander Eikichi 105

geisha 80, 85, 92, 103, 279
Genda, Minoru 264
General Headquarters of the Allied forces in Japan (GHQ) 252–3, 256, 266
GHQ (General Headquarters of the Allied forces in Japan) *see* General Headquarters of the Allied forces in Japan (GHQ)
Greater East Asia Co-Prosperity Sphere 36
Gripsholm 189
Guadalcanal 216, 219, 221, 269
Guangdong 64
Gunjin Chokuyu see "Imperial Rescript to Soldiers and Sailors"

Hagerty, James 274, 295
Hakuin, Ekaku 247, 294
Hawaii: climate 91–2; general overview 66–69; residents of Japanese ancestry 67, 76, 78, 81–2, 271, 277, 279
Hickam airfield 11–13, 70, 79, 97, 99, 104, 112, 131, 141–2, 150, 282

Index

Hikawa Maru 105
Hiraoka, Yoichi 193
Hitokappu Bay 116, 261
Hōjō school 47, 291
holly tree 173
Honolulu Star 12
Horiuchi, Captain 35, 38
Hotel New Grand, Yokahama 58
Hull, Cordell 224, 235

Imperial General Headquarters 237-8
Imperial General Headquarters-Government Liaison Conference 87, 105
Imperial Hotel, Tokyo 266
Imperial Japanese Navy Staff Office *see* Navy General Staff
The Imperial Naval Academy 23-6, 289
"Imperial Rescript to Soldiers and Sailors" 25, 290
Inner South Seas 92, 292
Iolani Palace 67
Ito, Vice Admiral Seiichi 256
Iwasa, Commander Naoji 153

Kamakura: period 293-5; shogunate 292
Kamakura Maru 190-5
Kamehameha I, of Hawaii 67
kamikaze aircraft 239, 293
Kanemitsu, Petty Officer Yū 221
Kaneʻohe Bay 94-7, 99, 100, 112, 114
Kannon 169, 173, 292
Kasumigaseki 32, 291
Kauai 66, 113, 127
Kidō Butai see Carrier Striking Task Force
Kimmel, Admiral Husband E. 127, 263
Kita, Nagao 63-4, 80, 97, 106-7, 111-2, 116-8, 129, 134, 138-9, 141-5, 147, 156, 159, 162-8, 170-4, 179, 183, 187, 202-3
Koga, Admiral Mineichi 236
Koiso, Kuniaki 238-9
Kōzui, Ōtani 35, 291
Kühn, Otto 118-9, 120-2, 143, 156, 181-2
Kurusu, Ambassador Saburo 224

Lahaina Roads 97-8, 102-3, 108, 114, 292
Lanikai Beach 118, 181
Lourenço Marques 183, 190, 193, 195
Lytton Report 53, 291

MacArthur, General Douglas 257
Maejima, Commander Toshihide 107
Makin Island 221
Manchukuo 27, 290
Manchuria Railway 226, 268, 290-1, 293
Manchurian Incident 31, 163, 290-1
Manila 41, 47, 114, 194, 222, 227, 229, 230-4

Maputo 293; *see also* Lourenço Marques
Marco Polo Bridge Incident 31, 99, 106
Matsuo, Sub-Lieutenant Keiu 105
Matsuyama 15, 23, 251
Matsuzuro, Captain Minoru 255
Meiji, Emperor 16, 25, 289
midget submarine *see* special midget submarine
Midway Island 96, 100, 113, 138, 194, 200, 217, 219, 225, 234, 275
Mikoyan, Anastas 274
Molokai 98, 292; *see also* Hawaii, general overview
Mongol invasion attempts 293-4
Morimura, Tadashi 2, 12, 14, 48
Mount Misen 26
Mukden Incident *see* Manchurian Incident

Nachi incident 222, 293
Nagano, Admiral Osami 23, 27, 289
Nagata Manor, Tokyo 41, 43, 206
Nagumo, Chūichi 261
Nakashima, Lt-Commander Minato 105
Nanboku-chō period 251, 294
Naozane, Kumagai 247, 294
national guard (U.S.) 164-5, 177, 186
National Institute for Defense Studies (Japan) 128, 155
Natsume Sōseki 23, 289
Naval Academy at Etajima *see* The Imperial Naval Academy
Navy General Staff 32, 34, 46, 48, 52, 87-9, 200, 211, 213-4, 218, 222, 225, 255
New York, NY 186-8
Nishin Maru 51
Nitta Maru 52, 58, 65
Nomura, Admiral Kichisaburō 52, 56, 190, 223
Nuʻuanu Pali 67, 92-4, 275
NYK Shipping Company 51

Oahu 66-7, 74, 92
obstruction balloons 108, 129, 130-131
Ōfuna, Japan 210
Okuda, Vice-Consul-General Otojiro 64, 166, 168-9, 179, 183
Otsuka Park (Numazu, Japan) 207
Overseas Japanese Residents' Association 76, 78

PA-K2 cipher 228, 234; *see also* cipher codes
Pacific Conference *see* Washington Conference
Panama 51, 107, 114, 131, 227, 229
PBY seaplanes 94, 96, 100-1

Index

Pearl Harbor 1, 11, 26, 39, 47, 66, 70, 73–4, 79, 84, 140, 223, 260, 265, 276
USS *Pennsylvania* 52, 260
Philippines 157, 225, 228, 239
Potsdam Declaration 242, 294
POWs (Prisoners of War) 210–1, 215–7
Prange, Dr. Gordon William 264
Proceedings (U.S. Navy periodical) 268, 270
Puunene Airport 98
Puyi 27, 290

Queen's Hospital, Honolulu 12

Rabaul 219, 220
radar 200, 216–7
"Remember Pearl Harbor" (wartime slogan) 160, 191, 292
Rice Riots 19, 289
Rinzai school 258, 294
Roosevelt, Franklin Delano 52, 56, 224, 235, 263

Saipan Island 236, 238–9, 269
Sakamaki, Ensign Kazuo 154
San Francisco Peace Treaty 254, 259
San Pedro, California 47, 160
Sankan Bay 153
Sasuke, Sarutobi 256, 295
Schofield Barracks 135
Secret Purple cypher coding 228; *see also* cipher codes
Self-Defense Forces (Japan) 269
Sengoku period 249, 293
"Shanghai Incident" 27, 290
Shikoku 15, 66, 284
Shimizudani Park, Tokyo 44, 273
Shinbashi District (Tokyo) 80, 291
Shinto 19, 28, 173, 292
Shivers, Robert 81, 143, 156, 234; *see also* FBI
Shizuoka 246–7
Shōwa, Emperor (or Emperor Hirohito) 24, 81, 86–7, 105, 194, 241, 289
Shunchoro Teahouse 79, 83–6, 103, 112, 135–7, 276, 279
Singapore 37, 194–5, 225
Solomon Islands 217, 219, 221–2, 236
Sorge, Richard 225, 293
Sōtō school 258
South Manchuria Railway Company *see* Manchuria Railway

South Seas 36, 84, 92, 163, 204, 213, 219
South Seas Development Corporation 226
South Seas Society 226
special midget submarine 149, 153–5, 259, 260, 277, 292
Stanford, Lt-Colonel Norman 269
Strike Force *see* Carrier Striking Task Force
Suzuki, Lt-Commander Suguru 107, 149
Sydney Harbour, Australia 105

Taishō, Emperor (or Emperor Yoshi-hito) 24, 289
Taiwan *see* Formosa
Taiyo Maru 93, 107, 149
Takeuchi, Rear Admiral Kaoru 211, 214–5, 255–8
Tatsuta Maru 105
Tavurvur Mountain 220
Tenru-ji 250, 294
Togetsu Bridge 251
Tomioka, Captain Sadatoshi 264
Toranomon Gate 268
Triangle T Ranch 165
Type-A Kō-hyōteki-class submarine *see* special midget submarine

U.S. Federal Committee for the Investigation of the Pearl Harbor Incident 226–7
U.S. State Department 160, 168, 177

Waikiki 66–7, 150, 276, 281
Wake Island 225, 234–5, 2a
Wang, Jing Wei 55
Warship March 205, 293
HMS *Warspite* 229
Washington Conference 289, 290
Wheeler Airfield 99, 282
Whitehead, Don 292

Yamamoto, Admiral Isoroku 87, 138, 153, 218–9, 220, 236
Yamato 256
Yokohama 30, 52, 58, 65, 105, 107, 195, 198
Yokoyama, Masaharu 154
Yonai, Admiral Mitsumasa 238
Yotsuya, Tokyo 44
Yura 30

www.ingramcontent.com/pod-product-compliance
Ingram Content Group UK Ltd.
Pitfield, Milton Keynes, MK11 3LW, UK
UKHW040610160426
5217IPUK00034B/326